THE PEOPLE OF ANGUISH

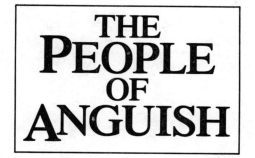

THE
PEOPLE
OF
ANGUISH

The Story Behind the Reformation

ANTHONY E. GILLES

Nihil Obstat: Rev. Lawrence Landini, O.F.M.
　　　　　　　Rev. John J. Jennings

Imprimi Potest: Rev. Jeremy Harrington, O.F.M.
　　　　　　　Provincial

Imprimatur: + James H. Garland, V.G.
　　　　　　Archdiocese of Cincinnati
　　　　　　March 13, 1987

The *nihil obstat* and *imprimatur* are a declaration that a book or pamphlet is considered to be free from doctrinal or moral error. It is not implied that those who have granted the *nihil obstat* and *imprimatur* agree with the contents, opinions or statements expressed.

Book and cover design by Julie Lonneman

SBN 0-86716-068-3

TO RICHARD AND LANIER MARIUS

THE PEOPLE OF GOD—FROM ABRAHAM TO US

A sweeping history of Judeo-Christian thought by Anthony E. Gilles

Volumes available:

The People of the Book: The Story Behind the Old Testament. SBN 268 $5.95

The People of the Way: The Story Behind the New Testament. SBN 365 $5.95

The People of the Creed: The Story Behind the Early Church. SBN 462 $5.95

The People of the Faith: The Story Behind the Church of the Middle Ages. SBN 765 $6.95

The People of Anguish: The Story Behind the Reformation. SBN 683 $7.95

In preparation:

The People of Hope: The Story Behind the Modern Church

PREFACE

Writing this book has been an agonizing experience. On the one hand, I felt the historian's call to depict this most quarrelsome era of Christian history as accurately as possible, leaving no wart or sore unexposed. On the other hand, my penchant for ecumenism kept tugging at my sleeve, insisting that I keep this sin hidden or let that error be laid to rest. This second impulse kept nagging at me, silently chanting all the while, "Why dredge all that up? Why bother about the failings of yesteryear? After all, we now live in an age when union among Christians is a real possibility."

I mention my interior struggle at the outset, because upon rereading the final draft of this book it seemed doubtful to me that you, the reader, would find much that is conciliatory in the pages ahead. I have not recorded pleasant times or events, and I have not been lenient on the principal characters in the drama. In one sense, I suppose, you could say that my respect for history won out over my desire for ecumenism.

Yet I trust that you will find me to have been fair. Where necessary, I have been as hard on the popes as I have been on Luther or Calvin or Knox. I present neither a sterilized Catholicism nor a disinfected Protestantism. In some cases you may feel that I am reopening wounds better left scar-covered or resurrecting fools, scoundrels and miscreants better left buried.

I write as I do not because I believe I would have acted more virtuously than the actual characters in the story, but because I believe that it is precisely in reliving the truth about our past that we best prepare ourselves for reconciliation in the present. In my estimation, nothing would be accomplished by writing an easygoing apologia whitewashing all the blunders and errors that were committed—writing, for example, "Yes, but after all we must look upon dear Pope So-and-so's avarice and corruption from his point of view and not ours," or, "Let's remember that, before burning these Catholics at the stake, sweet Queen So-and-so had the best of intentions, I'm sure."

Sugarcoated history such as this is, in reality, no history at all and serves no purpose in the quest for reconciliation. If we Christians are really serious about healing our divisions, then we must first face the truth about ourselves. Just as no individual who fantasizes that his early childhood in an orphanage was one wave of ecstasy after another can truly become whole, so too the Church cannot become whole if it does not first understand its adolescent unhappiness. Thus, anyone approaching a Protestant-Catholic dialogue aimed at reunion must first be prepared to do a little repenting and, after repenting, forgiving. There have been sins and mistakes on both sides. If either side is ignorant of its faults or tries to deny them, our dialogue will serve no useful purpose.

In the last analysis, therefore, the two impulses which motivated me to write this book—the historical and the ecumenical—both lead in the same direction: toward repentance, forgiveness and reconciliation. As a Roman Catholic, I ask forgiveness from my Protestant brothers and sisters for any conclusion I have reached which appears shortsighted or narrow-minded; I don't pretend to have left behind my Catholicism in preparing this book. Perhaps any negative evaluations of Protestantism in the pages ahead could be read as if preceded by, "In my opinion."

As for my fellow Catholics, I urge you to take a reconciliatory approach to reading this book. I suggest that you stand in the shoes of the Protestant reformers and ask yourselves if you would not have been at least tempted to respond to official Catholic arrogance and intransigence as they did.

To all Christians and seekers after God, I pray that this book will in some small way help us realize Jesus' promise:

"...you will know the truth,
and the truth will set you free." (John 8:32)

A Final Word

Just as the preceding two volumes in this *People of God* series were not works of original scholarship, neither is this one, nor is it intended to be. I am not a professional scholar but a writer who greatly admires the scholars and attempts to make their conclusions available to the average reader. What I have attempted in the upcoming pages is to popularize the work of several experts in the fields of Church history and the history of Christian thought.

I am particularly indebted (as I was in writing the two predecessors to this volume, *The People of the Creed: The Story Behind the Early Church* and *The People of the Faith: The Story Behind the Church of the Middle Ages*) to three masterpieces of scholarship and erudition: (1) Jaroslav Pelikan's four-volume *The Christian Tradition* (The University of Chicago Press, 1971); (2) Justo Gonzalez's three-volume *A History of Christian Thought* (Abingdon Press, 1971); and (3) the 10-volume *History of the Church* edited by Hubert Jedin (originally *Handbuch der Kirchengeschichte*, English translation, 1965; Crossroad Publishing Co., 1982).

This book then, in addition to being a popular introduction to the Reformation era, is also an introduction to the three works cited above, as well as to other scholarly treatises cited in the bibliographies of those works and on which I have also relied. Further, since Will Durant in his 11-volume *The Story of Civilization* likewise attempted to make otherwise inaccessible scholarship available to the ordinary reader, and since in doing this he provided quotations from many of the primary sources used by scholars in the field of Reformation history, I have made extensive use of Durant's work in the pages ahead. Anyone wishing to travel farther on the road of Reformation-era history than my introductory overview in this volume is encouraged to consult the authorities cited above.

If the upcoming pages make the experts' enormous contribution to our understanding of the Reformation era available to the average reader, I will have been amply rewarded.

CONTENTS

TIMELINE: THE REFORMATION

Secular Rulers	Events	Popes
		Nicholas V (1447-1455)
	1464: Erasmus of Rotterdam born	
	1483: Martin Luther born	
	1491: Ignatius Loyola born	Alexander VI (1492-1503)
	1492: Spanish Inquisitor-General orders Jews to accept Christianity or be exiled	Julius II (1503-1513)
Henry VIII (England 1509-1547)	1500: Pope Alexander VI declares a crusade against the Turks	
	1501: Pope Alexander orders burning of books deemed threatening to Church authority	
Francis I (France: 1515-1547)	1503: Martin Luther enters Augustinians; John Knox born	
	1506: John Tetzel sells indulgences in Germany 1507: Luther ordained an Augustinian priest	
	1509: Henry VIII becomes king of England, marries Catherine of Aragon; John Calvin born	Leo X (1513-1521)
	1517: Luther writes 95 theses, protests the sale of indulgences	
	1518: Luther refuses to recant 95 theses at Augsburg	
Charles V (Germany: 1519-1556)	1520: Thomas Munzer begins Anabaptist movement in Germany; Luther excommunicated by Pope Leo X	
	1521: Pope Leo declares King Henry VIII of England "Defender of the Faith" for his treatise condemning Luther; Luther, banned from Empire, retreats to Wartburg Castle and begins German translation of Bible	Adrian VI (1522-1523)
Thomas Munzer (1525)	1524: Peasants revolt in southern Germany; Zwingli abolishes Mass in Zurich	Clement VII (1523-1534)
	1527: Imperial troops sack Rome; Lutheran reform reaches Sweden	
	1528: King Henry VIII seeks divorce; Protestant reform begins in Scotland	
	1529: Thomas More made Chancellor of England; Luther and Zwingli debate the Eucharist at Marburg	
Ulrich Zwingli (1531)	1530: Philip Melancthon publishes Confession of Augsburg 1531: Zwingli killed in battle	
	1533: Henry VIII marries Anne Boleyn and is excommunicated	
	1534: Society of Jesus founded by Ignatius Loyola	Paul III (1534-1549)
Thomas More (1535)	1535: Thomas More executed by Henry VIII	
Desiderius Erasmus (1536)	1536: Catholic religious orders dissolved in England; first edition of Calvin's Institutes	
Andreas Carlstadt (1541)	1541: Calvin returns to Geneva from exile; John Knox assumes control of Reformation in Scotland	
	1542: Pope Paul III establishes papal Inquisition in Rome	
	1543: Pope Paul issues Index of Forbidden Books; Protestants burned at the stake by Spanish Inquisition	
Martin Luther (1546)	1545: Council of Trent convenes 1546: Religious Civil War in Germany; Martin Luther dies	
Henry II (France: 1547-1559)		
Edward VI (England: 1547-1553)		
Mary Tudor (England: 1553-1558)	1554: Catholics have civil rights restored in England under "Bloody Mary"	
Thomas Cranmer (1556)	1555: Religious Peace of Augsburg	Paul IV (1555-1559)
Ignatius Loyola (1556)		

1500

1550

Expanded edition of the *manuals*, now the "handbook of the Reformation"

Philip Melancthon (1560)

Francis II (France: 1559-1560)
Charles IX (France: 1560-1574)

John Calvin (1564)

1562: Third session of Council of Trent begins inaugurating real reform; French Huguenots massacred at Vassey and French Wars of Religion begin; *Thirty-Nine Articles* published in England
1563: Council of Trent ends; Puritanism appears in England   *Pius IV (1560-1565)*
1564: John Calvin dies; Philip Neri founds Oratorians in Rome

1567: Duke of Alba begins persecution of Protestants in Netherlands   1568: Jesuits establish mission in Japan

John Knox (1572)

1572: St. Bartholomew's Day Massacre; John Knox dies   1573: Huguenots granted temporary amnesty in France

Henry III (France: 1574-1589)

1577: *Book of Concord* prepared by Lutheran theologians
1579: John of the Cross writes "Dark Night of the Soul"   1580: Jesuit missionaries secretly arrive in England

Teresa of Avila (1582)
Charles Borromeo (1584)
Mary Stuart, Queen of Scots (1587)
Catherine de 'Medici (1589)
John of the Cross (1591)
Philip Neri (1595)
Peter Canisius (1597)

1588: Pope Sixtus V founds Vatican Library   *Sixtus V (1585-1590)*

1593: King Henry IV declares, "Paris is worth a Mass," and becomes a Catholic
1594: Richard Hooker's popular spiritual works appear in England
1598: Edict of Nantes grants freedom of worship and press to Protestants in France

Henry IV (France: 1589-1610)   *Clement VIII (1592-1605)*

1600

James I (England 1603-1625)

1606: Guy Fawkes and Catholic coconspirators sentenced to death in England

1611: King James Bible published

1615: Jesuits number 13,112 members in 32 provinces

1618: Thirty Years' War begins

Francis de Sales (1622)

1622: King James I dissolves English Parliament
1623: Blaise Pascal born in France
1624: George Fox, founder of the Quakers, born in England; Cardinal Richelieu becomes first minister of France

Charles I (England: 1625-1649)

1633: Inquisition forces Galileo to repudiate Copernican theories   *Urban VIII (1623-1644)*

Cornelis Jansen (1638)

1640: Jansen's *Augustinus* published posthumously

Galileo Galilei (1642)
Armand-Jean Cardinal Richelieu (1642)

1642: English Civil War begins

> Single dates in parentheses indicate an individual's date of death; dates spanning a number of years refer to time in office.

Secular Rulers

Richard Hooker (1647)

Louis XIV (France: 1643-1715)

Oliver Cromwell (1658)
Vincent de Paul (1660)
Blaise Pascal (1662)

Charles II (England: 1660-1685)

Peter the Great (Russia: 1682-1725)

George Fox (1691)

William and Mary (England: 1689-1702)

Auguste Francke (1727)

Jonathan Edwards (1758)

Voltaire (1778)
John Wesley (1791)

Innocent X (1644-1655)

Innocent XI (1676-1689)

Clement XIV (1769-1774)

Single dates in parentheses indicate an individual's date of death; dates spanning a number of years refer to time in office.

1648:	Peace of Westphalia ends Thirty Years' War
1649:	King Charles I of England beheaded
1653:	Cromwell becomes Lord Protector of England; Blaise Pascal joins Jansenist community at Port-Royal in France
1678:	Catholics excluded from both houses of English Parliament
1682:	King Louis XIV forces Huguenots in France to convert to Catholicism
1685:	Louis XIV revokes Edict of Nantes (1598) and exiles French Protestants
1686:	Pietist Auguste Francke organizes Bible study groups in Germany
1689:	William and Mary become king and queen of England; Peter the Great becomes Czar of Russia
1694:	Voltaire born
1703:	John Wesley born
1738:	Wesley's Aldersgate experience
1741:	Jonathan Edwards advances Calvinist theology in American colonies
1751:	French *Encyclopédie* published
1761:	Voltaire's collected works published
1773:	Pope Clement XIV dissolves Jesuits
1778:	Voltaire dies

1650

1700

1750

INTRODUCTION

The Reformation:
Re-Formation, Revolution or Reintegration?

This book represents the fifth installment of a six-volume series on the history of the people of God. While the book focuses particularly on the Reformation, it also continues the general story of God's people. As a result, we will not limit ourselves simply to the religious revolution of the 16th century, as many histories of the Reformation do. Instead, we will attempt to connect the Reformation to the ongoing story of God's people, focusing not only on the events of the 16th century but also on the Reformation's effect on European life and society in the 17th and 18th centuries—years not generally regarded by historians as part of the Reformation proper.

Notice that I said "European" life and society. In an effort to restrain myself from writing lengthy volumes beyond the interest and budget of the average reader, I have had to impose certain restrictions on myself. This book therefore ignores completely the development of the Church in the New World and concentrates instead on delineating the intellectual, spiritual and doctrinal origins and aftereffects of the Reformation in Europe—all of which, of course, had tremendous consequences on events unfolding in the European colonies abroad.

Thus American readers will miss a discussion of the interconnection between events in Europe and the shape which Christianity has assumed in its American setting. I apologize in advance for this shortcoming and encourage you to read the final volume in this series, *The People of Hope: The Story Behind the Church in the Modern World*, where I attempt to trace briefly the origins of the Church in the

New World. Even there, however, I have not abandoned the European setting entirely; I hope at some point to prepare a volume devoted entirely to the rise of the Church in the Americas.

DEFINING REFORMATION

That preamble aside, let's begin our analysis of the Reformation by taking up the question of what the word itself means. In my Catholic grade school one of the Sisters told us that we could always tell whether an encyclopedia was trustworthy by looking up this period of history and seeing exactly how it was listed. If the entry read "Protestant Revolt," Sister informed us, we could be assured of the author's sound historical training. But if the entry was labeled "Protestant Reformation," then we should be somewhat suspicious of what we were about to read.

This story illustrates two facts of historical life concerning the Reformation: (1) It proves the strength of the old adage, "Whoever writes the captions controls history," and (2) it demonstrates how our denominational upbringing colors our approach to the Reformation.

In my own Catholic boyhood in the South, for example, I never heard the Reformation spoken of by my Protestant friends aside from a recitation of gory details concerning the infamous Spanish Inquisition. It wasn't until I enrolled in my freshman history course at the state university that I discovered that many *Catholics* had also been burned at the stake or otherwise persecuted for their religious beliefs during the Reformation. Up until that time *Reformation* had meant for me nothing more than persecution of Protestants by the Catholic Church, about which I felt (and still feel) ashamed.

Our upbringing unquestionably affects how we look upon and define the Reformation and, as a result, the "captions" we add to our historical pictures are bound to be somewhat determined by our personal past. Acknowledging these two facts of historical life at the outset, let's proceed to what I hope will be an unbiased definition of the principal term with which we will be dealing in this book.

What does *Reformation* mean? Does it literally mean a process by which the Church was "re-formed"? If so, then one must first presuppose a "de-formation" of the Church. By this view the Church at some point stopped being Church and started being something else. All that was needed, then, was to discover the point at which this breakup occurred and re-form the Church according to its pattern before the point of dissolution.

If one were to believe the Protestant reformers themselves, this

2

is what *Reformation* means. The reformers did not see themselves as starting a new Church, but as recapturing the Church's golden age as it existed at some pristine moment in the past and reestablishing that pure Church in the present. Yet the fact that the reformers looked upon their activities in this way does not make this "re-formation" theory correct. If there is anything that modern historians have to offer to 16th-century historians (whether Protestant or Catholic), it is the modification of their somewhat limited historical perspective.

Today, for example, no reputable historian accepts the reformers' view that the true Church is found only in the pages of the New Testament and that everything after the New Testament era is a slide into perdition. Modern historical and biblical studies have shown that the process by which both Church and Bible developed was not so simple as the reformers supposed. For example, instead of basing all Church authority on the Bible, as the Protestant reformers attempted to do, the early Christians in actuality looked upon *apostolic* authority as their norm of orthodoxy. The early Christians found this norm in a slowly developing body of writings which they considered to be apostolic in origin (the New Testament), as well as in the teaching of their bishops and in their Creeds. Thus one is hard pressed to find in the first Christian centuries the "pure Church" (based solely on the Bible) which the reformers believed they were reestablishing.

In order to accept the Protestant reformers' view of history, one must believe something about the past that is not true of life itself—namely, that we can successively discard past moments as if they cease to influence the present. In reality, each moment of time builds on that which preceded it and carries that past moment along to the future. As in the human personality itself, all that has existed before a given age still exists, exerting its influence on the present and the future. It is thus inaccurate to speak of the Church as in need of *re-formation*—in the sense of being completely re-formed—especially if we are to believe Jesus' own words: "...know that I am with you *always*, until the end of the world!" (Matthew 28:20b; emphasis added).

Instead of the Protestant reformers' view of the Church's development, we would be better served by a view which sees the Church developing organically from its origins in first-century Palestine to the 16th century, incorporating into its life all the experiences which helped to shape its 16th-century form. This does not mean that everything that went into fabricating the 16th-century Church was good. Some elements adopted along the way have come to be seen, by both Catholic and Protestant standards, as unnecessary or even harmful to the Church's mission in spreading the gospel of Jesus Christ.

3

Looked at in this way, the Church does need ongoing *reformation*—in the sense of needing to be constantly reminded of its principal mission of spreading the gospel of Jesus Christ. The difference between Protestant and Catholic reformers in the 16th century concerned the question of *how much* reform—that is, did the Church's entire structure have to be overthrown or could reforms be made *within* the structure?

Yet simply because the 16th-century Church's makeup included inauthentic elements does not mean that it was no longer Church. Further, there is nothing to indicate that the Church which existed during those 16 centuries—however much it may have been beset by abuses—was anything other than the empirical, physical institution represented by Roman Catholic Christianity in the West and by Orthodox Christianity in the East.

In *The People of the Faith: The Story Behind the Church of the Middle Ages*, we traced the development of the Byzantine ("Greek Orthodox") Church to the mid-15th century, when the Byzantine Empire fell to the Turks. Although some Orthodox theologians dabbled in Protestant thought, the Reformation as a whole had little impact on the Greek Orthodox Church and its Russian Orthodox successor.

Thus "the Reformation" really means "the reformation of the Western Church" and, more specifically, of the Roman Catholic Church, burdened at times by conduct that made a mockery of Christianity, but nonetheless still existing as Church. The Church, then, had not ceased to exist at the turn of the 16th century; so *Reformation* as literal "re-formation" is not a helpful definition.

A WORD ABOUT THE RENAISSANCE

In many discussions of the period of history we are about to explore, the word *Reformation* is not mentioned unless it is associated with the Renaissance; many textbook discussions of this period, for example, are entitled "Renaissance and Reformation." Chapter Two will highlight briefly the interrelationship between the Renaissance and the Reformation, stipulating beforehand that since this book is about the Reformation and not the Renaissance we will give rather scant attention to the latter. My decision to treat the Renaissance in this fashion was another result of the concern to limit the size and scope of this book. It makes for a fascinating discussion to explore the many cultural, philosophical and theological interconnections between the Renaissance and the Reformation, but such a discussion would take us somewhat far afield of our main focus, which is to trace the development

4

of Church history. By way of introduction, however, let's note several key points.

The Renaissance represented the culmination of a centuries-long process in which the European person was coming of age—psychologically, spiritually, culturally, intellectually. The Middle Ages represented the era of Europe's adolescence, an age in which both Church and state still attempted to provide fatherly care and provision for their children. And during the Middle Ages it was in many respects indeed necessary for strong authority figures to arise—in both Church and state—in order to give cohesion and stability to a society struggling to regain the lost political and cultural unity of the Roman Empire.

Beginning in the 12th and 13th centuries, however, the citizen of the Middle Ages began to require less fatherly assistance from either prelate or prince. Arts and learning made a comeback; more and more people became literate and capable of thinking for themselves. With the influx into the West of long-forgotten Greek philosophical and scientific treatises, medieval men (and the few women who were given an education) began to realize that much of what the Church had had to say about the world and humanity's place in it was, at best, out of touch with a far superior classical Greek and Latin wisdom and, at worst, often completely at odds with contemporary philosophical and scientific innovations.

This new spirit of adulthood and independence naturally had its effect on religion. As we discussed in *The People of the Faith*, the 12th and 13th centuries were an age in which the laity came back into its own as a spiritual force in Christianity. All over Europe arose lay communities which demanded the right of self-determination in spiritual matters. Some of these groups broke completely with the Catholic Church, forming something of a seedbed for Luther's revolt. Other groups remained faithful to Catholicism, but asserted the right of the layperson to read and interpret the Bible without close clerical supervision and to practice forms of devotion and contemplative prayer previously reserved for priests and religious.

The impulse for more autonomy in spiritual matters was matched by a corresponding quest for independence in secular matters; artists, writers, philosophers, scientists and scholars of every type yearned for the intellectual freedom which had characterized classical Athens and Rome. The thinkers and artists of the past were venerated as paragons of virtue, wisdom, style and grace in contrast to the staid and inflexible culture of the recent medieval past. Thus, beginning in the 14th century in Italy and spreading to the Low Countries and to England, the spirit which we capsulize by the word *Renaissance*— "re-birth"—superseded

5

the spirit of the Middle Ages.

A new, more vibrant, more confident and optimistic outlook took hold of art, literature, philosophy and science. Renaissance culture came to be identified with "the new man," a creature capable of living without the paternalistic supports of the past. Renaissance man was supremely confident of his own power, a power that was entirely human, and suspicious of the Church's insistence on Divine Providence and grace as the foundations of human existence. With the coming of the Renaissance, Europeans felt that they could now provide their own answers to the great questions of life, and the form these answers took often diverged from the doctrine which the Church had long taught.

Given this environment it is not surprising that both Catholic and Protestant reformers hearkened back to a supposed golden age from which they could draw support and guidance for their program of restoring the Church to a condition of spiritual vigor. For Catholic adherents to the Renaissance, this "past" included the teachings of the Church Fathers, the Bible and that portion of the classical tradition which could be incorporated into the Christian worldview. Catholics who adopted the methods of the Renaissance—men such as Thomas More and Erasmus—tended to integrate the culture and wisdom of the non-Christian Greek and Latin past into traditional Catholic teaching. For them the Renaissance promised revitalization—not the destruction—of the Church's worn-out structures.

Protestant reformers, however, accepted only the *method* of the Renaissance—that is, the quest to bring the wisdom of the past into the present. Although most Protestant reformers were well-schooled in the Greek and Latin classics, they eschewed the Renaissance reverance for the supposed wisdom of the *non-Christian* past. For them the past meant simply the Christian past, which most believed could be found entirely in the Bible.

For the Protestants the Renaissance by and large stood for all that was wrong with the Church—namely, the attempt (as the Protestants saw it) to integrate non-Christian with Christian values. As the popes of the 15th and 16th centuries eagerly embraced the Renaissance, Protestant reformers denounced them for attempting to turn the Bride of Christ into the Whore of Babylon. In so doing the Protestant reformers at the same time castigated the entire spirit of the Renaissance, and especially the Renaissance emphasis on humanity's power to control its own destiny. Largely in reaction to this spirit, Protestant reformers created a theology which so overemphasized God's sovereignty that it virtually eliminated humanity's capacity to order its own existence—and hence we arrive at the celebrated controversy between faith and works and the Protestant definition of predestination.

An underlying theme of the Reformation—and of this book—is the differing emphases given by Protestants and Catholics to the role which humanity plays in its relationship with God. The Protestant reformers, influenced to a great extent by a negative reaction to the self-assured pride in human potential which the Renaissance spawned, tended to make humanity more passive in the God-human relationship. Catholic reformers, on the other hand, tended to remain with the more traditional "partnership" view which had characterized the fifth- and sixth-century Semi-Pelagian debates over St. Augustine's teaching on predestination. (See *The People of the Creed*, pp. 134-138.)

In other words, Catholic reformers wanted to assign humanity more of an active role in the God-human relationship. They insisted that humanity, through its own efforts, can *respond* to God's grace in contrast to many of the Protestants who simply asserted that God's grace in effect "conquers" the inert human soul without humanity playing any role in the process of salvation. This dichotomy between the passivity and activity of the human *will* is a theme to which we will constantly turn in the pages ahead. Further, the entire relationship in the Christian's life between that which is human and that which is divine will begin to occupy center stage toward the end of this book and into the following volume, *The People of Hope: The Story Behind the Church in the Modern World*. We will thus watch the development of this relationship closely as it is described by Protestants on the one hand and Catholics on the other.

The main point here is that both Catholics and Protestants during the Reformation saw themselves as going back to a past golden age in an effort to reform the Church, and in so doing they were influenced principally by the spirit of the Renaissance. Both Catholic and Protestant reformers, then, thought of Church reform in terms of a going-back rather than in terms of a going-forward.

Yet neither Protestants nor Catholics were entirely true to their principles in this respect: Both found it necessary to bring certain innovations to the rescue of their doctrine. By and large, however, the Catholic reformers adhered more closely to the past, and the Protestant reformers branched off into new directions. This leads us, then, to two understandings of the term *Reformation* which more accurately suggest the actual state of affairs during this period of history than the concept of "re-formation" discussed earlier.

Two Better Understandings of 'Reformation'

Reformation as Revolution

A more accurate definition of the Protestant phase of the Reformation is "religious revolution." *Revolution* here can be defined as a transformation of an institution's structure into an entirely new structure. In the 16th century, wherever the Protestant reformers succeeded, a religious revolution overthrew the old Catholic order in favor of a new order.

If you have read the previous volume in this series, *The People of the Faith: The Story Behind the Church of the Middle Ages*, then you have some idea of what the Catholic model of the Church looked like. To describe the model of the Church as the Protestant reformers envisioned it is one purpose of this volume. Without getting ahead of ourselves, we can simply say that their model was radically different from the Catholic model. This Protestant model essentially transformed Church structure. That is why we can say that the Protestant Reformation was more precisely a religious revolution than a reformation of the Church.

As we shall see, the Protestant model which emerged was anything but homogeneous and self-consistent. Yet it differed so extremely from the Catholic model that it is not really accurate to speak of the Protestant Reformation as simply a *going-back* to the Church's origins; rather, it was a *going-forward* to something new.

Religious revolution is not necessarily harmful. Christianity itself may be thought of as an example of a salutary religious revolution. Yet, for a revolution to be truly successful, that which provides the essential link to the past must not be discarded. In our own American Revolution, for example, while basic political structures were irrevocably changed, the revolutionaries nonetheless incorporated into their new system a healthy respect for such traditional English values as the common law and the right of private property.

Here, it seems to me, is where the Protestant reformers failed. Their impulse to go forward was a sound one. Catholic leaders themselves, such as Erasmus and Thomas More, wanted to bring the Catholic Church into the contemporary world of the 16th century. Such Catholics criticized the Church for clinging to past traditions for their own sake and for not adapting these traditions so as to make the gospel relevant to the new man and woman of the early modern era. Yet these Catholic critics realized the danger in going forward so recklessly as to destroy all ties with basic Christian traditions.

8

For reasons that we will discover in the pages ahead, the Protestant reformers were not as cautious. While Martin Luther himself tried to incorporate many traditional Catholic values into his revolution, the floodwaters which he released often washed away the entire edifice of traditional Christianity and eventually drowned the very concept of tradition itself.

Because of the Protestant flood, Catholic reformers hesitated to go forward and relied exclusively on going back, on reestablishing the ancient Catholic tradition. The Catholic phase of the Reformation, then, might be defined as "religious reintegration."

Reformation as Integration

By the start of the 16th century nearly everyone acknowledged that the Catholic Church was sorely in need of reform—"reform" meaning here the termination of abuses and the reinstitution of gospel values within the life of the Church. Whether Catholic reform would have taken place without the religious revolution undertaken by the Protestant reformers is something we will never know. My own conviction is that widespread and lasting Catholic reform would not have occurred without the spark of the Protestant revolution. Thus, in my opinion, Catholics can look upon the Reformation as something of a positive phenomenon.

Whatever the case, once the Protestant religious revolution began, Catholic reform also began to take place—and it took place in a way more in keeping with the spirit of the Renaissance than did the Protestant revolution. That is because the Catholic reform sought a reintegration and reestablishment of Catholic tradition as it had developed during the previous 16 Christian centuries. The Catholic reform, then, may be thought of more as a *going-back* than a *going-forward*.

So the Reformation really comprised two different impulses: a Protestant revolution and a Catholic reintegration, a Protestant going-forward and a Catholic going-back. Both going back and going forward are valid goals for anyone seeking Church reform. The tragedy of the Reformation was the lack of a consistent program of unified Church reform for integrating both impulses. Or, to put it another way, Protestants and Catholics failed to harmonize the two thrusts of the Renaissance—the emphasis on the past as a golden age and the quest to make of the modern world something radically different from the medieval world.

9

A Time of Anguish

This, it seems to me, is why we can look upon the Reformation as a time of the most profound anguish. Both Protestant and Catholic reformers were sincerely motivated to achieve something good. Protestants wanted to break the Catholic reliance on the medieval model of the Church and to bring the Church into modern times. Catholics wanted to preserve the traditional Christian values which had developed throughout the entire span of the Church's history, including the medieval period.

Protestants erred by ignoring the fact that the medieval Church—in the works of its greatest spokesmen, such as Thomas Aquinas—could establish its link to apostolic authority. Catholics erred, however, by being overly protective of the medieval model and by not acknowledging that authentic apostolic tradition could take on a new demeanor.

As a result, the Protestant reformers went forward with their revolution while the Catholics went back, reintegrating and reestablishing their ancient tradition. Neither recognized the value in the other's perspective, and the gap between them widened even further. In the end, Catholicism came close to being merely the *preserver* of apostolic tradition and not its *herald*, while Protestantism boldly proclaimed a gospel that departed increasingly from the one known by the apostles.

This situation engendered in the Western psyche an anguish which has colored the West's undertakings to the present day. Modern humanity badly needs to heal the division within the Church caused by the Reformation. Only a unified Christianity can authoritatively proclaim the gospel to a world which sorely needs to hear it.

CHAPTER ONE

BEFORE LUTHER

Secular and Religious Causes of the Reformation

It would be as inaccurate to say that Martin Luther caused the Reformation as to say that Herbert Hoover caused the Great Depression, or that the Japanese attack on Pearl Harbor caused World War II. In actuality no one person or event exerts sufficient control on an era to cause a drastic change in the course of history. Perhaps the only exception to that rule is Jesus of Nazareth, and that is because he not only began the religious revolution later known as Christianity but was also the very substance of that revolution.

The Reformation, on the other hand, had not one cause but many. Since we will devote ourselves in the pages ahead almost exclusively to the *religious* dimension of the Reformation, we should first say a word about the diverse *nonreligious* factors which contributed to its making. To come away from this book thinking that the Reformation was a purely religious phenomenon would be a great mistake. In reality, religious revolution was but one thread woven by the Reformation into the changing fabric of Western civilization.

NONRELIGIOUS FACTORS

The Growth of Nationalism and National Monarchies

European society about 1520 (see map, p. 13) was no longer dominated by the medieval two-power theory of government in which all earthly authority was thought to be divided between emperor and pope. By this time powerful nation-states (chiefly France, England and

Spain) had successfully consolidated their power under the rule of sovereign kings who asserted their independence from both pope and emperor.

Neither Italy nor Germany could accurately be called nations at this stage of their political development. Renaissance Italy, as we shall see more fully in Chapter Two, was a loose collection of city-states and duchies. As for "Germany," there really was no state with such a name. (Germany as a unified state did not come into existence until 1871.) Instead, in that area of Europe where German was spoken, there existed a somewhat fragmented entity known as the Holy Roman Empire. Despite the Empire's political disunity, however, German nationalism was a powerful force.

The German Empire of Luther's day was an aggregation of principalities, each seeking to advance its own interests. The princes of the Empire usually felt chafed by the emperor's attempt to bind their lands together into a united state.

In 1356 seven of the most powerful princes successfully asserted the right to be designated the emperor's *electors*. These seven electors consisted of the archbishops of *Mainz, Trier* and *Cologne*, the count of the *Palatinate* province (on the Rhine), the "margrave" (a noble ranking below a duke) of the province of *Brandenburg*, the duke of the province of *Saxony* and the king of *Bohemia*. Along with the emperor, these seven men held the destiny of the Empire in their hands; any given emperor had to treat them with respect so as to assure his family's hereditary control of the imperial office.

In addition to the German-speaking principalities, the Holy Roman Emperor controlled various principalities elsewhere in Europe. Imperial domination of European lands reached its peak when Charles V became emperor in 1519. By inheritance, Charles became sovereign ruler of the various German-speaking principalities, Burgundy (part of northern France and Belgium), what we call Holland, Spain (with all of its colonial possessions in America) and the kingdom of Naples (the southern half of Italy). It is easy to understand why such a powerful emperor was looked upon as a hostile threat by developing nation-states, like France and England, and also by the papacy, which was literally surrounded by imperial territory.

For our purposes the significance of Charles's accession to power lies in the fact that many of the lesser lords who lived in "his" lands looked upon these lands as "theirs." Further, no longer did the idea of empire universally appeal to many of Charles's ordinary subjects. Many people were coming to regard the sovereign of their *local principality*—not the emperor—as their true temporal ruler. Charles's

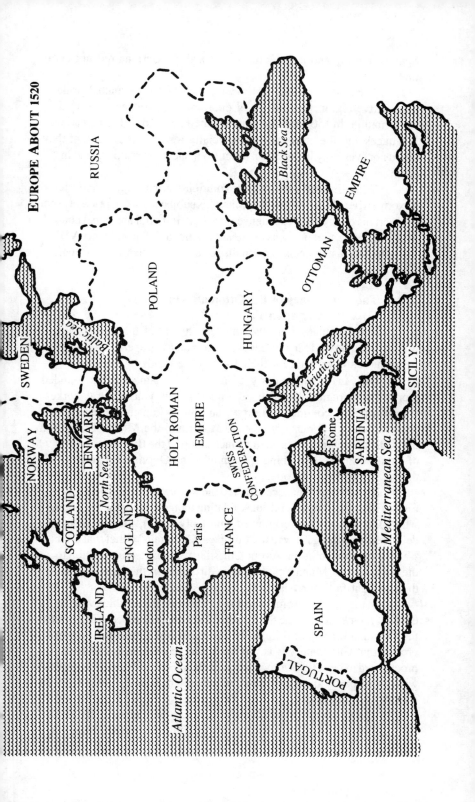

EUROPE ABOUT 1520

Spanish rearing and his ineptitude at speaking German did not help matters.

Thus, nationalistic sentiments, such as the Germans' pride in their native region, were to be of enormous significance during the Reformation. In 1500 people cherished their newly developing national languages and literatures. They especially resented the fact that they could not even pray in their own tongue but had to worship instead in Latin.

When Luther's religious revolution started, Duke Frederick of Saxony (where Luther lived) exploited his subjects' Saxon pride in order to assert his duchy's independence from both imperial and papal control. Much the same situation was to prevail in England, where Henry VIII manipulated his subjects' nationalistic fervor to establish his own Church.

The Supremacy of the Ottoman Turks
Over the Christian East

The Ottomans were the "nuclear threat" of the Reformation period. Just as we fear nuclear war, so many Europeans during the Reformation era feared for their lives at the hands of the Turks.

Early in the 14th century, a Turkish chief named Osman founded a principality named Osmanli (Ottoman) in Bithynia (central Turkey). Ottoman power continued to grow, and the Ottomans eventually achieved complete mastery of Asia Minor and the Middle East. From the mid-15th century on, after they had captured the Byzantine capital of Constantinople (renaming it Istanbul), the Ottomans regularly threatened Western Europe.

The Ottoman menace affected the Reformation in several ways. First of all, by capturing and consolidating their power in the very lands where Christianity had originated (the Holy Land), the Ottomans delivered a crushing blow to the European Christians' belief that theirs was the supreme religion. As one Christian region after another fell to the followers of Muhammad, many Christians in the East exchanged their ancient faith for Islam.

In the minds of some Western Christians, the terrible events in the East seemed to presage the Endtime. Yet other Europeans interpreted the Ottoman onslaught differently. To them, the Ottomans' success proved that Christianity was not the supreme religion it had been proclaimed to be. The Ottoman advance thus seemed to prove that there was at least parity among religious beliefs, if Christianity was not indeed inferior to other faiths.

The Ottomans were able to influence the course of the

Reformation in still another way. After Luther's revolt, European monarchs became more openly indifferent to Christianity. They not only ignored the pope's repeated call to fight the infidels; they even allied themselves with the Turks when expedience dictated. Christian soldiers would thereafter find themselves engaged in warfare against armies comprised of both infidel and Christian mercenaries. Evidently the only interest "Christian" princes wanted to serve was self-interest. The effect of this was devastating, both to Christian morale and to the concept of a unified Christian civilization.

The End of Scholasticism
During the Middle Ages every aspect of life was coordinated into a holistic Christian synthesis. This was especially true of intellectual activity. The great scholars of the Middle Ages, particularly Thomas Aquinas, had achieved an impressive synthesis of faith and reason. Yet barely three decades after Aquinas's death in 1274, William of Ockham developed a new method for approaching theology.

Aquinas had taught that natural law (the law God places within his creation) is based entirely on God's mind. Thus, since the all-perfect God cannot change his mind, natural law is *unchanging* and at the same time *knowable* by a rightly reasoning humanity. Ockham disagreed with Aquinas and taught instead that natural law is based not on God's mind, but on his will. And whereas God's mind cannot change, he said, God's will can. Thus the natural law is no longer absolutely fixed.

Such concepts as absoluteness and immutability, Ockham said, are merely humanity's way of circumscribing God. In reality, he continued, we know nothing certain about God, not even that he is omnipotent. Further, we cannot even say for sure if *any* absolute truth exists. The only things we can know for sure are individual things. For example, while we may know that John and Mary exist, we cannot reason from their individual existence to the existence of a universal reality called humanity.

Gabriel Biel, the last great Scholastic philosopher (1410-1495), elaborated upon Ockham's system at the University of Tubingen in Germany. Here he exerted great influence upon theological education throughout Germany—including Luther's own education. Like Scotus and Ockham, Biel believed in the supremacy of will over intellect. For him, human beings were not rational but volitional animals. Actions are right only because God wills them to be so, Biel said, and not because they are in accordance with God's purpose for his creation. Thus, he said, one cannot really know what is right; one must simply determine God's will and blindly follow it.

The irony of Biel's influence upon such reformers as Luther lies in the fact that while adamantly expressing their contempt for Scholasticism (having never really appreciated the true Scholasticism of Thomas Aquinas) the Protestant reformers nonetheless subconsciously adopted much of Biel's philosophy. We see this particularly in the Protestant doctrine of predestination, which Luther advanced and Calvin perfected. According to this doctrine, the inscrutable God in his salvific plan wills that only a fraction of humanity be saved. The irrationality of such a decision cannot be understood; it must simply be accepted.

Through Luther's and Calvin's efforts, Thomas Aquinas and the best of the Scholastic tradition, along with Ockham and Biel, were all lumped together by Protestant theologians under the heading of "damnable philosophy." This inadequate awareness of medieval Scholasticism started with Luther and affected all future Reformation theology.

Economic, Educational and Social Factors

Europe on the eve of the Reformation was ripe for a revolution—if not for a religious revolution, then any revolution. The lower classes everywhere were seething with unrest. Toward the end of the Middle Ages, as people gradually developed a sense of their own autonomy and self-worth, peasant and agrarian revolts became a common occurrence all over Europe.

At the same time in the cities, a new middle class had developed that was much more highly educated than the lower classes traditionally had been. These *bourgeoisie* (in French, or *burghers* in German) eliminated the economic basis of feudalism. The new middle class did not need feudal lords to guarantee its financial security as the peasants had; rather, the new urban classes could earn money quite well by themselves. Indeed, the middle class on occasion amassed fortunes that put their noble betters to shame. As a telling illustration, Emperor Charles V once was forced to borrow money from a burgher to pay for dinner.

From the middle class came new commercial barons and great banking families, such as the Fuggers in Germany, who replaced the nobility as the financiers of warfare and other state projects. Many princes and knights hated these newcomers on the social and economic scene, declaring—in the words of one prince—that they "should be driven out like wolves."

Yet the merchants, bankers and financiers transformed the culture of Europe into one based on education, hard work, earned wealth

16

instead of inherited wealth, and the right to unlimited advancement for the common man. To protect their interests the new classes insisted on new laws and new theories of government. Law and politics thus ceased to be based on Church law and developed instead along purely secular lines. The Church and Christian morality were superseded in the marketplace by commercial law and the profit motive.

The invention of a printing press with movable type in 1453 further contributed to the increasing independence and autonomy of the lower and middle classes. Once such classes could read they could think for themselves; they no longer depended on their lords and their priests for knowledge.

By 1500, therefore, the middle class and portions of the peasantry had achieved a dramatic improvement in their status. All that the new class of people needed was someone who could organize them for a common cause. Luther became for them that "someone," and his religious revolution became their "cause."

When Luther began to proclaim liberation from Rome, many Europeans heard him also proclaiming the dawn of a new day for them, a day in which the privileges of noble birth would be forever destroyed in favor of privileges which could be earned only by education and hard work.

RELIGIOUS FACTORS

In the next chapter we will discuss one religious factor which can be considered the immediate cause of the Reformation—the papacy's fascination with the Renaissance. But before reaching that discussion, let's summarize several other religious factors underlying the Reformation. Since we discussed several of these factors in greater detail in *The People of the Faith*, we will present only a brief summary here.

The Continuing Impact of Wycliffe and Hus

The Englishman John Wycliffe (1330-1384) and the Bohemian John Hus (1372-1415) had already tapped the deep resentment which the nationalistically-minded lower classes felt toward Rome's domination of their local Churches. Thus, before Luther arrived on the scene, the ground had been plowed by these proto-revolutionaries.

Wycliffe and Hus urged the Church in England and Bohemia, respectively, to give the vernacular Bible to the laity and to allow the Mass to be celebrated in the vernacular. Hus fought for the laity's right to receive Communion under both species. Both men spoke of the

Church not as an empirical institution but as a spiritual, unorganized society of those whom God had predestined for salvation. Each man would have replaced the hierarchical priesthood with the priesthood of all believers.

Luther succeeded where Wycliffe and Hus failed simply because the time was not yet ripe for the full acceptance of their views. A century after Hus was burned at the stake and Wycliffe's bones were disinterred from consecrated ground, however, the various forces we have already discussed combined to form a highly volatile compound of forces needing only a spark to ignite them into a widely popular movement. Luther provided that spark.

The Influence of the New Spirituality

As we saw in *The People of the Faith*, a new spirituality developed from the 14th century onward had brought the contemplative and mystical prayer traditions previously reserved to monks and nuns into the everyday lives of the laity. A prejudice against the possibility of lay sanctity had dominated Christian spirituality during the Middle Ages. With the formation in the 13th century of lay communities devoted to prayer, evangelization, poverty and service of others, however, it was amply demonstrated that priests and religious had no corner on holiness. As Christians for the first time in centuries heard lay evangelists preach the gospel, and as Christians witnessed the exemplary lives lived by new lay contemplatives, many people wondered why their priests were not as holy as their lay brothers and sisters.

In fact, the state of clerical sanctity was abysmal. Everyone in the late Middle Ages, loyal Catholics included, had horror stories to tell of priests blatantly violating the law of celibacy; of ignorant priests who could neither read nor preach an intelligible sermon; of priests and bishops who bought their offices and in turn leased them for profit to the highest bidder while they themselves went in search of more pleasurable ventures; of monks who lived like rajas in monasteries that were little more than bordellos; of clergy of all ranks who bled their flocks white for money which they spent not for the Church but on their own political projects.

It is little wonder that many Christians well before Luther had already lost confidence in the ordained clergy. By Luther's time a considerable population (especially in the Low Countries and along the Rhine) had proven, at least to itself, that it could lead a holy life without priests, sacraments or the institutional Church.

The Growing Disrepute of the Papacy

As we saw in *The People of the Faith*, the medieval papacy reached its lowest point with the episode known as the Babylonian Captivity, a name given to a period (1309-1377) in which the popes lived in Avignon, France, as puppets of the French king. As we shall discover in the next chapter, the shameful record established by the popes at Avignon was exceeded by the Renaissance popes. Thus the entire period from the mid-13th century to Luther's time was dominated by papal decadence.

Along with the usual category of personal vices, the popes during this period were especially afflicted by the inability to realize that the medieval theory of Church-state relations no longer exerted any influence on society. In the early Middle Ages, there had at times been valid reasons for popes to make political alliances with kings and emperors and to conduct their affairs in the way of secular princes. In earlier times, both Italy and the entire Western Church needed a strong centralizing force to stave off the disintegration which nearly destroyed Western society after the fall of the Roman Empire.

But by Luther's day strong monarchs and, in some countries, representative assemblies had arisen to provide political cohesion for Western society. The papacy was thus no longer needed as a political force. Everyone seemed to know this but the popes. Late-medieval Christians wanted their pope to be a spiritual father who led by moral example rather than a conspirator after political power, as was actually the case.

In addition, the popes deliberately blocked needed Church reform. After the Babylonian Captivity, Catholic leaders in every nation of Europe resolved to reform the Church, beginning with the papacy. Thus began the conciliar movement, an attempt to bring all the bishops, lesser clergy and noble laymen into the decision-making process of the Church. Yet the popes refused to cooperate with the various councils, seeking instead to sabotage those councils so that their own views of Church authority held sway.

In *The People of the Faith* we discussed the final attempt at medieval conciliarism—the ill-fated Council of Basle, a series of meetings to reform the Church attended by various bishops and abbots between 1432 and 1449. We learned from that discussion how the last medieval pope, Eugene IV, successfully diverted the Council from its agenda and dismissed it.

When the popes finally caught the conciliar spirit (lukewarmly) and convened the Council of Trent (1545-1563), Luther's revolution had permanently captured many Christians for Protestantism. By the time of Trent, the failure of conciliar reform, as well as general papal disrepute, had created a point of no return for many Christians in virtually every land of Europe. It became the papacy's anguish to learn too late the meaning of Hosea's prophecy,

> When they sow the wind,
>   they shall reap the whirlwind.... (Hosea 8:7a)

CHAPTER TWO

ON THE EVE OF
LUTHER'S REVOLT

The Renaissance Church

As we said in the Introduction, the Protestant revolutionaries saw themselves as re-forming the pure Church of early Christian times. One would think that for these people a "re-birth" of culture such as the Renaissance would have great appeal, because both the Protestant revolutionaries and the Renaissance humanists (a term we will define shortly) saw themselves as going back to a classical golden age and reviving it. Despite identical intentions, however, the advocates of religious revolution arrived at conclusions about the past which differed radically from those of the humanists. In order to understand this, let's discuss two main features of the Renaissance—its humanism and its morality—to see how they affected the Protestant revolutionaries.

RENAISSANCE HUMANISM

The underlying mind-set of the Renaissance was known as *humanism.* Beginning in the 14th century with Italians like Francesco Petrarch (1304-1374), Renaissance scholars began to study the Greek and Roman classics in order to bring classical wisdom to bear on contemporary culture. The writings which these scholars studied were known collectively as *studio humanitatis*, or "humanities"—hence, the words *humanism* and *humanist*. Petrarch summarized the goal of humanism as putting an end to what he called "this slumber of forgetfulness" so that people could now "walk forward in the pure radiance of the past."[1]

21

Humanism as a scholarly method or procedure became very popular. Going back to the ancient past rather than relying on recent opinion came to be thought of as the only sound means of education, and many Protestant reformers such as Luther and especially Calvin were heavily indebted to humanism in this sense. Yet a distinction must be made between humanism as a *procedure* for finding knowledge and humanism as a *substantive body of knowledge* in itself. Renaissance humanists did not simply republish the ancients; they entered into a dialogue with them, developing their own Renaissance humanistic philosophy in the process.

Italian Humanism

In the 15th century, humanists in Italy founded their own academies, considering themselves to be following in the footsteps of such classical educators as Plato and Aristotle. In these academies the humanists developed a distinctly Renaissance conception of humanity.

They tended to view human beings in much the same way as Ockham had—that is, as volitional rather than rational creatures. For the humanists, one's emotions and passions were seen as locked in a struggle with one's reason. Most humanists thus believed that it was the human will and not reason which guided humanity's destiny. Petrarch expressed this dichotomy between will and reason by saying, "It is better to will the good than to know the truth."[2]

This viewpoint, of course, differed both from Thomas Aquinas's belief in the supremacy of the intellect and from the entire Scholastic conception of human beings as rational animals who can know the truth and control their passions accordingly. Whereas the Scholastics had put God, intellect and moral order at the top of their hierarchy of values, the humanists gave first place to human beings, freedom and human creative potential. And, whereas the Scholastics had been primarily religious in their orientation, the humanists were primarily secular.

Yet many humanists were Christians who often supplemented the pagan classics with the teachings of Augustine and the other Fathers. Thus began the tradition of "Christian humanism." Pico della Mirandola (1463-1491), for example, stressed in his *Oration* humanity's creative freedom, but placed that freedom within Christian parameters by reminding his readers,

> You will have the power to sink to the lower forms of life, which are brutish. You will have the power, through your own judgment, to be reborn into the higher forms, which are divine.[3]

By and large, however, the Italian humanists, while professing to be Christian, advanced frankly non-Christian themes in their writings. Niccolo Machiavelli (1469-1527) in *The Prince*, for instance, openly praised deception, deceit, trickery and any other vice that would serve his ideal prince's interests. As he put it, "When the very safety of the country is at stake there should be no question of justice or injustice, of mercy or cruelty, of honor or disgrace."[4] *The Prince* was a shocking but realistic testimony to the humanist belief in the ability of human willpower and initiative to master the forces of fate and nature. The artists, sculptors and scientists of the Italian Renaissance likewise demonstrated in their works this belief in an invincible human potential.

Desiderius Erasmus

The greatest Christian humanist, and the greatest scholar of his age, was born not in Italy but in Holland. Desiderius Erasmus (1469-1536) had received both a contemplative and a classical education, having studied in his youth with the Brethren of the Common Life (see *The People of the Faith*, p. 161) and then at the Universities of Paris and Oxford, where he became a master of classical Greek. Throughout his life Erasmus was to maintain (perhaps better than anyone since Augustine) a unique balance between classical learning and Christian faith.

Erasmus developed in his writings what came to be called "the philosophy of Christ." In this philosophy Erasmus criticized late medieval Ockhamism as a sterile and inflexible system of thought which had stripped Christianity of its mystery and passion. Erasmus placed the Bible at the center of Christian thought, declaring that the laity were sufficiently independent and intelligent to understand Scripture through their own reading.

For Erasmus, the core of Christianity was the love of Christ. He thus considered many devotional practices which had arisen during the Middle Ages, such as indulgences and relic worship, ridiculous distortions of the true gospel. In his most famous book, *The Praise of Folly*, Erasmus excoriated such practices: "What can be said bad enough," he asked, of those who "by the fumbling over their beads" pretend "they shall procure riches, honors, pleasure, long life, and lusty old age, indeed, even after death a seat at the right hand of the Savior?"[5] He condemned the popes for "their riches, honors, dispensations, indulgences, excommunications and interdicts."[6] And he wrote of the prostitute who counted "swill-bellied monks"[7] as her best customers.

Yet in the heat of his fury Erasmus still managed to display his reverence for the Catholic tradition which, he asserted, he was only trying to save from ruin. "What would Jerome say," he wrote, "could

23

he see the Virgin's milk exhibited for money..." and "the portions of the true cross, enough, if collected, to freight a large ship?"[8] The overriding theme of Erasmus's critique was the institutional Church's perversion of true Christianity. Commenting on Matthew 11:30, he wrote, "Truly the yoke of Christ would be sweet, and his burden light, if petty human institutions added nothing to what he himself imposed."[9]

Humanism's Effect on the Revolutionaries

Luther and the other reformers did admire Erasmus and the *northern* humanists greatly. In sampling Erasmus we can well appreciate the adage, "Erasmus laid the egg that Luther hatched." Erasmus, for his part, while at first approving of Luther's revolt, eventually broke with Luther, expressing his reasons in a letter he wrote to a cardinal in Rome: "I would rather see things left as they are than see a revolution that may lead to one knows not what...."[10]

With respect to *Italian* humanism, the Protestant revolutionaries regarded its philosophy as a perverse belief in the perfectibility of human nature. Thus, while humanism as a method was something they could accept, they rejected humanism as a substantive body of knowledge—or at least they rejected the Italian form of that body of knowledge. In place of the Italian humanists' belief in unlimited human potential, the Protestant reformers posited the utter depravity of human nature. And in place of the Italians' worship of human freedom, the reformers imprisoned humanity in the pit of predestination.

Since the worst of humanism, in the reformers' opinion, emanated from Italy and was fostered by the popes, the reformers eventually came to regard the entire achievement of the Italian Renaissance—its art, literature and science—as inimical to their ends. Consequently, the Protestants quickly came to have a negative view of all secular learning. One of Luther's lieutenants, Philip Melancthon (1497-1560), himself an educated humanist, bemoaned the correlation between the spread of Luther's revolution and the deterioration of learning.

RENAISSANCE MORALITY

The Renaissance belief in human potential and creativity ran contrary to the somber assessment of human nature that one finds in Paul's Epistles and in the writings of Augustine. Augustine's view on free will and grace (discussed in *The People of the Creed*) was the dominant moral theology of the Middle Ages. In a sense, what the humanists accomplished (or attempted to accomplish) was the liberation of Catholicism from Augustine's theology. The Protestant reformers, on the other hand, relied greatly on Augustine and reinterpreted his theology for their own purposes.

The problem with the humanists' emphasis on human freedom was that they had no moral theology of their own to replace Augustine. As a result, at the same time that learning and culture reached new peaks, morality reached perhaps the lowest point in all of Christian history.

The ideal of Renaissance humanism was not morality, but power and achievement. Had this ideal been reflected only in the lives of *lay* humanists, it would have perhaps not been so bad. What actually happened, however, was that much of the *clergy* also eagerly embraced the humanist ideal. That is one reason why the Renaissance may be thought of as a "cause" of the Reformation.

Clerical Corruption

When Luther visited Renaissance Rome in 1510 he was scandalized by the behavior of his fellow priests, several of whom frankly admitted to their serious German visitor that they didn't believe a word of Catholic doctrine and remained in their offices only because of the wealth and privilege these offices brought them. It is little wonder, then, that Luther went back to Germany fuming over the corruption which the Renaissance had brought to the Church. And it is also little wonder that he and other reformers took a very dim view of the art, culture and learning which came out of Italy.

Other Renaissance writings, too, illustrate how immoral much of the clergy had become. Giovanni Boccaccio (1313-1375), for example, had written a century before Luther of "the lewd and filthy life of the clergy."[11] And the satirist Pietro Aretino (1492-1556), demonstrating that conditions had not improved by Luther's time, wrote, "truly it would be easier to find Rome sober and chaste than a correct book."[12] And the historian Francesco Guicciardini (1483-1540) described the papal court as "an example of all that is most vile and shameful in the world."[13]

Lest one doubt the testimony of these non-saintly observers, the words of St. Catherine of Siena (1347-1380), a Doctor of the Catholic Church, would seem to substantiate the general report:

> On whatever side you turn—whether to the secular clergy of priests and bishops, or to the religious orders, or to prelates small or great, old or young, you see nothing but offenses; and all stink in my nostrils with a stench of mortal sin. Narrow, greedy, and avaricious, they have abandoned the care of souls. Making a god of their belly, eating

and drinking in disorderly feast, they fall thence forthwith into filth, living in lasciviousness, feeding their children with the substance of the poor. They flee from choir service as from prison.[14]

Catholic Reform Before Luther

We can perhaps now sympathize with Luther, writing from his monastery in staid and devout Germany, fulminating against the abuses which he had seen in pagan Italy. Yet Luther had seen only half the picture. It is characteristic of moral behavior that vice shouts while virtue whispers. Had Luther probed beneath the surface of Italian Catholicism, he would have found that Christianity had not disappeared and that the Church had not died. While public Catholicism was at times doing its utmost to betray the gospel, privately many Catholics were fighting against the moral decline. Even before Luther, then, the seeds of Catholic reform were being planted.

Throughout Italy, for example, Catholic preachers denounced abuse in high places. The Franciscan John Capistrano (1386-1456) preached penance and apostolic poverty throughout Italy and in Eastern Europe, and Bernardino of Siena (1380-1444) almost single-handedly reformed the moral climate in many Italian cities and towns. Pope Paul II believed that people were as impressed by Bernardino's words as the early Christians had been by the preaching of St. Paul.

A Dominican preacher, Vincent Ferrer (1350-1419), preached successful reform missions in France, Germany and Switzerland, performing great miracles and calling many souls to repentance. Another Dominican, Archbishop Antoninus of Florence (1389-1459), personally nursed back to health those struck down by plague. His reputation for sanctity was so great that popes and statesmen alike sought his guidance.

All of these men were eventually canonized as saints by the Catholic Church—an admission, in effect, that both saints and sinners of the Renaissance could find a home within Catholicism.

In addition to the reforming efforts of the established religious orders, new congregations were founded for the express purpose of reforming the clergy. The Theatines, for example, founded by Cardinal Gian Pietro Caraffa (the future Pope Paul IV) and Anthony Maria Zaccaria, called many priests to repentance. Over 200 Theatine priests themselves became bishops, thereby spreading the cause of pre-Lutheran Catholic reform throughout Europe.

Bishops, too, were called to repent of their sins. Archbishop Claude de Seyssel (1450-1520), in his *Treatise of the Threefold State of the Wayfarer*, vigorously condemned episcopal abuses. And Cardinal

Gasparo Contarini (1483-1542), in *On the Duty of the Bishop*, criticized bishops for ignoring their teaching responsibilities while too readily absorbing the humanist philosophy.

The principal abuse which these and other Catholics attacked was clerical greed. Everywhere priests, bishops, cardinals and popes were reviled for their avarice. Simony was commonplace: Priestly offices were on sale publicly, and young noblemen in every country lusted after the rich episcopal benefices and red hats which the papacy put up for auction. Bishops who had themselves bought their sees in turn parceled off parishes to the highest bidder.

Many dioceses had absentee bishops who never once visited the sees they had bought. It was not at all uncommon for noblemen to buy several sees at once and to live as bishop in only one or in none of them. Indeed, a famous example of this existed in Luther's Germany: The 23-year-old Prince Albert of Brandenburg was bishop of both Magdeburg and Halberstadt, in addition to being imperial elector of Mainz.

To counter such flagrant perversions of the priestly and episcopal offices, many Catholic preachers called the clergy to repent and to accept a life-style of apostolic poverty. Thomas Aquinas, who had taught that poverty was the only way to Christian perfection, was quoted to recalcitrant priests and bishops as Catholic authority for the reform position.

The Franciscan Friars Minor in particular (see *The People of the Faith*, p. 96ff) sought to turn the clergy's eyes from money and back to the gospel. The friars' preaching brought down upon them the wrath of many a wealthy prelate and, ironically, the condemnation as well of both Franciscan and Dominican generals and university rectors. The Church's moral life had sunk so low that the very followers of Francis and Dominic had succumbed to the lure of wealth, as is evidenced by Chaucer's stinging satire of the English friars.

Thus a great battle had been joined *within* the Catholic Church, well before Luther, between the partisans of evangelical poverty and the partisans of clerical wealth and privilege. Perhaps the greatest source of anguish for Catholics during the Reformation arose from the fact that this battle for too long was waged more successfully by partisans from the latter group. The principal reason for this predicament lay in the fact that the proponents of wealth and privilege were led by able generals—the very men who claimed to stand in the shoes of St. Peter.

THE RENAISSANCE POPES

Nicholas V

Like the other great cities of Renaissance Italy, Rome was beset by factional rivalries between great noble families. The Colonna and Orsini families controlled Rome and often made life miserable for the popes. A great part of the popes' energy was spent trying to gain security for the Papal States in an age when secular princes had ousted ecclesiastical lords as the great powers of Italy.

Into this maelstrom came Pope Nicholas V (1447-1455), a man determined to restore the papacy to its greatness—and to do so by capturing Renaissance culture for the Church. Nicholas reasoned that, since this culture was the greatest force of his day, the Church should not resist the Renaissance but embrace it—and, he hoped, co-opt it.

As a result, Nicholas spent the resources of his papacy to achieve this end. "All the scholars of the world," a contemporary observer noted, "came to Rome in the time of Pope Nicholas, partly of their own accord, partly at his request."[15] Nicholas spent a fortune on books, initiating a project that would culminate in the world-famous Vatican Library. He offered enormous rewards to any scholar who could best translate both the pagan classics and the Fathers of the Church into modern Latin and the vernacular. So grandiose was Nicholas's undertaking that one observer remarked, "Greece has not perished, but has migrated to Italy!"[16]

Looking around at Rome's shabby architecture, Nicholas resolved to beautify the city and to turn it into a showpiece befitting the "capital of the Renaissance," as he hoped the world would soon characterize Rome. Thus Nicholas began to build, as he put it, "noble edifices combining taste and beauty with noble proportions [that] would immensely conduce to the exaltation of the chair of St. Peter."[17]

So began the greatest refurbishing of Rome since imperial days—an undertaking so enormously expensive that Nicholas used the Jubilee Year of 1450 to entice the thousands of pilgrims coming to Rome to part with their money for indulgences, blessings, Masses and artifacts. One historian has discovered that in just one bank Nicholas deposited the 1986 equivalent of $25 million. As for other banks and for his own treasury, no one knows how much Nicholas earned for his beloved beautification project.

As we look at the magnificent Eternal City today, we may think that whatever amount Nicholas accumulated was well spent. Yet in those days Christians beyond the Alps had their doubts. They questioned the huge sums being spent—not just on churches, but on purely civic restoration projects as well. Particularly in Luther's Germany, the land with the greatest resources in Europe, good Catholics deeply resented the drain of wealth to support the pope's expenditures.

Calixtus III

Pope Calixtus III (1455-1458) succeeded Nicholas. He reigned for only three years, during which time he initiated a scandalous practice that would soon become a papal tradition: *nepotism*. A member of the Spanish Borgia family, Calixtus raised his unscrupulous nephews to high positions in the papal court. His nephew Rodrigo would become Pope Alexander VI.

Pius II

The Italians hated Calixtus and his Spanish entourage. They celebrated lavishly when he was succeeded by a refined and educated Italian humanist, Enea Silvio de' Piccolomini, who took the name Pius II (1458-1464).

Before becoming pope Pius had been a man of his times. Much like Augustine, he had resisted a Church career because of his preference for sexual promiscuity. Also like Augustine, he eventually turned from the promiscuous life and became a priest; he did not, however, relinquish his love for scholarship and the classics. Yet Pius did not imitate Nicholas V. Instead of spending like a profligate, Pius lived simply and spent little. Morally, he was above reproach. He even made public repentance for his earlier sins.

Pius's significance for the Reformation lies in his failure—despite his high degree of intelligence—to read the signs of the times. Princes, nobles and in many cases native bishops continually called for a reform of the papacy and Curia. When German bishops, sensing their flocks' restlessness, demanded another reform council, Pius sternly prohibited it. The popes still did not appreciate the force that nationalism exerted on Churches beyond the Alps.

Yet Pius himself constantly pleaded for reform. He was well aware of the tragic consequences in store for a Church plagued by corruption. In 1463, sensing that death was near, Pius sketched his own picture of the papal court:

> People say that we live for pleasure, accumulate wealth, bear ourselves
> arrogantly, ride on fat mules, trail the fringes of our cloaks after us,
> and show round plump faces beneath the red hat and white hood,
> keep hounds for the chase, spend much on actors and parasites, and
> nothing in defense of the Faith. And there is some truth in their words:

many among the Cardinals and other officials of our court do lead
this kind of life. If the truth be confessed, the luxury and pomp at
our court is too great. And this is why we are so detested by the
people that they will not listen to us, even when we say what is just
and reasonable. [18]

It would be the later papacy's great anguish to look back on Pius's
words as a prophecy that had not been heeded.

Paul II

Pius's reign represented the best which the pre-Luther
Renaissance papacy had to offer. In 1464 Cardinal Pietro Barbo became
pope. Before he took the name Paul II, he proposed that he be called
Formosus, "the good-looking one," thereby indicating the depth of his
narcissism. With Paul II (1464-1471) the expensive tastes of Nicholas
V returned to the papal throne. For example, he raised the cardinals'
yearly income to roughly the equivalent of $1 million and adorned
himself with a tiara that cost a fortune. Yet Paul did make an attempt
at reform by regulating the sale of indulgences.

Sixtus IV

Paul II was succeeded in 1471 by Cardinal Francesco della
Rovere, who became Pope Sixtus IV (1471-1484). A scholarly humanist
like Pius II and a nepotist like Calixtus III, Sixtus sought to aggrandize
both his own family's interests and the interests of Renaissance Rome.
Sixtus made his decadent 25-year-old nephew a cardinal and gave him
$1.5 million yearly to spend on his mistresses and other frivolous
pursuits. A second nephew, Giuliano della Rovere, would become Pope
Julius II.

Sixtus became a warrior pope, dedicating most of his energies
to restore the weakened Papal States to their medieval power. As a
result, Sixtus led all of Italy into a prolonged war that nearly lost the
Italian peninsula to the Turks. Sixtus's wars and his many art projects
(for example, the Sistine Chapel—named for him) nearly bankrupted
the papal treasury. When Sixtus died, the papal court owed debts of
$37.5 million (in today's equivalent).

The pope's military ventures, his practice of nepotism and
simony, the flaunted immorality of his relatives, the restoration of the
Papal States as a secular power—all these nearly destroyed respect for
the papacy outside of Italy and contributed greatly to making the
Reformation more and more inescapable.

Innocent VIII

Upon Sixtus's death mobs ruled Rome, running wild through the Vatican offices and stealing everything in sight. The conclave of cardinals which met in this hostile atmosphere to elect a new pope chose the placid and dignified cardinal-bishop of Genoa, Giovanni Battista Cibo, who became Pope Innocent VIII (1484-1492).

Innocent was a good father and family man although he had never bothered to marry. The kindly old "grandfather pope" spent his papacy doting on his children and grandchildren, arranging their marriages and celebrating their weddings in lavish parties at the Vatican, generously spending the Church's resources on wedding presents and honeymoons. In 1487 when he arranged for his son Franceschetto to marry Maddalena de' Medici (daughter of the powerful magnate Lorenzo de' Medici of Florence), Innocent at the same time concluded an alliance in which Lorenzo the Magnificent became the arbiter of papal policy. Until Innocent's death in 1492, the papacy's interests became those of the house of Medici.

It is little wonder that during Innocent's reign the papal court became the joke of Europe. To raise revenue the pope sold meaningless Vatican jobs to Roman social climbers, such as the 52 papal appointees who did nothing more than seal papal documents. Two of these "dedicated Church servants" revealed that during their two years in office they had forged over 50 official papal decrees.

Papal justice became a mockery. The Curia once sold a verdict of acquittal for the equivalent price of $2 million to a man who had raped and murdered his own daughters. Cardinal Rodrigo Borgia, who supervised the case, explained the travesty by intoning, "God desires not the death of a sinner, but rather that he should pay and live."[19] On that note of pious hypocrisy Innocent's pontificate ended and the saddest chapter in papal history began.

Alexander VI

The conclave of cardinals which met to elect Innocent's successor succumbed to the bribes of the Spanish Borgia family. They elected that family's champion, Rodrigo. He chose the name, as he put it, of the "Invincible Alexander."[20] Thus began a pontificate (1492-1503) appropriately dedicated not to the memory of the Christian saints but to the greatest warlord of antiquity.

Alexander's perversion of his papal calling became proverbial. He was known throughout Europe as the perpetrator of the most fiendish evils, and he appointed his own corrupt relatives and in-laws to positions of curial power. A contemporary witness said that "10 papacies would

31

not have sufficed for all of Alexander's cousins."[21]

Alexander also had no scruples about making deals with the Church's enemies. A letter to Alexander from the Turkish sultan promised the pope the equivalent sum of nearly $40 million, "with which Your Highness may buy some dominions for your children."[22] One of the most popular jingles of the day, sung throughout Italy, contained these words:

> The keys, the altars, Alexander sells, and Christ;
> with right, since he has paid for them.[23]

Further examples of Alexander's foul reputation are superfluous. It is enough to say that his papacy was but the culmination of a long process of papal decline. Yet toward the end of his reign Alexander had a change of heart. When his son Giovanni was murdered, Alexander interpreted the deed as God's chastisement. He openly confessed himself to be a fornicator, a power-hungry militarist and a simonist.

His remorse ran so deep that he even pledged to begin Church reform, telling a meeting of cardinals:

> We on our part are resolved to amend our life, and to reform the Church....Henceforth benefices [episcopal sees] shall be given only to deserving persons, and in accordance with the votes of the cardinals. We renounce all nepotism. We will begin the reform with ourselves, and so proceed through all ranks of the Church till the whole work is accomplished.[24]

It was a noble gesture which Alexander quickly forgot once the memory of his slain son grew faint.

Julius II

Guiliano della Rovere followed Alexander VI, adopting the name of another ancient warlord by calling himself Julius II (1503-1513). Julius was not so much a pope as a general. For 10 years he rode about Italy clad in armor, defending the interests of his Papal States.

At the same time, he was a great patron of Renaissance art. Thanks to Julius we have Michelangelo's Sistine Chapel ceiling. It was Julius who destroyed old St. Peter's and began the one that stands today. And, as we shall soon see, Julius's scheme for financing the construction of the great basilica—by granting indulgences to those who contributed to its cost—would, under his successor, provide the spark that ignited Luther's revolution.

While Julius was occupied in warfare, several cardinals were trying desperately to convene a reform council. When Julius got wind of the plan, he deposed the cardinals who had signed the document calling for a council. Yet some 27 cardinals and bishops met anyway, first at Pisa and then at Milan (1511). Undaunted, Julius convened a rival council in his palace, the Fifth Lateran Council, which he encouraged to dawdle along so as to accomplish nothing.

Leo X

The pope when Luther began his religious revolution in 1517 was Giovanni de' Medici, called Leo X (1513-1521). It was Leo who uttered those infamous words, so full of significance for Luther's revolt: "Let us enjoy the papacy, since God has given it to us."[25]

Leo epitomized all that was wrong with the Church on the eve of revolution. At age eight he had become an abbot. By the age of 13 he had been absentee bishop or abbot of 16 benefices. At 14 he was made a cardinal, and at age 37, still unordained, he was elected pope. He then proceeded to spend the equivalent of $25 million on his papal inauguration. The motto of Leo's papacy became, "I will think the matter over and see how I can satisfy everybody."[26]

Leo's papacy provides a study in contrast to Luther's religious sensibilities. Fulfilling the dream of Nicholas V, Leo turned Rome into the capital of the Renaissance world. The art and culture of antiquity was truly reborn under the pope's tutelage—all at a frightful price both economically as well as spiritually. It cost the papacy whatever spiritual credibility still remained.

The Spark of Revolution

In 1510 a German Augustinian priest, Father Martin Luther, was sent by his religious superior to the Curia to seek certain concessions for his Order. Years later Luther recorded his memory of the visit:

> At Rome I was a fanatical saint; I hurried through all the churches and clefts and believed everything that is fabricated there. I suppose I celebrated one or 10 Masses at Rome and was then almost sorry that my father and mother were still alive, for I should have been happy to rescue them from purgatory by my Masses and other excellent works and prayers.[27]

Elsewhere Luther described his "main purpose" in going to Rome as "my desire of making a complete confession from my youth and to become devout."[28]

A few years after Luther paid his visit to Rome, Pope Leo

initiated the scandal which precipitated the Reformation in Germany. Unable to pay for his enormously expensive and vain pursuits—even though he sold 1,353 newly created papal offices for over $110 million—Leo turned his avaricious eyes north to rich and faithful Germany. There he found the archbishop-elector of Mainz, Prince Albert of Brandenburg, seriously in arrears on his payment of various papal taxes.

A deal was struck: Leo needed money to complete construction of St. Peter's basilica begun under Julius II. He would authorize Albert and his agents for eight years to sell plenary indulgences—absolving from their sins all those who bought indulgences—with the understanding that Albert could keep half the proceeds and satisfy his debt to Rome with the rest.

Albert hired indulgence preachers who went forth carrying out Leo's scandalous enterprise. Some of the indulgence preachers even sold certificates which guaranteed absolution for all *future* sins. One preacher, the Dominican John Tetzel (1465-1519), preached the indulgences near the border of Luther's Saxony. When members of Luther's own parish crossed the border to purchase indulgences, Luther exploded in rage.

On October 31, 1517, he wrote to Prince-Archbishop Albert complaining that the preachers' "promises about indulgences lull the people into security and lack of fear."[29] Luther enclosed in his letter 95 theses (written in scholarly Latin) illustrating how erroneous the sale of indulgences was—according to *Catholic* theology. Luther also sent his theses to the various bishops involved in the indulgence scheme. When these bishops did not respond, Luther then sent his theses to theologians all over Germany. (There is insufficient evidence to support the popular story that Luther nailed the 95 theses to the door of the Wittenburg church.)

The revolution had begun.

CHAPTER THREE

FAITH VERSUS WORKS

The Evolution of Luther's Theology

Martin Luther, Augustine and Thomas Aquinas are the three pillars upon which postapostolic Christianity rests. Further, it is Luther more than any other figure who is responsible for the beginning of modern Western civilization. He was the conduit through which flowed the transforming energies that turned the Middle Ages into the early modern epoch. Of course Luther had help in initiating this process. The demise of Scholasticism, the rise of nationalism, the Renaissance—such forces as these preceded Luther and conditioned the environment into which he came. But it was Luther's religious revolution which drew all of these preparatory forces into a recognizable and irresistible movement for change.

EARLY DAYS

Martin Luther (1483-1546) traced his ancestry back to the peasantry of Thuringia, the vast forest territory which the Merovingian Franks had subjugated a thousand years before his birth. His father, Hans Luther, had sought to rise from the peasant class, by giving up farming to become a copper miner. The young Martin respected his parents' reverence for hard work and discipline. In later years, with perhaps a touch of unrealistic nostalgia, Martin reminisced, "They endured hard work. Now the world no longer does it. My parents kept me in the strictest order, even to the point of intimidation."[1]

Good German Catholics, Martin's parents provided the best

35

Christian education possible for their son. Martin excelled in Latin and liturgical music. His teachers were stern and strict, exceeding that "point of intimidation" which had characterized Martin's life at home. "From childhood I was so trained," Martin later wrote, "that I could not but turn pale and become terrified if I merely heard the name of Christ mentioned, for I was taught only to regard him as a stern and angry judge."[2] A brief period under the tutelage of the Brothers of the Common Life softened the harsh experience of his earlier education, but that early experience had nonetheless indelibly marked Luther's pysche.

At the University of Erfurt, Luther studied the then prevalent Ockhamist rendition of Scholasticism. In 1502 he received his bachelor of arts degree and, in 1505, a master's degree. Then, despite his father's opposition, Luther gave up higher studies in law and joined the hermits of Saint Augustine at Erfurt. His decision was perhaps prompted by an incident in which he promised St. Anne to become a monk if she would intercede for his deliverance from a lightning storm.

Ordained a priest in 1507, Luther was still gripped by the fear of God's anger; he almost fled from the altar in panic during his first Mass. Nonetheless, Luther's Augustinian superiors saw in the young priest a good candidate for a professor of theology. So Luther prepared for the doctoral degree in theology at the University of Erfurt, where he continued to experience Scholasticism under the Ockhamist guise. It was there also that Luther came under Gabriel Biel's influence (see pp. 15-16).

In 1508 Luther took a part-time position as lecturer in moral theology at the University of Wittenberg. During this period he began to experience the confusion which Ockhamism—with its skepticism of absolute values—would naturally produce in a serious scholar. Thus he began to teach that only Scripture could bring certainty to theological inquiry. In 1510 Luther made his visit to Rome, and in 1512 he became a doctor of theology and a professor of Sacred Scripture.

LUTHER'S QUEST FOR HOLINESS

From his earliest lectures on Scripture, we find in Luther that churning, tempestuous struggle to bring the wrathful God under control which would characterize his later theology. We find his concern with that principal question which motivated all of his study and preaching: How does humanity become holy in the presence of the all-consuming Fire? From Luther's earliest writings, the central theme of his later polemic is already stressed: "For not he who thinks himself humble, but he who thinks himself to be abominable and worthy of damnation is just."[3]

Luther's Spiritual Problem

Luther's struggle was principally a spiritual struggle: He was not primarily motivated by scholarly or theological interests. For Luther the Bible did not give knowledge *about* God, but knowledge *of* God. For that reason Luther threw himself into the Bible exclusively for the purpose of solving the great problem of his own existence which, as Luther might have posed it, was: "How can I, the unholy and miserable sinner, approach the wrathful God and appropriate his holiness?" This question dominated all Luther's biblical and theological study, all his teaching as a professor and his preaching as a priest, all his mental and emotional energies. Out of his struggle to resolve this dilemma evolved both Luther's theology and his religious revolution.

Luther saw the solution to his problem encased in Paul's discussion of *justification*. By justification Paul had meant something like "the being made holy." Luther felt that, if he could comprehend Paul's analysis and somehow apply that analysis to his own life, then *he* could become holy. Yet Luther yearned not just for an intellectual understanding of this holiness, but first and foremost for the *experience* of that holiness. Only then, Luther felt, would the nagging sense of his own sinfulness disappear.

Let's look briefly at the process by which Luther undertook his quest for subjective holiness, a quest, incidentally, which had colored much of late medieval lay spirituality before Luther ever approached the issue.

Justification and Imputed Righteousness

Luther began to develop his theology of justification—his understanding of how one could personally experience God's holiness—in several lectures delivered in 1515 and 1516 on the subject of Paul's Epistle to the Romans. Luther read Romans in what we could call an exclusively negative light. This is not to criticize his analysis; Romans does present a somewhat negative view of human nature. But Luther was so attracted to the negative elements in Paul's theology—finding a "kindred spirit" in Paul—that he virtually lost sight of the other, differing theological viewpoints presented by the New Testament. Finding in Romans the "justification" (pardon the pun) for his own sense of depravity, Luther held up Romans as the New Testament's principal theological statement.

The central conclusion of Luther's analysis involved the concept of *imputed righteousness*. Since this concept is so essential to the understanding of future Lutheran and Protestant theology, let's take a moment to discuss it in detail.

The starting point for Luther's theology is humanity's sin and God's holiness. To grow from sin to righteousness is the purpose of Christian life. The means by which one makes this inner transformation is faith. "If faith does not enlighten man and love does not free him," Luther wrote, "he cannot will or possess or do anything good; he can do only evil, even when he does good."[4]

This, of course, was pure Augustine and consistent with the position of the majority of other Catholic theologians of the day. But Luther went further, ignoring the tempering of Augustine's position by the Synod of Orange in 529 (see *The People of the Creed*, p. 137) as well as the interpretations given to Augustine by the Scholastics. Luther wanted Romans to be read strictly in the light of Augustine's unmitigated teaching on grace—the "pure" Augustine, Augustine at the very height of his counterattack against Pelagius, who had taught that human nature in itself possesses enough grace to achieve salvation.

In restoring God's sovereign grace as the be-all and end-all of Christian existence, Luther gave Augustine an interpretation that was Luther's own, an interpretation that squared with Luther's ongoing experience of God's work in his life:

> Therefore I struggled with myself without knowing that forgiveness was *indeed real* but that there was no taking away of sin *except in hope*, that is, that sin must be removed by the gift of grace, which begins to take it away so that henceforth it is no longer *reckoned* as sin.[5] (Emphasis added.)

Here we find in Luther's earliest discussions the doctrine of imputed righteousness. Notice that Luther says forgiveness is "indeed real," but sin is taken away only "in hope," so that it is no longer "reckoned" as sin. In other words, Luther is saying, God forgives humanity's sin by *imputing* to humanity God's own holiness.

Imputation is a legal concept which means to attribute or to credit to someone else one's own responsibility for an action or condition. The further connotation of the word is that the attribution or crediting is effected unjustly or without merit. Thus, in saying that God no longer "reckons" humanity's sin as sin, Luther means that God has unjustly (unjustly to God) *credited* humanity with the divine holiness.

The obvious question about Luther's theory of imputation is: Does God in forgiving our sin in fact *make* us holy, or does he only *reckon* us to be holy? Luther's answer was that God only reckons us to be holy—that is, God acts *as if* we have been made holy even though we have *not* objectively been made holy. In Luther's own words, "human nature justified is like a dung heap covered with snow."

Perhaps now it is clearer why I said earlier that Luther based everything on a personalistic and subjective reading of Romans, to the exclusion of other New Testament theology. How, for example, does Luther's theory of imputation square with Paul's words: "...if anyone is in Christ, he is a new creation. The old order has passed away; now all is new!" (2 Corinthians 5:17)?

Did Paul mean that God only "reckons" the Christian to be a new creation? Or did he mean that through the power of the Holy Spirit humanity is in fact raised to an objectively new level of existence? From his own experience, Paul seems to have understood the latter rather than the former. He writes elsewhere, "...the life I live now is not my own..." (Galatians 2:20a), suggesting strongly that justification works an empirical, objective change in the human soul. Paul was not saying that God acts *as if* there were now a condition of holiness in the soul, but that there is *in fact* a new holiness within the soul. For Paul, Luther's "dung heap covered with snow" was no longer a dung heap; rather, God had turned it into a mound of freshly fallen snow.

Luther's interpretation was obviously more in keeping with ordinary human experience—we rarely *feel* like "new creations," especially when we keep right on sinning after professing our belief in Christ. Luther addressed himself to this latter problem also.

'Simul Peccator et Justus'

Luther's early biblical lectures and writings introduced his teaching that a justified individual is "simultaneously a sinner and just" (in Latin, *simul peccator et justus*). Luther described such an individual as "a sinner in reality, but just by virtue of the consideration and the sure promise of God that he will redeem him from sin until he *completely* saves him"[6] (emphasis added). So, although he believed that one's *justification* by God occurred at a specific moment in time, Luther did not believe that one's *salvation* could be thought of as a finished result.

Catholicism likewise taught that salvation is a continuing process in which we are somehow both just and sinful at the same time. Where Luther differed from most Catholic theologians of his day was in denying the existence of *sanctifying grace*. Sanctifying grace was defined as God's own life within human beings enabling them to perform good works—that is, works of virtue and charity. The Scholastics had taught that this grace was normally attained through the sacraments.

Luther, however, based everything on *justifying grace*—that is, the grace of God enabling persons to become sanctified even *before* reception of Baptism or the other sacraments. Luther's rejection of sanctifying grace was a function of his attempt to construct a theology in which people were not involved in their own salvation. This reflected Luther's view that humanity was entirely passive before God, which, in turn, was a reaction by Luther to the Renaissance ideal of unlimited human potentiality.

Faith and Works

For Luther, then, justifying grace was the key to salvation, and the only way to receive this grace was through faith in Jesus Christ. Just as Jesus had been fully united to the eternal God and thus victorious over death, so too by faith we become united to Christ and victorious over sin. Justifying grace thus accomplishes our salvation, even if this salvation takes our entire lifetime to become fully realized.

As a result, Luther saw no need for "the sacraments of grace" which, he said, "help no one, but rather they harm anyone who does not approach in full faith. No, faith is already a justifying grace."[7] Elsewhere he wrote, "it is not the sacrament but *faith in the sacrament* that justifies"[8] (emphasis added).

Most Catholics would look upon the sacraments as expressions of faith. The reception of Baptism, for example, would be seen as an expression of faith in God's power to grant new life through the sacramental sign of poured water. But Luther saw the sacraments as expressions of human initiative, or "works." In his view, persons receiving the sacraments believed that God gave grace because they had first performed the "work" of going through the sacramental ritual, as if they had done their duty and now God "owed them" grace.

Whatever individual Catholics may have believed in Luther's day (or might believe now), Catholic theology did not teach that God "owed" anyone grace for going through a sacramental ritual. Luther was no doubt motivated to assume his position largely by the excesses of the indulgence controversy. For him the sacraments—like indulgences—represented one more means of "earning" salvation, one more "work" condemned by St. Paul as irrelevant to salvation.

Luther did not condemn all works, but works insofar as they were inspired by human initiative rather than by God's initiative. For Luther works were the *result* and not the source of justification—and with this Catholic theology agreed. Where Luther eventually parted company with Catholic teaching was in his denial of the efficacy of any human action toward good that was not preceded by justifying grace.

The Scholastics would have agreed with Luther on two points: that justification is by faith, and that faith is an unmerited gift of God. But the Scholastics had spoken of a "faith informed by love"—that is, a faith motivated by the natural human desire to know and serve God. This innate human impulse, the Scholastics said, could bring a person to *seek* the faith which justifies. Luther rejected this idea of faith informed by love. For him, faith was *a priori* to love or even the desire to love. Love could come only after one had been given the gift of justifying faith. Thus Baptism, for example, was not a *means* to that faith, but merely a *sign* of one's faith already received.

Without realizing it, Luther was actually positing faith in faith as the source of salvation, rather than faith in God's power to save through the ministry of the Church and its sacraments. In other words, Luther saw faith as the catalyst, as it were, to justification, but he so emphasized one's expression of faith that he turned that expression *itself* into the means by which God saves us.

In actuality, it is not our faith which saves us, but God. *Through* one's faith in Jesus Christ, God saves us, not *because* of our faith in Christ. God does not owe us salvation because of our expression of faith any more than he owes us grace because we have received the sacraments. As the apostle Peter put it, "Our belief is rather that we are saved by the favor of the Lord Jesus..." (Acts 15:11). Yet Luther virtually made the expression of faith a "work" by tending to make faith, rather than Christ himself, the means to salvation.

Luther's Position as Catholic

Luther's fundamental teaching—his insistence on the priority of God's grace before any human action which leads to salvation—was consistent with the Scholastic theology that Luther condemned. Both Augustine and Aquinas, the twin pillars of Catholic orthodoxy, had taught that any human action which moves toward God is in actuality but a *response* to God's prevenient grace (*prevenient* literally means "coming before"). Even Ockham, who stressed the freedom of the human will, stressed even more the absolute freedom of God, who was not "required" to honor human actions.

Therefore, when Luther condemned the Scholastics—"O Fools, O piggish theologians!"[9]—he was not really condemning the best in Catholic teaching. And up to the time of the indulgence controversy, Luther—insofar as his teaching on the priority of grace was concerned—was just another Catholic theologian expressing himself within the parameters of orthodox doctrine. As the indulgence controversy became more intractable, however, Luther adopted positions which clearly departed from the apostolic tradition.

THE INDULGENCE CONTROVERSY

The Early Stage

In his 95 theses, Luther developed his theology of indulgences. Written in Latin so that only well-educated theologians could understand them (Luther did not want to cause a public spectacle), the theses in themselves did not necessarily require an unorthodox reading. For example, Luther upheld the efficacy of acts of penance, did not reject indulgences *per se* but only their elevation above works of mercy and prayer, and acknowledged the validity of intercession for the souls of the dead. (Some people had bought indulgences for departed loved ones.)

Indeed, Luther even acknowledged in Thesis 6 the pope's authority to specify that sins can be forgiven upon satisfaction of certain conditions. Further, the general tone of the 95 theses was not one of rebellion against Catholic authority. Luther stressed again and again that he was merely proposing his theses for debate, emphasizing that he would accept correction if proven wrong. Bishop Adolf of Meresburg even remarked that Luther's theses should be translated into the vernacular and posted for the laity to read in order to warn them against "Tetzel's humbug."[10] (Tetzel was a leading preacher of indulgences; see p. 34.)

Spurred on by such support, Luther translated his theses and expounded upon them in his *Sermon on Indulgences and Grace* (1518). In this and in *Resolutions*, another treatise of the same year, Luther still showed himself to be a faithful son of the Church, declaring his purpose to be the preservation and not the destruction of Church authority. In an introduction to one of his works he wrote, "I intend to say and to assert nothing except what is contained primarily in Holy Scripture and then in the Church Fathers...and in canon law and the papal decrees."[11]

At this early stage of the indulgence controversy, a religious revolution could certainly have been avoided through compassionate and brotherly dialogue between Luther and the hierarchy. That such a dialogue never took place was not Luther's fault but the fault, in the last analysis, of Pope Leo X, who dismissed the German indulgence controversy as "the squabble of monks" and returned to his pleasures.

The Point of No Return

Rome's understanding of the controversy in Germany was colored by the fact that Tetzel and other indulgence preachers were Dominicans while Luther was an Augustinian—supported, incidentally, by most of the priests of his order. Since acrimonious theological debate between rival religious orders was nothing new, the Roman Curia erroneously assumed that Luther's complaints would soon be forgotten—as had all previous calls for reform.

As a measure of caution, however, Cardinal Thomas Cajetan (1469-1534), the powerful Dominican general in Rome, wrote a treatise in 1519 condemning "certain preachers" who arrogantly presumed to speak for the Church on the issue of indulgences. It is unlikely that Cajetan at this point had even seen Luther's 95 theses. At any rate, he was certainly incorrect in saying that Luther presumed to speak for the Church.

Spurred on by their general, the Dominicans in Rome rallied to the cause of Luther's condemnation. They were instrumental in having Luther summoned to Rome for a hearing. When Luther received the summons he took a fateful step. Instead of responding through ecclesiastical channels, he asked his prince, the elector Duke Frederick the Wise of Saxony, to ask the emperor to have the hearing moved to Germany. From that moment on the indulgence controversy became inextricably involved with the political situation in Germany.

After complicated negotiations, Frederick arranged for Luther to appear before Cardinal Cajetan in the town of Augsburg in the province of Swabia. Luther later remembered that Cajetan received him "very graciously...almost with too much deference."[12] Yet, instead of engaging Luther in debate, Cajetan simply demanded that Luther recant the position taken in his theses and in his corollary writings.

A Theological Digression: What Is the Church?

The only theological issue discussed at Augsburg was the question of how human beings appropriated the merits of Christ. Cajetan maintained that the merits of Christ and the saints were coextensive with the "treasury of the Church" and that the Church was the dispenser of these merits through such means as the sacraments and indulgences. Luther rejected this position. He argued that, while the Church may contain the "treasury of indulgences," it does not contain the "treasury of the lifegiving grace of God." This he said, was to be found not in the Church but only in Christ.

The key issue of the indulgence controversy, therefore, involved two fundamentally different conceptions of the Church: Cajetan saw the Church as the Body of Christ on earth and the institutional Roman Catholic Church as coextensive; thus the Church's ministry of salvation is the same as Christ's. For Luther, the institutional Church and the Body of Christ may or may not be coextensive, depending on the actual conduct of the institutional Church. If that conduct contradicts the gospel, the institutional Church becomes simply another earthly authority, incapable of ministering in Christ's name.

Since Vatican II Roman Catholic teaching no longer insists that the institutional Church and the earthly Body of Christ are completely coextensive; but it does still teach that even sinful people ministering in Christ's name, through the authority of the Church, nonetheless minister efficaciously. For Luther it was not a question of what ministers in the Church did or did not do; it was the faith of the believer, and only that, which made the Church the Body of Christ on earth. For him the ministry of the Church is *received* through faith; it is not given by ordained ministers.

The Church's Teaching on Indulgences

Since the meeting between Luther and Cardinal Cajetan at Augsburg ended with neither man making concessions, Luther asked for a clarification of indulgence theology directly from Pope Leo X. Leo's response, drafted by Cajetan, affirmed in no uncertain terms that the pope has the authority to allocate merits from the treasury of the Church to whomever he wills and, further, that the pope can remit the punishment arising from sins by granting indulgences.

In reality this was but a reaffirmation of the Church's ancient teaching on indulgences—namely, that indulgences do not in and of themselves absolve people from their sins (confession is required for this), but that indulgences remit the *punishment* arising from such sins.

This distinction had been blurred by Prince Albert of Brandenburg's indulgence preachers. Instead of stressing that confession and penance were the necessary prerequisites for forgiveness of sins, these preachers frequently made it sound as though the indulgence itself forgave sins, and thus uneducated persons thought they were buying licenses for "free sins," as it were.

Charles V Becomes Emperor

Shortly after Leo X issued his statement on indulgences, Emperor Maximilian I died, and the election of a new emperor became the greatest concern of the day. Pope Leo X showed his true colors when he realized that the election of Charles V would encircle the Papal States by imperial lands: Leo dropped the attack against Luther altogether in order to curry favor with Luther's prince, Duke Frederick, whom Leo urged to seek the imperial crown for himself. Thus, when Pope Leo X should have been attending to the now-raging theological controversy in Germany, he could think only of his political interests, and so he ignored Luther for the time being.

Such a cavalier attitude toward the indulgence issue surely convinced Luther that he had been right all along in considering the Church merely another worldly institution. As the hierarchy continued to fritter away every opportunity for reconciliation, he systematized his theological position and steadily consolidated his support among an ever-growing body of German Catholics. When Charles V was actually elected emperor in 1519, Leo X tried to dissociate himself from Frederick and resume the proceedings against Luther, but by now it was too late to regain lost papal credibility in Germany.

LUTHER'S THREE PAMPHLETS OF 1520

By 1520 Luther was no longer limiting his theological writings to the indulgence controversy. He had become more than an obscure monk engaged in an arcane theological debate; he was now a national hero standing up to the oppressive Italian hierarchy. Everywhere Germans hailed Luther as the man who would help them achieve their deepest national aspirations. The religious controversy had thus become a means for Germans to express their pent-up nationalistic fervor. Luther capitalized on this burst of national pride. In 1520 he wrote three pamphlets which further politicized the controversy and made reconciliation with Rome increasingly impossible.

'An Open Letter to the Christian Nobility of the German Nation'

In the first of these pamphlets, Luther wrote to the German princes not so much as a theologian but as a German patriot urging his lords to join the revolt:

> Some have estimated that every year more than 300,000 guldan* find their way from Germany to Italy. Here we come to the *heart of the matter*. How comes it that we Germans must put up with such robbery and extortion of our property at the hands of the pope?[13] (Emphasis added.)

Luther had indeed come to the "heart of the matter." For the nobility to join the revolt—as Luther well knew—they would have to be motivated by political and economic factors.

Luther coupled his call to patriotism with a new and more daring doctrinal attack: He declared all Christians to be priests and thus proclaimed the ordained priesthood to be invalid. Each Christian, he

---

* An enormous amount, perhaps as much as $75 million in today's terms.

said, is an authoritative interpreter of Scripture.

'The Babylonian Captivity of the Church'

In the second pamphlet written in 1520, Luther compared the Church's captivity by Rome to the Jews' Babylonian captivity. Because of this captivity, he said, all the doctrines promulgated by Rome during the last thousand years were invalid.

Even though he had now clearly broken with the Catholic Church, Luther could somehow still bring himself to respect the papacy. In a letter to Leo X he wrote,

> I have always grieved, most excellent Leo, that you have been made pope in these times, for you were worthy of better days....Do not listen, therefore, my dear Leo, to those sirens who make you out to be no mere man but a demigod....In short, believe none who exalt you; believe those who humble you.[14]

'A Treatise on Christian Liberty'

In his third pamphlet of 1520, Luther set forth in simplified form his previous theological reflections on faith, works and justification. Written for the average German Catholic, Luther used simple metaphors to drive home his message. In order to emphasize the relative priorities of faith and works he wrote, "The tree (faith) bears fruit (works); the fruit does not bear the tree."[15]

Here Luther developed his understanding of Christian freedom. True freedom in Christ, he wrote, does not come from fastidious attention to religious duties, but from a renewed life based on justifying faith. This was clearly a doctrine that Catholic theologians could comfortably discuss with Luther. Yet Leo's agents did not think in terms of dialogue but only in terms of intimidation.

While Luther was urging Christians to free themselves from the yoke of the law, curial officials were busy posting throughout Germany Pope Leo's bull (*Exsurge Domine*, June 15, 1520) excommunicating Luther. Their actions were interpreted by Germans virtually as an act of war by foreign invaders. Luther's response to the pope's inflexible attitude was to convene a group of his students at Wittenberg to burn the papal bull in a bonfire which likewise consumed the university's library of Scholastic treatises and various curial decrees. It was an appropriate symbolic gesture by which the revolution broke all ties with the past. On January 3, 1521, Luther was formally excommunicated from the Catholic Church.

THE DIET OF WORMS

Pope Leo's agents reported back to him that the bull of excommunication had met with fierce resistance throughout Germany. One of these men, Girolamo Aleander, wrote to the pope,

> All Germany is in an uproar. For nine-tenths "Luther" is the war-cry; for the rest, if they are indifferent to Luther, it is at least "Death to the Roman Curia," and everyone demands and shouts for a council. [16]

Leo finally realized that the religious controversy in Germany was far more than a monks' squabble. He called on Emperor Charles V to enforce the secular penalties attached to a papal bull of excommunication: namely, to arrest Luther and burn him at the stake.

But Charles vacillated. In order to gain the imperial throne, he had promised the electors that no one would be subjected to imperial punishment without a hearing. Consequently, when Charles asked Elector Frederick to bring Luther before the Diet of Worms,* the emperor phrased his summons to Luther in the most conciliatory language. He greeted Luther as "Honorable, dear and pious one" and stated the purpose of the summons to be simply the emperor's desire "to obtain information from you."[17] Finally, the emperor guaranteed Luther safe-conduct to and from Worms.

Luther set out confidently for Worms, proclaiming, "Even though there were as many devils at Worms as tiles on the roof, I still would go there."[18] On April 17, 1521, he appeared before the emperor and the diet in the palace of the local bishop. When asked whether he was prepared to recant his heretical writings, Luther wavered, asking for time to think the question over. The next day Luther was asked again if he recanted. This time he answered in no uncertain terms, with words that were to shake the Catholic Church to its foundation:

> If I do not become convinced by the testimony of Scripture or clear rational grounds—for I believe neither pope nor councils alone, since it is obvious that they have erred on several occasions—I remain subjugated by the scriptural passages I have cited and my conscience held captive by the word of God. Therefore, I neither can nor will recant anything. For to act against conscience is difficult, noxious,

---

* A "diet" was a legislative assembly. Worms, pronounced "Vorms," was the town where the assembly met.

47

and dangerous. May God help me. Amen. [19]*

A few weeks later, on May 25, 1521, Emperor Charles reluctantly signed the Edict of Worms, declaring Luther to be a heretic and subjecting him to imperial arrest and punishment. Meanwhile Luther, protected as much by enthusiastic popular support as by the emperor's guarantee of safe-conduct, was taken by comrades to the castle of Wartburg near Eisenach in Saxony where Elector Frederick advised him to lay low for a period of time. The events at Worms brought Luther and his revolution international fame. While Luther "rotted," as he put it, at the Wartburg, his teachings began to spread.

The Wartburg Writings

From May 4, 1521, to March 6, 1522, Luther stayed in his dank, self-imposed prison, throwing ink bottles at the devil and fine-tuning his theology. Let's sample some of Luther's writings during this Wartburg period.

On *private confession*: "I regard private confession as a very precious and salutary thing...but it is a bad thing that the pope makes it a compulsory institution."[20] On *celibacy*: "I have resolved now to take up the question of religious vows and to free young people from this infernal celibacy."[21] On the *priesthood and the Mass*: "Everyone knows on what the whole kingdom of priests is based and built: on celebrating Mass, in other words, on the grossest idolatry on earth."[22] On *infant Baptism*: "To bring a child for Baptism signifies nothing else than to present it into Christ's open hands of grace. Since he has proved to us by many examples that he accepts what is offered to him, why do we doubt here?"[23] (In other words, Luther approved of infant Baptism.)

Luther and the Bible

The greatest achievement of Luther's Wartburg period was his translation of the Bible into German. He translated the New Testament in 11 weeks; his Old Testament translation, which required the assistance of collaborators, was not actually finished until 1534. Although his was not the first German-language Bible—Catholic scholars had prepared a

---

* The original transcript does not have the words, "Here I stand; I cannot do otherwise." This sentence was apparently added by an enthusiastic editor to a later reprint of the transcript.

total of 18 versions since 1461—Luther's translation became the most widely read. The dialect he used was that spoken at Elector Frederick's court in Saxony. Luther's translation played a key role in the process by which the various German dialects became unified into a single German tongue.

In translating the Bible, Luther did not hesitate to bring his own experiences to bear on the translated text. He had no compunction, therefore, in altering the original text to suit his purposes. Thus he translated the phrase "justice of God" as "justice valid before God." And in the key passage of his entire theology, Romans 3:28, he added the word "alone" after "faith," so that his version read, "For we hold that a man is justified by faith *alone* apart from observance of the law."

Further, Luther established his own canon of Scripture; he rejected the Letter of James and the Book of Revelation, and only begrudgingly accepted the Epistle to the Hebrews.

For Luther the principle of *sola scriptura* ("the Bible alone") meant not only that the Bible was superior to Church authority, but also that it was only the Bible which should guide one's reading of the Bible. One should interpret Scripture, Luther said, so as to "enhance Christ,"[24] by which he meant that, if a given passage was troublesome, it should always be read so as to glorify Christ rather than to detract from his glory. In the last analysis only the individual believer could decide what a passage meant. Luther saw Scripture scholarship as a concession to paganism. "Reason is the greatest enemy that faith has,"[25] he once wrote, and he characterized as atheism the scriptural studies of scholars like Erasmus.

Further Theological Expression

From his Wartburg period Luther's theology gained impetus for further expression. His earlier thoughts on justification, faith and grace led him to develop a full-blown doctrine of predestination. Like Augustine, Luther believed that "few are saved, infinitely many are damned."[26] Elsewhere he wrote, "We are the children of wrath, and all our works, intentions and thoughts are nothing at all in the balance against our sins"[27]—a statement which could easily have been made by any medieval Catholic theologian.

As for good works, Luther stated that anyone who could find Christ requiring good works in the Gospels was a liar, perhaps forgetting when he said this such passages as Matthew 7:21-27 and 25:31-46. The most detestable of all "works" for Luther were the sacraments. He reduced their number from seven to two—Baptism and the Eucharist—and changed the meaning of these two entirely.

According to Luther, Baptism does not *effect* one's justification; it is merely a *sign* of justification already received. As for the Eucharist, he believed in the Real Presence, but not in *transubstantiation*—that is, he disbelieved that the substance of the bread and wine is transformed into Christ's body and blood. For Luther, Christ is present in the bread and wine *along with* the substance of bread and wine, a position known as *consubstantiation*. He further denied that a priest is necessary to change the eucharistic elements into Christ's body and blood. Not words of consecration, in Luther's opinion, but Christ's own desire to come down from heaven change bread and wine into his body and blood.

Whereas the Catholic Church taught that the sacraments are signs which actually effect that which they signify, Luther considered the sacraments as signs in the sense of *pledges* of God's promises. For example, the Eucharist is a sign which substantiates Jesus' words, "This is my body....Do this in memory of me...," and Baptism is the pledge of Christ's promise to give eternal life to all those who believe in him.

With the sacraments virtually eliminated, the Church itself obviously had to be defined differently. Luther eventually denied papal authority, calling the pope's power of the keys (see Matthew 16:19) "not keys but husks and shells of the keys."[28] The only Church authority Luther would accept was the Bible, and the true Church, he said, exists only where the Bible is preached and believed.

Yet Luther was not an anarchist. He appreciated the need for Church structure, order and discipline, and he was not willing to throw out all Church traditions. In his new "Mass," Luther kept everything virtually the same as the Catholics had had it: His ministers wore vestments, elevated the host and said all the Catholic prayers, omitting only words referring to "sacrifice."

The typical German Christian attending Luther's service would likely have noticed nothing different about it (Luther at first even kept the Latin language) except that the preaching of the Gospels was now given more attention and was undoubtedly vastly superior to most Catholic sermons. Since he was concerned for the "weak consciences" of some German converts to his beliefs, he did not force them to abandon everything they had believed for years.

In Luther's vision of the Church, every person was a priest of equal status; though, in practice, men rather than women continued to lead the new Church. Luther defined his universal priesthood of all believers in terms of ministry to others: "As priests," he wrote, "we are worthy to appear before God to pray for others and to teach one another divine things."[29] If not set in opposition to the ordained priesthood, this position was clearly consistent with Catholic doctrine.

When Luther left the Wartburg in 1522, and returned to Wittenberg to resume the leadership of his religious revolution, he found it had headed in a new direction. As he tried to regain control, he turned from a revolutionary into a reactionary.

CHAPTER FOUR

THE 'CRAZY MOB'

The Revolution Turns Violent

While Luther hid himself away in the Wartburg Castle, other religious revolutionaries took up his cause. Some of these men were close associates of Luther and, like him, more interested in writing and preaching reform doctrines than in organizing and spreading the revolution. A second group of reformers, however, were more organization-minded than Luther and his fellow theorists. They were also more insistent in demanding that the "purified" Church which the theorists had described be established at once. As this second group of reformers began implementing Luther's theories by creating radical reform communities, the religious revolution turned violent.

After a word about some of the reformers in Luther's circle, we will take up the story of the violent revolution.

LUTHER'S ASSOCIATES

George Spalatin

One of Luther's closest friends was George Spalatin (1484-1545), who tutored the sons of Elector Frederick of Saxony. Spalatin met Luther in 1511, learning from him much about the Bible and adopting Luther's doctrine of *sola scriptura*.

Spalatin more than anyone was responsible for winning Elector Frederick to the Protestant cause. Frederick, a clever politician, had at first avoided personal contact with Luther; thus Spalatin was an invaluable go-between. Spalatin's intercession was crucial to the success of the religious revolution since, without the support of a powerful prince, Luther's revolt no doubt would have come to nothing. Spalatin was also a humanist who brought a cultural and refined scholarship to the Lutheran cause.

Philip Melancthon

The greatest humanist involved in Luther's revolution and the true founder of Lutheran theology (in that he systematized Luther's doctrines) was Philip Melancthon (1497-1560). Melancthon, who had been professor of Greek at the University of Wittenberg, came as close as anyone to bringing the spirit of the Renaissance to bear upon Luther's revolution.

With Luther confined in the Wartburg, Melancthon became the spokesman for the new movement. In 1521 he composed his famous *Loci Communes* (*Common Themes*) in which he systematized the key elements of Luther's theology. Melancthon—who was not a professionally trained theologian—focused in his *Loci* on the Epistle to the Romans and its central themes of faith, law, sin and grace.

Melancthon did not share Luther's stern suspicion of all religious "works." He had originally followed Luther closely, writing as Luther had on the supremacy of justifying grace and the futility of works of charity aside from faith. Yet, largely because of the violent disturbances which we are about to describe, Melancthon had a change of heart concerning Luther's theology in his second edition of the *Loci* (1522).

He thus spoke of certain good actions which sinners can achieve even before they receive justifying grace. Although Melancthon did not say that ungraced actions earn salvation (neither did Catholics), he nonetheless did praise reason and tradition as guides to right conduct. Because he took this position, some of Luther's followers considered Melancthon a traitor. Nevertheless, it was Melancthon who succeeded to the leadership of the Lutheran movement after Luther's death and largely determined the future course of Lutheran theology.

John Bugenhagen

After leaving the Catholic priesthood and marrying in 1522, John Bugenhagen (1485-1558) became pastor of Luther's parish church in Wittenberg and served as Luther's confessor. (Luther went to confession regularly, even years after the revolt had started.) Bugenhagen officiated at Luther's marriage to a former nun, Catherine von Bora (June 27, 1525). He was instrumental in spreading the Lutheran movement to northern Germany and Denmark.

Justin Jonas

Justin Jonas (1493-1555) joined Luther's revolt in 1521 after accompanying Luther to Worms. Elector Frederick named Jonas professor of canon law at the University of Wittenberg. As a law professor, Jonas's talents were useful in forming the Lutheran concept of Church organization. Jonas was also the "publicity agent" of the Lutheran movement. He translated Luther's and Melancthon's German writings into Latin for distribution to scholars in other countries, and he translated Latin writings into German for the less educated in Germany.

Nikolaus von Amsdorf

Having assisted Luther in his translation of the Bible, Nikolaus von Amsdorf (1483-1565) became the first Protestant bishop. He was ordained by Luther as Bishop of Naumburg in 1542. Von Amsdorf represents the conservative wing of Lutheran theologians. He adamantly opposed Melancthon's compromise position on faith and good works and communicated the "pure Luther" to future ages.

LUTHER'S SOCIAL DOCTRINE AND THE RADICAL REFORM PREACHERS

Five months after he left the Wartburg, Luther wrote a fiery pamphlet entitled *Against the Falsely Called Spiritual Order of the Pope and the Bishops*. His purpose in writing was to defend himself against the charges of heresy brought against him by various German bishops. "It were better that every bishop were murdered," he thundered. "All who contribute body, goods and honor that the rule of the bishops may be destroyed are God's dear children and true Christians."[1] That Luther himself later ordained Nikolaus von Amsdorf a bishop is simply another of his inconsistencies.

Luther's pamphlet condemning the bishops was read by the average German—who was more interested in political and economic freedom than in religious revolt—and seen as the long-awaited assault on the privileged higher classes. Luther encouraged this sentiment by writing another pamphlet, *On Secular Authority: To What Extent Should It Be Obeyed?* There he unleashed the full resentment of his own peasant ancestry and, at the same time, unwittingly made himself the firebrand of a social revolution. He called princes "God's jailers and hangmen," and he summarized the lower classes' rising expectations by declaring, "the common man is learning to think, and contempt of princes is gathering forces among the multitude and the common people." He warned the princes, "The world is no longer what it was when you hunted and drove people like so much game."[2]

Princes who read these words were of course horrified, but they were unable to stir Elector Frederick to take action against Luther. It is debatable whether Luther truly harbored revolutionary social views or whether he was simply venting his own pent-up anger against the German religious-political system. In a letter written in 1524 he takes a very radical stance: "I believe that in Christendom all things are in common, and each man's goods are the other's, and nothing is simply a man's own."[3]

Luther's radical pamphlets coincided with the increasing popularity of two radical reform preachers, Andreas Carlstadt (1480-1541) and Thomas Munzer (1490-1525). Yet, as interaction with these radicals would show, Luther was at heart a stodgy conservative, if not a belligerent reactionary.

Andreas Carlstadt

Carlstadt (his given name was Andreas Bodenstein) had published in 1518 his own theses, which he labeled as "Protestant"—that is, "protesting" against Catholic belief. Unlike Luther, who believed in gradual reform of the liturgy, Carlstadt sought the immediate extirpation of anything Catholic from Christian worship services. On Christmas Day 1521 Carlstadt presided over a Communion service dressed as a layman. He allowed the other communicants to pick up the consecrated bread with their own hands—a daring innovation even by Luther's standards.

Encouraged by popular support, Carlstadt persuaded the Wittenberg city fathers in January 1522 (Luther was still in Wartburg Castle) to issue a decree removing images from the parish church. When Luther heard of this, he condemned Carlstadt. Carlstadt reacted by calling Luther a "neopapist" and leaving Wittenberg for the town of Orlamunde. When Luther reported to his prince that Carlstadt was preaching seditious doctrines from the pulpit, Carlstadt was expelled from Saxony.

Moving to south Germany, Carlstadt grew increasingly bitter over Luther's rejection of him and began to develop a distinctly radical, anti-Lutheran theology. For example, he rejected the doctrine of the Real Presence in the Eucharist, which Luther accepted.

Far from discrediting him, Carlstadt's writings increased his popularity. Luther wrote to a friend in 1524, "You will not believe how that man Carlstadt is succeeding in Switzerland, Prussia, Bohemia and everywhere...."[4] What bothered Luther the most—apart from Carlstadt's eucharistic teaching—was the ever-growing lower-class support for Carlstadt, a group of people whom Luther now characterized as "the crazy mob."[5]

Because of Luther's attacks against him, Carlstadt eventually suffered a collapse of will, abandoning his pastorate and returning to university teaching. He died in 1541 an abandoned and lonely man, the first Protestant casualty of a religious revolution supposedly based on freedom of conscience and unrestricted personal interpretation of the Bible.

Thomas Munzer

Thomas Munzer was even more radical than Carlstadt; in fact, Carlstadt tried to dissociate himself from Munzer's teachings. Munzer had been a priest but converted to Luther's cause some time in 1519. In his preaching he called for both religious and social revolution, proclaiming himself the personal oracle of the Holy Spirit.

Before Munzer had spoken of such matters openly, Luther had recommended him for the pastor's job of a Church in Zwickau. When the elector who ruled this region of Germany expelled Munzer because of his socialist preaching, Munzer emigrated to Bohemia but found little support there. We hear of him again in 1523 when he had returned to Germany and become pastor in the town of Allstedt.

Toward the end of 1523, Munzer wrote two pamphlets viciously attacking Luther and his doctrines, especially Luther's acceptance of infant Baptism. Eventually Munzer rejected Baptism entirely, calling it a mere "external" which did nothing to transform a person spiritually. Only the direct action of the Holy Spirit, he said, could truly bring one to salvation. With this revolutionary teaching the Reformation completely departed from the apostolic tradition's most basic doctrine—namely, that Baptism is the means to new life in Christ and that the Church administers Baptism on the authority of Christ.

When the local count forbade Munzer from further preaching, he responded by preaching a "sermon to princes" (July 13, 1524) in which he called for the full establishment of the Kingdom of God on earth—a call for Christians to form an egalitarian, communistic society. The princes who heard of Munzer's sermon were shocked, but feared taking action because they regarded Munzer as a devotee of Luther.

Luther, however, completely broke with Munzer, calling him "Satan" and urging the princes to punish him in order to "check disorder and forestall revolution."[6] Luther the revolutionary thus gradually became a reactionary who supported the old social order in the face of anarchy. Munzer responded to Luther's about-face by publishing a pamphlet in which he called Luther "Dr. Liar" for preaching grace and freedom for the nobility, while demanding law and order for the lower classes.

In 1525 Munzer assumed the pastorate of a congregation in the town of Muhlhausen and began to call for the establishment of a radical commune to be led by himself and a like-minded preacher, Heinrich Pfeiffer. All over Germany (as we shall discuss shortly) peasants were revolting against the established order. These two preachers urged their flock to join the social revolution, characterizing the general uprising as God's holy war against the powers of darkness.

Luther lashed out at Munzer again, calling him "a murderous and bloodthirsty prophet."[7] Munzer traveled around Germany with roving bands of peasants until he was finally arrested, tortured and executed (May 27, 1525). His life and writings illustrate the cleavage which existed in Protestant eschatological thinking: On one extreme stood Luther, who by his later social writings showed himself to believe in strict submission to the established order until the final day of history; on the other extreme stood Munzer and fellow radicals, who called for the full establishment of God's Kingdom here and now.

THE PEASANTS' REBELLION

As our discussion of Carlstadt and Munzer suggests, Luther's revolution was threatening to slip away from him as early as 1522—only five years after he had composed his 95 theses. All over Germany (indeed all over Europe, partially as a result of the Renaissance awakening), people were rebelling against some form of ancient tyranny—whether economic, political, social or religious—and many of them claimed Luther as their champion. Emperor Charles V's brother, Archduke Ferdinand, wrote to the emperor, "The cause of Luther is so deeply rooted in the whole Empire that not one person in a thousand is free from it."[8]

Throughout Germany self-proclaimed preachers arose, throwing out priests and taking over their Churches. Monks and nuns fled from their monasteries. Even great princes, whose Catholicism had been part and parcel of their feudal ancestry, converted to Luther's new brand of Christianity. Along with Elector Frederick of Saxony, the princes of Hesse, Brandenburg and Wurttemburg abandoned their Catholic faith, as did the emperor's own sister. Rome's repeated demands for Luther's arrest fell on deaf ears, and the popes' agents in Germany were themselves now put in peril.

While everywhere more and more people declared themselves "Lutheran," few converts knew anything about Luther's revolt other than that it promised freedom from Rome's oppression. At this time there was hardly a consistent Lutheran theology being taught throughout Germany, nor was there a standardized liturgy. All that mattered to Germans inebriated with the liquor of rebellion was that Rome's domination had come to an end.

The lower classes who got wind of Luther's social pronouncements understood him to be calling on them to destroy the old social order. Now that every man was a priest, every man was thought to be equal. Luther's widely circulating German New Testament was read as a charter for social change: The greed of both secular and religious rulers was tried and condemned by the tribunal of evangelical poverty.

An anonymous pamphleteer calling himself "Pitchfork John" allied the peasants' interests to Luther's. Another writer demanded universal (male) suffrage and popular election of all rulers. Traditional values were stood on their heads. Some preachers proclaimed that only peasants could gain salvation, while the upper classes were damned. The communistic theology of Munzer and Pfeiffer was said by some to be Luther's own teaching.

When a disastrous hailstorm ruined the crops in south Germany in 1524, a spark was ignited and the peasantry rebelled. A man named Hans Muller formed the "Evangelical Brotherhood," a radical Christian movement calling peasants to revolution and freedom. In four months some 30,000 armed peasants had joined Muller.

Luther at first blamed the rebellion on the princes' past selfishness, but at the same time he retreated from his earlier social teachings, now defending social inequality and serfdom. Confused, the peasants' leaders nonetheless pressed on for radical social change. A group of them published "Twelve Articles" of dissent which, if heeded, would have drastically altered German society.

The nobles' violent reaction was not slow in coming. When an ex-priest named Jakob Wehe and his band of 3,000 peasants took the town of Leipheim in south Germany, a mercenary general hired by a league of princes attacked the ill-trained "army," beheaded Wehe and dispersed the peasants. Peasants elsewhere reacted vengefully, prompting one observer to write, "Robbing and plundering became so common that even pious men were tempted thereto."[9]

Shocked by the peasants' excesses, Luther now broke with them entirely; in May 1525 he wrote the pamphlet *Against the Robbing and Murdering Hordes of Peasants*. In it he allied himself completely with the princes, urging them to "smite, slay and stab, secretly or openly," the rebellious peasants. "It is just," Luther proclaimed, "when one must kill a mad dog; if you do not strike him he will strike you, and a whole land with you."[10]

The princes took Luther at his word. Not two weeks after the publication of Luther's pamphlet, 5,000 peasants were slaughtered. Others were spared only when they agreed to stone their leaders to death in exchange for their own lives. A week later another 20,000 peasants were killed, and nobles all over Germany chopped off the hands and gouged out the eyes of any peasant suspected of revolutionary behavior. In all, over 130,000 peasants died in the rebellion, and another 50,000 were dispossessed of their homes and property, creating a permanent class of beggars. The Catholic emperor blamed Luther directly for the chaos, and many princes either reneged on their previous conversions to Lutheranism or publicly reavowed their Catholic faith.

Luther was now condemned on all sides—by peasants for his betrayal, by princes for stirring up the rebellion with his dangerous doctrines. For five years Luther dared not leave Wittenberg, the only city where he was still safe. "Now lords, priests and peasants are all against me," he wrote, "and threaten my death."[11]

Seeking to disclaim all ties with the rebellion, he wrote another pamphlet condemning the peasants. "A rebel," he declared, "is not worth answering with arguments, for he does not accept them. The answer for such a mouth is a fist that brings blood from the nose."[12] The effect on the peasants of Luther's disavowal was to drive them to cynicism and resentment. While many of them returned to the Catholic Church, others joined the more radical Protestant Churches, and still others simply became irreligious.

THE ANABAPTISTS: 'LEFT WING' OF THE REVOLUTION

Many Protestants who parted company with Luther now accepted the radical, "left-wing" gospel that had been preached by Munzer. Yet, owing to the horrendous consequences of the peasant rebellion, such people renounced the use of violence and abandoned the cause of social reform.

A collective name given to these peaceful, left-wing revolutionaries was "Anabaptists"—from the Greek for "re-baptizers," since they rejected infant Baptism to the point of rebaptizing adults. (Despite some parallels, there is no strict correlation between the Anabaptists and the later Baptists.) The Anabaptists wanted to establish the Kingdom of God here and now, in small, elite groups of believers.

They dedicated themselves to simple life-styles in strictly disciplined communities governed by penance and sealed by the sign of adult Baptism.

They rejected infant Baptism entirely. For them people were first "saved" through a demonstrable, communicable conversion experience. Only then did Christians accept Baptism as a *sign* of their faith that salvation had already taken place. Thus began an entire strand of Protestant theology based on the notion of a single moment of salvation. This idea differed radically from both Catholic and Lutheran beliefs in salvation as a process continuing throughout the Christian's life.

The first Anabaptists came from Switzerland and were led by Conrad Grebel (1498-1526) and Felix Mantz (1500-1527). These men taught that the Church is not a society of saints and sinners alike, but an elite company of the elect who fully demonstrate in their lives the precepts of the gospel. Along with their followers, Grebel and Mantz were expelled from Switzerland by more conservative Protestants in 1525 for refusing to have their infant children baptized.

This Protestant intolerance reached its peak when the Zurich town council (a group dominated by Protestant elders) decreed drowning as a punishment for anyone who was rebaptized. In 1527 Mantz himself was drowned. In south Germany Protestants burned Anabaptists to death. Observers no doubt wondered how Luther's revolution had improved upon the excesses of the Catholic Inquisition. Religious toleration, unknown in the Middle Ages, remained unknown during the Reformation.

Toward the middle of the 16th century, the Anabaptist movement became increasingly Gnostic and spiritualistic, developing a dualism in which the flesh was condemned as impure compared to the "pure" spirit. This dualism was applied to the Church, which in Anabaptist circles was now stripped of all impure "externals," such as sacraments, liturgy and organizational structure. The Church was said to be an entirely spiritual entity dispersed secretly throughout society. The Anabaptists also developed a new view of Church history which taught that "the visible Church of Christ was ruined and destroyed right after the Apostles."[13] But it was political history that the Anabaptists, together with the other reformers and the traditionalists, were about to write.

PROTESTANT VERSUS CATHOLIC WARFARE

When Emperor Charles V issued the Edict of Worms in 1521, his political control over Germany had been tenuous and uncertain. He had been emperor for only two years, and the princes and electors of Germany supported him only tentatively. Should Charles have insisted on his full imperial prerogatives, his vassal lords could easily have deserted him. It took eight years and the terrible strife of the Peasants' Rebellion to give Charles enough incentive and confidence to assert himself fully in the religious controversy.

His opportunity came in 1529 at the Diet of Speyer. At that assembly a committee appointed by him to study the growing religious diversity recommended: (1) that the new Lutheran religion not be forbidden; (2) that Anabaptists and similar sects be banned; and (3) that celebration of the Catholic Mass be permitted throughout the Empire.

Given the growing animosity between Catholic and Lutheran princes, this recommendation was strikingly tolerant and balanced. Yet certain of the Lutheran princes formally *protested* against the committee's proposal, thereby earning for themselves the name "Protestant"; thus they brought Carlstadt's term into popular usage for the first time.

Despite this protest, the emperor and the Catholic princes signed an edict on April 22, 1529, incorporating the three items listed above. Further, to assure the Protestant princes that the emperor would not favor the Catholic princes, the following language was added to the Speyer declaration:

> We, electors, princes, prelates, counts and estates, have unanimously agreed and loyally promised one another that no one of a spiritual or a secular estate is to offer violence to another or compel or attack him because of faith...."[14]

It was a promise that proved impossible to keep.

The Failure of Religious Dialogue

Although in theory the princes who left the Diet of Speyer had bound themselves to maintain a policy of religious toleration toward Catholics and Lutherans, in practice they continued to advance whichever religion best served their political interests. This was particularly true of the Protestant princes, who continued to find Lutheranism more economically profitable than Catholicism. Luther's disciple, Philip Melancthon, wrote of these princes: "They do not care in the least about religion; they are only anxious to get dominion into their hands and to be free from control of the bishops."[15]

More and more princes and free cities (cities not controlled by princes) began to realize the economic boon of Lutheranism with its abolition of the oppressive Roman taxes; and so they held steadfastly to the new religion. Erasmus observed in 1530 that "the people everywhere are for the new doctrine."[16] And Melancthon offered an additional reason why the new doctrines succeeded: "Under cover of the gospel," he wrote, "the princes were only intent on the plunder of the churches."[17] The new adherents to Lutheranism became increasingly intolerant of Catholics, and thus—in spite of their promises at Speyer—Catholics and Lutherans gradually grew more suspicious of each other.

When Emperor Charles V realized that the Speyer declaration had not achieved religious peace in Germany, he convened another diet to meet in Augsburg in 1530. He hoped to achieve a more detailed agreement on religious toleration than had the Speyer declaration.

Meanwhile, Luther had already begun to compose a Lutheran confession of faith which Melancthon elaborated upon in his *Confessio Augustana*, or *Confession of Augsburg*. In this *Confession* Melancthon used moderate language to express the Lutheran position. He listed 28 articles which, in effect, summarized the various points of Luther's theology that we have already discussed.

The emperor presented the *Confession* to certain Catholic theologians at the Diet of Augsburg and they in turn issued a *Confutation*, or rebuttal, of Melancthon's document. It is to Melancthon's credit and the Catholics' discredit that the Lutheran position was stated in "a dignified, moderate and pacific tone,"[18] while the Catholic rebuttal was put forth in bellicose and condemnatory language. Because of the Catholics' attitude, the attempt at dialogue completely failed, and the emperor ordered the Protestant princes to accept the *Confutation* or prepare for war.

Religious War

With the Turkish threat in the East momentarily occupying his energies, Emperor Charles delayed the start of the religious civil war. This gave the Protestants time to consolidate their position. In January 1540 Luther and Melancthon dictated terms to the emperor, demanding that he accept the Augsburg *Confession*. Luther intensified the animosity by writing, "If it is permitted to wage war against the Turk and to defend oneself against him, it is all the more permitted against the Pope, who is worse."[19]

Faced with the prospect of a Turkish war, a religious civil war and the growing threat of French aggression, Charles momentarily retreated from his adamant position at Augsburg. He convened a meeting at Regensburg in 1541 at which Protestant and Catholic theologians tried to settle their differences. Although the theologians reached consensus on the issues of married priests and the reception of Communion under both species (agreeing to permit both of these practices), they could not resolve the issues of papal authority and the manner by which the Real Presence in the Eucharist took place (transubstantiation or consubstantiation). Once again dialogue failed and war became more certain.

By 1545 the Turks had turned away from Europe and the emperor had subdued the French. Backed by the pope's money and mercenaries, Charles now felt confident to attack the Protestants. The irony of the war was the pope's fear of imperial victory. Pope Paul III (we will discuss his papacy in Chapter Seven) wanted Emperor Charles to win—but not decisively, because of the threat which Charles's land holdings posed to papal interests (see map, p. 65). Thus, at a crucial moment in the war the pope betrayed the emperor by ordering his papal mercenaries to desert Charles.

The Protestants rejoiced at this act of back-stabbing and went on to force Charles to submit to negotiations for a lasting religious peace. Bitterly dejected by the pope's betrayal, Charles turned the peace conference over to his brother, Archduke Ferdinand of Austria. In 1556 Charles V, Catholic Holy Roman Emperor and loyal son of the Church, broken in spirit by religious hatred, abdicated his throne to Ferdinand and became a monk in Spain.

'Cuius Regio Eius Religio'

At Augsburg in 1555 with Archduke Ferdinand presiding, Protestant delegates demanded toleration of Protestantism in Catholic territories while insisting on the prohibition of Catholicism in Protestant territories. There was not a trace of theological discussion at the conference; it was a purely diplomatic meeting concerned only with political claims. By 1555 religious revolution had completely destroyed any chance for religious reconciliation.

On September 25, 1555, "The Religious Peace of Augsburg" was proclaimed. The delegates promulgated a purely pragmatic *Formula* expressed in Latin as *cuius regio eius religio*—"whose region, his religion." In other words, the *Peace Formula* stipulated that each prince had the right to decide which religion (Catholic or Lutheran) his subjects would follow. To ensure the possibility of religious freedom, Germans were given the right of emigration to a principality of their choosing.

In Protestant principalities the *Formula* effectively elevated the respective Protestant princes to the status of "bishop" of the local Church. Because of this, each Protestant principality developed a Church which conformed to the prince's beliefs, not necessarily to the

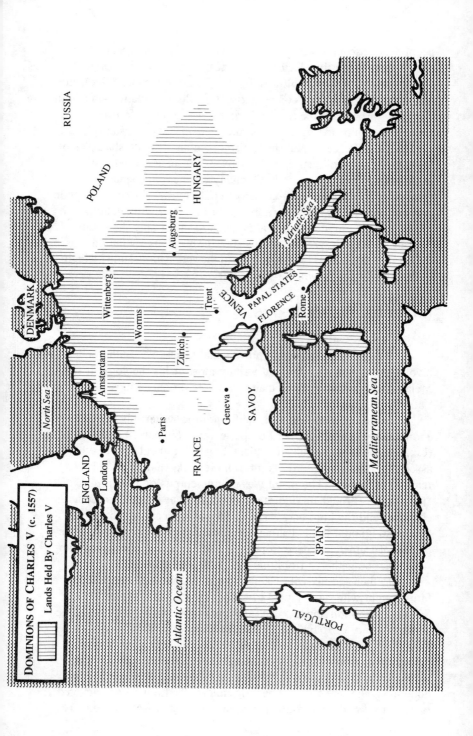

DOMINIONS OF CHARLES V (c. 1557)

Lands Held By Charles V

RUSSIA

POLAND

DENMARK

HUNGARY

Augsburg

Wittenberg

North Sea

Amsterdam

Worms

Trent

ENGLAND

London

Zurich

VENICE

Adriatic Sea

PAPAL STATES

Paris

FLORENCE

Rome

FRANCE

Geneva

SAVOY

Atlantic Ocean

SPAIN

Mediterranean Sea

PORTUGAL

people's. Consequently there came to be not one Lutheran denomination but dozens. When the elector of the Palatine territory converted to Calvinism in 1563 (we will take up Calvinism in Chapter Five), the existence of diverse and competing sects within Germany—and from Germany throughout the rest of Europe—was assured forever.

In addition to fragmenting Protestantism into a thousand pieces, the Religious Peace of Augsburg also made an absolute shambles of the Empire as a political unit. Now over 300 separate and distinct principalities and free cities in Germany claimed independence and autonomy. In the future the emperors could muster concerted support only in times of dire crisis or through bribery and intimidation. The "Holy Roman Empire" in actuality came to mean only the duchy of Austria. Perhaps the greatest anguish that the religious revolution caused the German nation was the destruction of the very national unity which Luther had hoped to win for his people.

LUTHER'S LATER YEARS

'Table Talk'

By 1530 the Protestant princes had taken over Luther's revolution. By then Luther had written most of his theology; it was Melancthon and other theologians who now produced most of the Lutheran treatises.

Luther nonetheless remained a prolific writer; his books were enormously popular all over Europe, earning his publisher a fortune (Luther himself refused any royalties). Beginning about 1529, Luther's associates began to record his informal remarks and small talk with family and friends. The result was a large corpus of *Tischreden*, or "table talk." Through this table talk we get a unique insight into Luther's character and thinking on a wide variety of subjects which he had otherwise ignored in his learned treatises. In order to round out our picture of Luther, we need to present some of the details about him which can be gathered from this informal conversation.

Luther and his wife Catherine had six children and lived on a farm bought with money paid to Luther by the various electors of Saxony. For continuing to preach and teach in Wittenberg, Luther earned a yearly salary of roughly $75,000, in today's terms. Though Luther loved "my Lord Katie," as he called his wife, he was very much a conservative man of his day in matters involving the sexes. "Take women from their housewifery," he remarked, "and they are good for nothing....They are made for bearing children."[20] Luther was a devoted father and, in addition to their own brood, he and Katie raised 11 nephews and nieces whose parents had died. These adopted children recorded many of Luther's spiciest off-the-cuff remarks for posterity.

Luther's youthful biographers depicted him as a portly man given to slight excess in food and drink. Decrying the Germans' love of beer, he nonetheless imbibed the national beverage frequently, proclaiming that God could "bear with him for taking a good drink to honor him."[21]

His anger at Rome and its institutionalized religion expressed itself in increasingly caustic insults. Papal decrees were "dung"; the pope himself was "the Devil's sow"; bishops were "ignorant apes"; monks were "fleas on God Almighty's coat."[22] He excused the un-Christian tone of his speech by saying that fits of anger sharpened his concentration.

Luther was an earthy man, a Christian who would have scoffed at later centuries' prudishness. "Women wear veils because of the angels,"[23] he joked; "I wear trousers because of the girls." He once upbraided a remorseful Melancthon by advising him, "Sin powerfully; God can forgive only a hearty sinner."[24] Luther sought joy wherever he could find it. He considered music the greatest art form after theology, and he wrote numerous powerful hymns, perhaps the most famous being his *Ein feste Burg ist unser Gott*—"A Mighty Fortress Is Our God." He encouraged youngsters to dance and rebuked preachers who forbade attendance at plays.

All in all, the Luther we find in the table talk seems an entirely different man from the scowling, brooding figure who lurks beneath the pages of his theological treatises.

Luther's Intolerance

After sampling the table talk, it should not surprise us to learn that Luther's emotions frequently got the better of him in his relations with other Christians. While his vitriolic denunciation of Catholic clergy (though never of laypersons) was proverbial, Luther was every bit as virulent in his condemnation of other Protestants who departed from his doctrine.

In *On Secular Authority* (1522) he proclaimed, "Faith is a free work, to which no one can be compelled....Faith and heresy are never so strong as when men oppose them by sheer force...."[25] Yet he virtually crowned himself the Protestant's pope by declaring, "My doctrine cannot be judged by anyone, even by the angels. He who does not receive my doctrine cannot be saved."[26]

As the number of contradictory Protestant doctrines proliferated—doctrines tracing their origins to Luther's teaching—Luther fiercely condemned these innovations. Imitating the very Catholic tradition which he had denounced, Luther now sanctioned the use of nonbiblical creeds and doctrinal definitions. Yet he declared that only Scripture as he interpreted it was authentic Scripture, and by his interpretation the Bible provided ample sanction for persecution of heretics.

Commenting on Psalm 82, he urged the princes to kill Anabaptists and other Protestant heretics, and he exhorted the princes to require mandatory attendance at his new Lutheran liturgy. Following Luther's lead, Protestant rulers all over Europe asserted their control of the Christian's conscience.

Last Days

In his old age Luther suffered from a number of physical ailments, but his wits remained sharp and his barbs grew even more stinging. As John Calvin's theology threatened to outstrip his own in popularity, Luther increased his attacks on Calvin and the other reformers, often publicly humiliating even loyal disciples like Melancthon. Suspicious that the common people were deserting him for the new sects, he developed a totalitarian fondness for government-sponsored suppression of religious dissent. A return to slavery, he wrote, was the only way to control the heretical religious impulses of the common people.

So submissive to princely power did Luther himself become that he condoned the bigamous marriage of Prince Philip of Hesse, who in 1540 wedded his mistress. When Melancthon expressed shock at this scandal, Luther congratulated himself on his "tough Saxon skin" which, he said, "has grown thick enough to bear such things."[27]

A month before his death, Luther wrote of himself as "old, decrepit, sluggish, weary."[28] He increasingly had visions of the devil and confessed to doubts about the success of his movement. Yet when asked on his deathbed if he stood by his doctrine, he answered with an emphatic yes.

CHAPTER FIVE

THEOCRACY IN SWITZERLAND

The Reformed Faith

Luther's revolt against the established Church in Germany was not the only religious revolution at the time. In this chapter we introduce Ulrich Zwingli and John Calvin as well as their theological innovations in Switzerland.

ZWINGLI AND THE REVOLUTION IN SWITZERLAND

Ulrich Zwingli (1484-1531) initiated the religious revolution in Switzerland. Ordained a priest in 1506, he gradually developed a taste for politics. When the papacy recruited Swiss mercenaries to assist in its various Italian wars, Zwingli went to Italy as the soldiers' chaplain, receiving a yearly stipend from the Curia for his services.

Zwingli's transformation from loyal Catholic to religious revolutionary was not as dramatic as Luther's. He developed his new religious beliefs slowly and gradually, through an educational process which depended as much on the humanities as it did on the Bible. His education was less theological than Luther's.

Zwingli considered himself to have broken with Catholic teaching five years before the publication of Luther's 95 theses. In 1523 he wrote, "Before anyone in our area knew anything of Luther's name, I began to preach the Gospel of Christ in 1516."[1] When Luther broke with the Church, Zwingli kept his distance, stating that it was he and not Luther who was the true founder of the Protestant revolt.

'Grossmunster' of Zurich

In 1518 Zwingli accepted a call from Catholics in Zurich to become *Grossmunster* or "People's Preacher." In Zurich, as in most of Switzerland, a highly educated citizenry usually ignored the demands of the Catholic hierarchy. The Church in Switzerland had succumbed to the basest forms of corruption. One Swiss bishop levied a yearly tax on his priests for each child they fathered and counted the revenue thus collected as his principal source of income. And because the popes sorely needed Swiss mercenaries, they increasingly allowed the 13 Swiss "cantons" (provinces and cities) to assert secular control over the Swiss Church.

By the time Zwingli assumed his post as *Grossmunster* of Zurich, the city had already declared its independence from Rome in matters of religious discipline—three years before Luther's revolt in Germany. As Zwingli prepared his weekly sermons for Zurich's Catholics, he gradually developed his own theological position, moving farther and farther away from Catholic tradition.

While it is true that Zwingli's revolt predated Luther's, it is inaccurate to regard Zwingli as the father of the Protestant Reformation. There had been several reform efforts similar in substance to Zwingli's a century and a half before Luther (Wycliffe's, for example) which had come to nothing; and Zwingli, too, probably would have failed had it not been for Luther. Once Luther's revolt gained momentum, however, Zwingli's reform theology took hold in Switzerland.

In 1523 the Great Council of Zurich, a body of elders which governed the city, convened a meeting for the purpose of airing Zwingli's opposition to Catholic doctrine. The Council felt assured of its autonomy largely because of Luther's success in Germany. The elders urged the Swiss bishops to send delegates, making it clear that the Council and not the bishops would be the final arbiter of religious policy in Zurich.

On January 25, 1523, Zwingli stood before some 600 delegates in Zurich's city hall and defended 67 theses he had composed. By way of summary, he denied that the Church was the authoritative interpreter of Scripture; proclaimed the Bible alone as the source of truth; asserted the autonomy of the secular power vis-a-vis the spiritual power; called for the marriage of priests (a year later he married his mistress, Anna Reinhard); denied the existence of purgatory; and called on the hierarchy to repent of its sinfulness, warning them that "the axe is laid to the root."

The city fathers approved Zwingli's theses and issued a decree requiring the city's priests to "preach nothing which they cannot justify

70

by recourse to the Holy Gospels and the rest of divine Scripture."[2] Thus the secular government in Zurich endorsed the principle of *sola scriptura* and made it the law of the canton. All priests in the canton now had to choose either to follow Zwingli or to remain loyal to the Catholic Church.

Theocracy and Warfare

Firmly in control of the Church in Zurich, the Great Council gradually asserted more and more control over the canton's political life. Theocracy—the complete integration of Church and state—became the principle of city government. The Council commissioned Zwingli to draft a statement of acceptable religious doctrine and practice, which he did in 1524. In this statement, and in two later pamphlets, Zwingli's new "reformed"* religion took shape.

Zwingli rejected the concept of original sin as defined by Augustine and the Catholic tradition (the hereditary transmission of the guilt arising from Adam's fall). Zwingli considered original sin merely an inclination toward unsocial behavior. At the same time, however, he accepted Luther's doctrine of predestination, but tempered it by writing that Christian parents' unbaptized children who are too young to know the difference between right and wrong will be saved.

In the Eucharist, Zwingli said, Christ was not present in any real sense but only symbolically. In Zwingli's new liturgy the Eucharist was celebrated four Sundays a year; sermons replaced the Eucharist during the rest of the year. Zwingli and the Great Council reestablished the supremacy of the Old Testament along with its prohibition of "graven images"; they thus decreed the destruction of religious icons, statues and art. For good measure the Council also banned music from services as a form of idolatry. Catholics who attended Mass were fined; it became illegal to fast on Friday; monasteries were closed and the Catholic liturgical calendar was abolished.

When the other Swiss cantons heard of the events in Zurich, five chose to follow the new Reformed religion and five others formed a Catholic League to suppress all Protestant movements. As in Germany, religious warfare ensued. Erasmus, who was teaching in Basle at the time, described the feverish emotions which had gripped the opposing factions, writing of "men possessed, with anger and rage painted on their faces...."[3]

Zwingli assumed control of Zurich's military forces and at the

---

* This word gradually became a proper adjective, distinguishing Zwingli's, and eventually Calvin's, Reformation theology from Lutheran theology.

town of Kappel frightened the Catholic forces into submission without a fight. The factions concluded a peace treaty that lasted for two years. Then in 1531 the Protestant cantons reopened the war when they demanded that the Catholic cantons give Protestant preachers free access to all Catholic pulpits. Again the opposing forces met at Kappel, but this time the Catholics prevailed, killing Zwingli and over 500 of his troops. As in Germany, the religious war in Switzerland split the country in two. Seven cantons remained Catholic, four chose the Reformed faith and two were ambivalent.

When Luther heard of Zwingli's death, he proclaimed it a "triumph."[4] Let's look briefly at the reasons why Luther rejected Zwingli and his doctrines.

Zwingli and Luther's Differences

German Protestant Prince Philip of Hesse hoped to unite the religious revolutions in Germany and Switzerland (with himself as the political beneficiary). He thus arranged for a meeting between Luther and Zwingli at the German town of Marburg on September 29, 1529. Since Zwingli had made no secret of his dislike for Luther's "neo-Catholic" tendencies, Luther and his associates arrived at the meeting suspicious and defensive. When Zwingli offered Luther his hand, the latter refused, saying, "Your spirit is not our spirit."[5]

The chief topic of debate at Marburg was the Eucharist. Luther picked up a piece of chalk and wrote on the table which separated him from Zwingli, "This is my body." For two days the two men and their disciples debated, with Luther insisting on the doctrine of the Real Presence and Zwingli demanding a purely symbolic interpretation of the words Luther had written. Luther held fast: "Those words, 'This is my body,' hold me captive," he told Zwingli. "Do away with the text for me and I am satisfied."[6] Zwingli, on the other hand, insisted that the words be taken spiritually. Zwingli insisted that Jesus did not say "'This is my body' essentially, really, corporeally....The soul is spirit. The soul does not eat flesh; spirit eats spirit."[7]

Here Zwingli, no doubt unintentionally, was proposing a radical break with the apostolic tradition and a return to the Platonizing heresies that led the early Church into a constant fight to keep Christianity from turning into a purely "spiritual" religion similar to the mystery cults of the day. The early apostolic tradition had insisted on the dignity of created matter as the focal point of God's presence among humanity. By speaking of the Eucharist as purely "spiritual," then, Zwingli was returning Christian theology to the early docetic heresies which denied the reality of the Incarnation and its ennoblement of created matter.

Thus not only the Eucharist was at stake at Marburg. Zwingli disbelieved generally in the worth of material creation as a means of grace. In a famous exchange he told Luther, "Do not hang so much to Christ's humanity and flesh, but raise your mind to Christ's divinity." In a reply that succinctly summarized 15 centuries of Catholic teaching, Luther responded, "I know no God except him who became man, and I do not want any other."[8]

The conference at Marburg was a failure. Luther and Zwingli signed an ambiguous compromise formula presented to them by Philip of Hesse, but each man interpreted the document in his own way. Two weeks after the conference Lutheran and Reformed preachers were again damning each other for their respective heresies. Luther urged Duke Albert of Prussia to forbid any Zwinglian from coming into Prussian territory.

The real loser at Marburg was not Protestant concord but the apostolic tradition and its belief in the goodness of God's creation. Had Luther remained in charge of the Protestant revolution, Catholic teaching on the worth of created matter would have suffered only a slight setback, and the early reconciliation of Catholics and Protestants would have remained a real possibility. As it turned out, however, Luther's revolution was captured by Zwingli's theological successor in Switzerland—a man whose teachings converted more people to Protestantism than Luther's, a man who put a stamp on Protestantism which turned it irrevocably away from the apostolic tradition, making future reconciliation with the Catholic Church a seemingly insurmountable obstacle.

CALVIN: THE BIOGRAPHICAL EVENTS

John Calvin (1509-1564) was born in France, the son of a bishop's secretary excommunicated for questionable handling of the bishop's money. When John later entered the University of Paris, he changed his name from Jean Chauvin to Johannes Calvinus. John's father told him to terminate his studies in Paris and enroll in law school (exactly as Luther's father had told *him* to do), and he obeyed, transferring to the University of Orleans. Calvin liked his new course of study and earned the Bachelor of Laws degree in 1531. Like Zwingli, Calvin was an avid student of the classics and a self-made humanist.

At some point in 1532, Calvin happened on Luther's writings and found their boldness exhilarating. When he and a friend helped write a speech for the new rector of the Sorbonne, they laced the man's remarks with a call for toleration of Luther's doctrines. In politically centralized France (unlike in decentralized Germany), the French crown and the Paris *Parlement* took swift and decisive action against the radical lawyer and his associates. Arrested, freed and threatened again with arrest, Calvin fled to Protestant Basle in Switzerland, barely escaping the terrible persecution of French Protestants by King Francis I.

From 1534 to 1536 Calvin worked on his monumental theological treatise, *The Institutes of the Christian Religion* (known popularly as *The Institutes*), in which he developed his unique brand of Protestant theology. We will discuss Calvin's theology in more detail shortly. For the moment, however, let's skip over his theology and follow the events of his life to their conclusion.

Religious Transformation in Geneva

In 1536 Calvin made his way to the French-speaking Swiss city of Geneva (Zwingli's Zurich was German-speaking). Like Zurich, Geneva was governed by a council of elders, the Council of Sixty. Also as in Zurich, this Genevan council controlled both the religious and the political affairs of the city, even before Luther's revolt. (The local bishops were noblemen disinterested in the tedious affairs of Church life.)

Shortly before 1520, certain members of the Council of Sixty had sought to win freedom from both episcopal and princely rule by swearing an oath of independence with the citizens of other Swiss cities. The French word for these "oath comrades" was *Huguenots*, a term that would acquire great significance later, as we shall see.

Just before Calvin arrived in Geneva the city council had repudiated the city's allegiance to Catholicism and chosen Zwingli's Reformed faith. Thus when Calvin arrived he found the city undergoing the strain of religious transformation. The Mass had been outlawed, churches had been looted of relics and images, and a stern Old Testament theocracy—enforcing the Ten Commandments as civil law—was being established.

The leader of Geneva's religious revolution, William Farel, met Calvin and persuaded him to begin preaching in the former Catholic cathedral. Heavily influenced by Farel's Old Testament-style moral theology, Calvin helped persuade the city council to issue laws enforcing a strict moral code. Prominent citizens rebelled, and the council eventually expelled both Farel and Calvin from Geneva.

The two men went their separate ways, Calvin going to Strasbourg to pastor a small Protestant congregation. The Genevans' expulsion of Calvin and Farel meanwhile precipitated an ill-fated comeback attempt by the Catholic bishop. When this enterprise failed, the Genevan council changed its mind about Calvin and invited him back. He returned in 1541, never to leave Geneva again.

Calvin's Theocracy

The Genevan council commissioned Calvin and other reformers to draft a code of Church discipline, and in 1542 the resulting *Ecclesiastical Ordinances* was completed. In this document Calvin laid the groundwork for the *presbyterian* form of Church government (that is, leadership by a body of pastors) which characterizes many Protestant denominations to this day. All religious matters in Geneva were to be governed by a "Presbytery" of five ordained pastors and 12 lay elders. Calvin became the head of this body in 1541 and retained control until his death in 1564. During that time he was literally the dictator of both religion and politics. Whether he was a benevolent or a malevolent dictator depends upon one's point of view.

Calvin and his fellow presbyters believed themselves guided directly by God to govern every aspect of the Genevans' lives. Completely outstripping Zurich in its efforts to integrate politics and religion, Geneva became a theocracy the likes of which had not been seen since the days of ancient Israel. In fact, never have Church and state been so completely united as in Calvin's Geneva.

For example, the Genevans were required by law to attend Sunday sermons. They were obligated to accept only Calvin's brand of Protestantism (Calvin rejected Luther's principle of personal interpretation of the Bible). The practice of religious beliefs contrary to Calvin's was made a capital offense. The Presbytery regulated such minute matters as the length of women's dresses, the color of clothing and the number of dishes the Genevans could use at their meals. In addition, the Presbytery forbade jewelry and lavish hairstyles, banned the secular theater, censored the press and banned books, and jailed any citizen who spoke ill of the Presbytery.

As in the Ayatollah's Iran so too in Calvin's Geneva, fornicators and adulterers were put to death. A child was executed for showing disrespect to parents; and blasphemers, idolators and "witches" were burned in public. Torture became a policy of state. Between 1542 and 1564 the records reveal 414 prosecutions for moral misbehavior, 76 banishments and 58 executions in a population of 20,000.[9] Those who point accusingly to the excesses of the Spanish Inquisition cannot fairly ignore the reign of terror which existed in Calvin's Geneva. Yet most Genevans adulated Calvin and willingly accepted his theocracy.

Why? Because through Calvin the developing European middle class gained respectability. Calvin combined his stern morality with the promotion of capitalism. For Calvin, sobriety, temperance and morally correct behavior flourished where people worked hard and used the fruits of their labors to build lives of order and discipline. Although he did not invent the "Protestant ethic" (which, beginning in the 17th century, equated hard-earned wealth with God's favor), he certainly paved the way for it.

Largely because of Calvin the middle class replaced the nobility as God's favored people in popular thinking. With Calvin the notion was born that hard work and unlimited wealth were Christian virtues. The medieval belief in evangelical poverty disappeared from non-Catholic society.

The Servetus Affair

Calvin was not without his detractors. Lutheran theologians denounced his views on predestination (which we will cover shortly) as well as his teaching on the Eucharist. Swiss libertarians condemned his dictatorial control of Genevan society, seeing him as a French usurper who threatened Swiss independence and autonomy. Calvin responded to his detractors with vitriolic abuse, calling them "Luther's apes."

Calvin increasingly felt that his critics' attacks threatened his control of the Genevan Church. This is illustrated by his handling of the conflict with Miguel Servetus (1511-1553). Servetus was a Spaniard who had been attracted to the Protestant cause after meeting Melancthon on a trip to Germany. At the age of 20 he wrote a learned treatise denying the existence of the Trinity. The publication of this work led Lutheran reformers to reject him.

After studying medicine in Paris, he wrote another treatise, *The Restitution of Christianity*, in which he denied the divinity of Christ. Servetus sent his work to Calvin, hoping to initiate a dialogue. Calvin responded to Servetus simply by sending him a copy of *The Institutes*, and Calvin told friends that if Servetus were ever to come to Geneva, "I will not suffer him to get out alive."[10]

When Servetus became a hunted heretic in Catholic France, he traveled for unknown reasons to Geneva, where he was shortly arrested. After a trial for heresy in which he was accused of "defaming the doctrines of the Gospel of the Church of Geneva,"[11] the Genevan council found Servetus guilty and ordered him burned at the stake.

The burning of Servetus brings into focus once again the intolerance which characterized the Reformation. Clearly, Protestants were equally as capable of murder for the sake of the gospel as Catholics had been. In fact, Calvin's rationalization for the use of violence would have satisfied the most fiendish of medieval inquisitors:

76

Whoever shall maintain that wrong is done to heretics and blasphemers
in punishing them makes himself an accomplice in their crime....There
is no question here of man's authority; it is God who speaks, and it
is clear what law he would have kept in the Church even to the end
of the world.[12]

And when others questioned Calvin's use of violence and his intolerance
of religious differences, he responded in words that would have
delighted the most ardent advocate of an exaggerated understanding of
papal infallibility:

...I am sure that what I have taught and written did not arise in my
head, but I have it from God and I must hold it fast, if I do not wish
to become a traitor to the truth.[13]

Calvin died in 1564 supremely confident of his salvation.
Because of Calvin, many thinking people throughout Europe
wondered whether the vines of state-sponsored intolerance which the
Protestants had supposedly uprooted had not just been replanted in the
Protestants' own garden. The simple gospel of peace preached by Jesus
seemed no closer to fulfillment after four decades of Protestantism than
at the close of the Middle Ages. Slowly and gradually the seeds of
religious cynicism were sprouting and taking root in the soil of European
thought.

CALVIN: THE THEOLOGY

During the years of his Genevan dictatorship, Calvin became a
skilled preacher and theologian. He greatly expanded the first edition
of his *Institutes*—from six chapters in 1536 to 80 chapters in 1559. By
the time it reached this final stage of development, *The Institutes* had
become the principal handbook of the Reformed faith. The final edition
gives us Calvin's fully matured theology, a theology destined to
influence Protestantism more than any other book ever written, with
the possible exception of the Bible. Let's turn now to an analysis of
this monumental achievement of Protestant thought.

'Sola Scriptura'—Almost

Although all persons have an intuitive awareness of God, Calvin
said, this awareness is clouded by the evil of sin. As a result, we cannot
truly know God as he is but only as the Bible reveals him to us. Calvin
thus defined the Bible as the one and only means of knowledge about
God—eliminating in one stroke the entire spiritual tradition of infused
contemplation begun with the desert fathers of the early Church.

So although Calvin relied heavily on Augustine for other aspects of his theology, he implicitly rejected Augustine's spirituality. For Augustine, the "Trinitarian vestige" (see *The People of the Creed*, pp. 125-126) which is present in all creation is also present within the human heart; therefore, even beyond the knowledge of God we find in the Bible, there is a mystical knowledge gained in prayer which deepens and fulfills scriptural revelation. For Calvin, on the other hand, there is no knowledge of God other than the written pages of Scripture.

For Calvin, the eternal Word—the *logos*, or Second Person of the Trinity—is fully comparable to the "word" of Scripture; therefore, we can know nothing either *about* the Word or *through* the Word that is not in the Bible. The Church is thus seen not as an organism which grows up around the eternal Word's ongoing revelation throughout time, but as an entity which springs fully formed, as it were, out of the Bible.

It is uncertain what Calvin would have said in response to later historical findings that the canon of Scripture was not formed until several centuries after Pentecost. It *is* certain that no reputable scholar today believes the early Church formed itself from the Bible, as if the first Christians looked on the Bible as a "how-to" manual for Church organization. Thus Calvin's theoretical first premise—upon which his entire theology rests—would seem to be fallacious by the standards of modern scholarship. Although Calvin imagined himself as *going back* to the pure Church of the first century and re-forming it, he was actually *going forward* with the formation of a new Church.

Calvin's insistence that we can know about God only what we read of him in Scripture must have caused Calvin some uncertainty when Servetus sent him his treatise denying the existence of the Trinity. According to Calvin's own principles, since neither the word *Trinity* nor the Augustinian elaboration of the Trinity (which he accepted) were found in the Bible, he logically should not have condemned Servetus for denying the Trinity. Despite his insistence on *sola scriptura*, however, Calvin could not bring himself to discard the Catholic tradition's most significant theological achievement.

Fallen Humanity

Calvin interpreted Scripture's words, "Let us make man in our image" (Genesis 1:26), to mean that God's likeness is hidden in the human soul. This purely spiritual interpretation denied the worth of the human body and its inherent reflection of the divine.

Again Calvin in one stroke rejected centuries of Christian tradition. In confronting the Gnostics the early Christian apologists (see *The People of the Creed*, pp. 30-36) had striven to show the dignity of

78

the human body as well as of the soul. When Irenaeus of Lyon in the second century had written, "The glory of God is man fully alive," and when Clement of Alexandria in the third century had written, "God became man so that man may learn how to become God," they were each talking about humanity in body and soul.

Although Calvin could speak of Adam's original purity before the Fall, he is most concerned with Adam *after* the Fall. Here we find Calvin at his best, describing humanity as a "frightful deformity" because of its infection by original sin. Calvin defines original sin as "a hereditary depravity and corruption of our nature, diffused into all parts of the soul, which first makes us liable to God's wrath, then also brings forth in us those works which Scripture calls 'works' of the flesh."[14]

Here Calvin relies heavily on Augustine. Yet Calvin lacks the hopeful optimism which comes out clearly in Augustine's mystical writings. Whereas Augustine after his conversion finds great joy in his relationship with God, Calvin—even after he writes of the justifying work of Jesus Christ—still seems suspicious of God, regarding God as someone to be kept at bay. Whereas Augustine relishes and delights in his newfound freedom in Christ, Calvin—no matter how much he writes of the Christian's election to salvation and glory—never sounds truly convinced that God *likes* humanity. For Calvin God seemingly holds saved humanity at arm's length between the thumb and forefinger of one hand while holding his nose with the thumb and forefinger of the other hand.

While the starting point for Calvin's *soteriology* (theology of salvation) is humanity's utter depravity—as it was for most Catholic theologians—Calvin cannot really bring himself to believe that justification in Christ truly reestablishes the divine likeness in humanity. Like Luther, Calvin taught the doctrine of imputed righteousness, the process whereby humanity "*appears* in God's sight not as a sinner but as a righteous man"[15] (emphasis added). For Calvin justified human nature resembles Luther's "dung heap covered with snow." Catholic theology, on the other hand, saw Christ's act of justification as an *objective* remaking of human nature—not just a *subjective* experience of salvation.

Theory of Predestination

Calvin defined predestination as "God's eternal decree, by which he determined with himself what he willed to become of man."[16] Calvin's doctrine of predestination is, like Luther's, based on God's decision to save some persons and damn others in a way completely unrelated to human conduct. Thus merit has nothing to do either with God's salvation or his damnation of particular persons. When objections were raised to Calvin's doctrine, he admitted that predestination to damnation was "a horrible decree"; but he asserted, nevertheless, that predestination is "in conformity to the clear doctrine of Scripture"[17] and "promotes our admiration of God's glory."[18]

Unlike Luther, who based his theory of predestination on God's foreknowledge of the future (the traditional Augustinian approach), Calvin makes predestination more horrible than anyone before had ever dreamed of doing. Breaking new ground, he does not simply teach that God damns those whom he foresees rejecting divine grace; Calvin teaches that God *wills* for certain people to reject his grace, and thus wills their damnation. It is doubtful that a more perfidious distortion of the gospel has ever been conceived.

Reconciling Calvin's theory of predestination with his doctrine of *sola scriptura* is difficult if not impossible. (Reconciling the theory with his belief in justification by faith is likewise difficult. How can one who is predestined truly be said to have voluntarily believed in Christ?) One gets the general sense from studying the Bible that God wants all of his creation to be saved. The image of God that Jesus presents in the Parable of the Prodigal Son, for example, is hardly Calvin's malevolent monster scheming to damn humanity to eternal punishment. Further, individual verses of Scripture mandate categorically against Calvin's doctrine:

> Rather, he shows you generous patience, since he wants none to perish but all to come to repentance. (2 Peter 3:9b)

> ...for he wants all men to be saved and come to know the truth.
> (1 Timothy 2:4)

> He is an offering for our sins,
> and not for our sins only,
> but for those of the whole world. (1 John 2:2)

> The grace of God has appeared, offering salvation to all men.
> (Titus 2:11)

Perhaps the only reason why anyone would leap at the opportunity to accept Calvin's theory of predestination is for the reason Calvin himself once let slip indiscreetly from his pen. Predestination, he wrote, "is productive of the most delightful benefits"[19] for the elect. Perhaps predestination as Calvin saw it simply grew out of the spirit of the times in which a rising middle class needed some theoretical assurance of its status as independent from the nobility. What better way to soothe one's status-anxiety than to proclaim, "I'm predestined to heaven, but you're predestined to hell"? In other words, Calvin's theory of predestination becomes the ultimate guarantee of one's superiority. With it the "saved" Christian can flaunt his elitist status in the face of the damned.

And how does one identify the damned on the one hand and the saved on the other? Calvin's followers devised what they thought was the perfect test: The saved are those who live respectable, comfortable, middle-class lives of civic virtue. In the most astonishing distortion of the gospel in all of Christian history, the very Savior who proclaimed, "Blest are you poor; the reign of God is yours....But woe to you rich, for your consolation is now" (Luke 6:20, 24)—that very Savior was held up by later Calvinists as the sponsor of middle-class civic piety.

Predestination became for future generations of American Calvinists the ultimate verification that they had "made it," the divine sanction of their lust for wealth and power. They failed to notice that the gospel in which they professed to believe had gotten lost somewhere along the way.

Calvin's Church

Calvin's doctrine of predestination naturally affected his concept of the Church, which he defined as the sum total of those whom God predestines to salvation. This Church, then, is invisible; only God knows it members. In the visible, institutional Church—the "church in respect to men,"[20] as Calvin called it—there "are mingled many hypocrites who have nothing of Christ but the name and the outward appearance."[21]

Yet Calvin did not denigrate the role of an institutional Church; it could serve as a sign of the invisible Church. He even quoted the Catholic Fathers (perhaps in a momentary lapse of memory as to the principle of *sola scriptura*) by saying that no one can be saved who does not have the Church for his mother.[22] Calvin's visible Church is a sign in that it identifies and points to the elect, showing the world who they are while guiding them toward heaven. The Church carries out this mission in two ways: It preaches the Word of God and it administers the sacraments.

The Sacraments

Calvin defines a sacrament as "a testimony of divine grace toward us, confirmed by an outward sign...an outward sign by which the Lord seals on our consciences the promises of his good will toward us in order to sustain the weakness of our faith."[23] While this may suggest that Calvin regards the sacraments simply as pledges or testimonials of God's promises (rather than as God's actual implementation of his promises), Calvin shows elsewhere that he regards the sacraments as efficacious means of grace, although in ways that differ from Lutheran and Catholic theology.

For example, Calvin denies that Baptism removes original sin. Yet he professes that in Baptism the Church efficaciously declares the baptized person to be united to Christ, although it does not actually unite the person to Christ. The important distinction to keep in mind here is this: For Calvin Baptism is a sign of justification having *already* taken place, while for Catholics Baptism is a sign of justification *presently* taking place.

As for the Eucharist, Calvin rejected both the Catholic and Lutheran versions of belief in the Real Presence. For him, Christ is not present in the bread and wine; he is present only in heaven. Yet, when receiving the bread and wine, Calvin says, one does receive Christ's body and blood—through the power of the Holy Spirit acting in the sacrament and uniting the communicant to Jesus' body in heaven. Thus Calvin rejected both the Zwinglian and Anabaptist positions (which interpreted the Eucharist purely as a memorial service) as well as the Lutheran and Catholic positions (which located the body of Christ in the bread and wine themselves).

With this brief look at Calvin's theology, we conclude our discussion of Protestantism's most influential theologian. How shall we evaluate a man who introduced such striking innovations into the Christian gospel? Perhaps it is better not to try. Let's simply end by repeating a left-handed compliment which Pope Pius IV paid to Calvin. "The strength of that heretic," Pius said, "consisted in this, that money never had the slightest charm for him. If I had such servants my dominion would extend from sea to sea."[24]

CHAPTER SIX

BOTH SIDES OF THE CHANNEL

England, Scotland and France Join the Religious Revolution

T he revolutions in England, Scotland and France differed from those in Germany and Switzerland. The latter were theological revolutions which became politicized, while the former were political revolutions which became theologized. In order to understand this statement, let's begin with the famous reign of King Henry VIII (1509-1547) in England.

THE REIGN OF HENRY VIII

When Henry became king of England in 1509, a more loyal Catholic sovereign could not have been imagined. In writing to his friend Erasmus, Thomas More hailed the young king's accession to power as the dawn of an era of Christian humanism and enlightenment.

Many English people looked upon the king as an exemplar who would lead the English clergy out of corruption and return them to their true mission, for the hierarchy in England was indeed corrupt from top to bottom. The usual priestly immorality was combined with the immense wealth of abbots and bishops who owned, at the very least, 20 percent of all land in England.

The celebrated humanist dean of St. Paul's in London, John Colet (1466-1519), preached frequently to his fellow priests on the urgent need for clerical reform. "Nothing has so disfigured the face of the Church," wrote Colet, "as the secular and worldly living on the part of the clergy."[1] Colet was accurately expressing the mood of the average

English Catholic. Emperor Charles V's ambassador to England reported on the English situation by saying, "Nearly all the people hate the priests."[2]

When Luther's revolt broke loose in Germany, Henry VIII composed his own theological response, *Assertion of the Seven Sacraments Against Martin Luther* (perhaps anonymously coauthored by Henry's chancellor, Cardinal Thomas Wolsey). In this treatise, the king condemned Luther in terms that would later come back to haunt him. "The whole Church," wrote Henry, "is subject not only to Christ but to Christ's only vicar, the pope of Rome."[3] Delighted by the king's treatise, Pope Leo X conferred upon Henry the title "Defender of the Faith."

Encouraged by the pope, Henry moved to squelch the popular reform movement which had been steadily gaining momentum in England. The king forbade the publication of a newly translated English Bible (Tyndale's version of 1525) and prohibited heretical reform writings. Cardinal Wolsey headed a secret police force which scoured the countryside for heretics and reform-minded polemicists.

Yet, in one of the most striking reversals in all of history, the very king who had most devotedly protected the hierarchy's interests would soon seize control of the Church and begin his own version of reform. The catalyst for this turn of events was Henry's unfulfilled desire for a male heir.

Henry's Marital Difficulties

At the age of 12 Henry's father had arranged for him to marry his deceased brother's widow, 18-year-old Catherine of Aragon, daughter of the king and queen of Spain. Since the Old Testament defined such a marriage as incest (Leviticus 20:21), Henry's father had applied to Pope Julius II for a dispensation from the Levitical prohibition. Julius interrupted his wars long enough to agree, but only reluctantly and for purely political reasons: He needed English support in his contest with the French.

In fairness to Henry, one should not have expected a marriage contracted for a 12-year-old boy to be successful. Henry himself, at the age of 14 and while still a prince, valiantly tried to extricate himself from the union by seeking an annulment, but he was deterred for reasons of state.

Seven months after he became king, Catherine bore Henry a son who quickly died. This misfortune was repeated twice. Then, in 1516, Catherine bore a daughter, Mary (the future "Bloody Mary"). At age two Mary was betrothed to the heir of the French crown. This meant that if Henry died without a son, a despised French prince would become king of England. Henry's counselors began to warn the king of the impending disaster.

A French king would mean political catastrophe for England. This, plus Queen Catherine's degenerating sex appeal, motivated Henry to seek again an annulment of his marriage. In 1527, the same year in which he began writing love letters to Anne Boleyn, Henry petitioned Pope Clement VII for the appointment of a papal legate who would hear his case and decide on the validity of his marriage.

Pope Clement complied, agreeing to abide with whatever decision his legate Cardinal Lorenzo Campeggio and Henry's chancellor Cardinal Wolsey would reach. Failing to persuade Catherine to abdicate (Catherine stubbornly insisted that her prior marriage to Henry's brother had never been consummated), Campeggio convened a marriage tribunal on May 31, 1529. After an emotional appeal by Catherine, Campeggio vacillated and persuaded the pope to remove the tribunal to Rome.

Henry was furious and took out his anger on Wolsey who, the king believed, should have orchestrated a proper outcome to the hearing. Deposing Wolsey as chancellor, Henry replaced him with the most celebrated humanist and lawyer in the realm, Thomas More.

Meanwhile, Pope Clement deliberately delayed a decision on Henry's marriage case until he could determine the political consequences of the proposed annulment. As the king's anger turned toward Rome, he openly united himself for the first time with the popular hatred of the Roman Curia and the corrupt English prelates. Parliament now felt confident to express its pent-up nationalistic fury. In an "Act of Accusation" it presented the king with a list of grievances against the clergy and implored him to reform the English Church.

The English Reformation

Thus began the English Reformation, a political revolt on the part of Henry and Parliament against the medieval Church-state system in which the papacy had played a dominating role. Because of their more sophisticated political institutions, the English were able to bypass the violent phase of revolution which had characterized the German Reformation and proceed directly to a political solution. With Parliament's support, Henry in 1531 required the English clergy to acknowledge him as "the protector and only supreme head of the Church and Clergy of England." The "Defender of the Faith" thus founded a new state-sponsored Church of England. When the English bishops realized the seriousness of Henry's purpose, they quickly abandoned

Rome, piously urging Henry in 1532 to withdraw "the obedience of your Highness and of the people...from the See of Rome."[4]

There were notable Catholic dissenters, the most famous being the Lord Chancellor himself, Thomas More, who resigned his post. Thomas Cranmer, the archbishop of Canterbury, succeeded More as chancellor. Cranmer provided theological justifications for the king's new policies and decreed Henry's marriage to Catherine invalid. On June 1, 1533, Anne Boleyn became Queen of England; a month later Pope Clement excommunicated Henry. In September Queen Anne gave birth to a daughter, Elizabeth. As future queen, Elizabeth would finalize her father's revolt and irrevocably separate the Church of England from Rome.

By the Act of Succession (1534), Parliament required all English subjects to swear an oath of loyalty to their king in his new role as head of the Anglican Church and to accept Elizabeth over Mary as the true heir to the English throne. When Thomas More, Bishop John Fisher of Rochester and a handful of other Catholic leaders refused to take the oath, Henry had them beheaded. More became England's most famous Catholic martyr, assuring the spectators at his execution that he died "in and for the faith of the Holy Catholic Church."[5]

Henry's Legacy

In the latter days of his reign, Henry was besieged by troubles on every side. When Queen Anne bore Henry a stillborn child, Henry began to believe himself cursed. When he turned his amorous eyes to another woman, Queen Anne's fate was sealed. In 1536 Henry had his queen beheaded and married Jane Seymour, who at last gave Henry a son (the future Edward VI). Jane died shortly after giving birth and Henry married three more times, earning the contempt of his still overwhelmingly Catholic subjects who disapproved of their king's marital acrobatics.

With Henry's reputation sinking, many of his loyal Catholic subjects began to question his far-reaching policies of Church reform. While most English Catholics had wanted clerical reform, they were not willing to go so far as to allow a secular monarch to become chief bishop of their Church. Throughout England Catholic rebels joined together and demanded the suppression of the heretical theology promulgated by Henry's advisers, the restoration of Princess Mary's right of succession to the throne and the resubmission of the English hierarchy to papal authority. Faced with the prospect of civil war, Henry lashed out against the rebels and disbanded them.

Since the English monasteries served as focal points for Catholic tradition, Henry felt he could prevent rebellion only by confiscating all monastic property in England. The revenues from this policy totaled today's equivalent of roughly $75 million. With this money Henry rewarded his most ardent supporters—namely, the rising class of newly rich merchants and lawyers who had no ties to the Catholic nobility and who became England's future political leaders. Thus by 1540 monasticism had virtually come to an end in England.

Henry's religious policies remained strangely ambivalent until his death. Although he outlawed Roman Catholicism by requiring all English Catholics to disaffirm their belief in papal authority, he at the same time persecuted Protestants who deviated from his State-sponsored religion, which was still Catholic in its external features. In 1531 Henry ordered burned at the stake a Protestant who preached against religious icons; he ordered arrested, tortured and executed another Protestant who advanced a symbolic interpretation of the Eucharist.

In 1539 with the "Act of the Six Articles," Henry and Parliament proclaimed as orthodox doctrines the Real Presence in the Eucharist, the validity of Masses for souls in purgatory, confession of sins to priests and other traditional Catholic beliefs. Priests who married were jailed as felons, and two bishops who opposed the Act were replaced by more "Catholic" bishops. Henry died of an ulcer and syphilis, leaving a huge bequest for Masses for his peaceful repose.

Henry had severed England's ties with the Church of Rome and created a Church ruled by the English crown. Theologically, however, his revolt against Rome changed little in the English Church. His break with Roman authority, however, eventually led English theologians to provide a theoretical base for his policies. During the reign of Henry's son, Edward VI, and especially during the reign of his daughter, Elizabeth I, the English crown was able to consolidate its grasp on the Church and formulate a uniquely English style of Christianity.

ANGLICAN THEOLOGY

When Edward VI became king, he was only nine years old and sickly. Thus the government of England passed into the hands of two dukes who served separate terms as regents. During the regency, Archbishop Thomas Cranmer (1489-1556) became England's theologian-in-chief. Earlier, on a diplomatic mission to the court of Emperor Charles V, Cranmer had secretly married the niece of a leading German reformer. While in Germany he had also adopted many Protestant doctrines, but had to repress the less orthodox of these while Henry VIII reigned. Cranmer began to advance his true beliefs, however, during the regency. It was Cranmer more than anyone who laid the foundation for Anglican theology.

Cranmer first arranged for the abolition of Henry's "Act of the Six Articles," which had required Cranmer himself to put aside his wife (whom he had smuggled into England hidden in a box). He also encouraged publication and reading of English translations of the Bible. Cranmer's most significant achievement, however, was his editorial leadership on the *Book of Common Prayer*, which abolished Henry's Catholic theological tendencies once and for all. The *Book*, for example, rejected both transubstantiation and consubstantiation and denied that the Eucharist was a sacrifice, thereby doing away with the Mass as an element of the Anglican faith.

Cranmer's policies received a temporary setback when the Catholic princess, Mary Tudor ("Bloody Mary"), succeeded Edward VI to the throne in 1553. Queen Mary put Cranmer to death and tried to erase his Protestant reforms, but to no avail. In 1558 Mary died, having executed some 300 Protestants for adhering to their new faith. During the long reign of Mary's successor, the Protestant Queen Elizabeth I (1558-1603), royal persecution continued, but this time Catholics were burned at the stake—roughly half as many as the number of Protestants executed by Mary.

The Thirty-Nine Articles

Elizabeth's success in establishing the Anglican Church rested not only on persecution of Catholics but on the growth of Anglican theology as well. The chief development in this process was the publication of the *Thirty-Nine Articles of Religion* in 1566. The *Articles*, in their final form, based themselves on the principle of *sola scriptura*, but in a way not inconsistent with Catholic belief. For example, the *Articles* stated that "Holy Scripture containeth all things necessary to salvation" (Article 6) and that "it is not lawful for the Church to ordain any thing that is contrary to God's word..." (Article 20). Certainly, Catholics could not have disputed such wording, although their interpretation may have differed.

With respect to liturgy, ceremonials and devotions, the *Articles* took a conciliatory posture. In Article 34 the authors "rebuked openly" anyone who rejected "traditions and ceremonies of the Church which be not repugnant to the Word of God." The Articles went on to state that the "national Church" has the prerogative to change ceremonies and rites, since such things were not found in Scripture in the first place.

Although most of Elizabeth's subjects appreciated her policy of toleration for traditional practices, certain radical reformers resented it.

Such persons favored Calvin's theology in which ceremonials and liturgical rites were seen as departures from Scripture. These dissenting Englishmen—who insisted on the "pure" Church—gave birth to the *Puritan* movement.

In Article 12 of the *Thirty-Nine Articles*, the Anglican Church placed itself squarely behind Luther's doctrine of justification by faith, defining good works as the "fruits of Faith...which follow after justification"—language with which Catholic theologians could certainly also have agreed. Unlike Henry VIII's "Six Articles," the *Thirty-Nine Articles* rejected purgatory, confession to priests for the absolution of sins, indulgences and the use of religious images.

In its definition of the Church, the *Articles* adopted some elements of Calvin's thought, positing the distinction between a visible and an invisible Church. As for Calvin, the sign and mission of the Anglicans' visible Church was the preaching of the Scriptures and administration of the sacraments. The *Articles* also followed Calvin's sacramental teaching. For example, Article 28 reads, "the Body of Christ is given, taken and eaten in the Supper only after an heavenly and spiritual manner."

Taken as a whole, the *Thirty-Nine Articles* represent something of a compromise between traditional Catholic theology and the more radical doctrine of the Swiss reformers. Elizabeth hoped her compromise position would win her Catholic subjects to the new faith, and indeed the *Articles* did gain many Catholic converts to Anglicanism. Yet many other Catholics refused either to accept Elizabeth's *Articles* or to take the required oath of supremacy acknowledging her as the "Supreme Governor of England" in religious matters.

Anglican Intolerance

Some 50,000 of these Catholic "recusants" ("refusers") adhered to their faith, illegally celebrating Mass in their homes. Many other English Catholics emigrated to France. William Allen, a future cardinal, founded a seminary for English priests in the French town of Douai. Here Catholic scholars later published their own "Douay" English Bible a year before the King James Version was published in England. Priests from Douai were smuggled back to England to celebrate Mass and hear confessions on the sly. When the newly formed Jesuits joined ranks with these secular priests, Anglicans began to reconvert to Catholicism in such large numbers that Parliament in 1581 decreed conversion to Catholicism a capital offense.

Elizabeth and Parliament likewise persecuted the newly formed Puritans. Rejecting the queen's compromising theology, these English

Calvinists brazenly condemned Elizabeth in public. Elizabeth, described by one historian as "totally destitute of the sentiment of religion,"[6] abhorred the Puritans more than the Catholics. To her the Puritans were wild-eyed Gnostics. Elizabeth's move to compel acceptance of the *Thirty-Nine Articles* only stiffened Puritan resistance, so she sanctioned the execution of Puritan leaders. Like the Catholics, English Puritans fled England, traveling to Holland and eventually to the new English colonies in America.

THE KIRK OF SCOTLAND

Scotland's overriding purpose had always been to keep itself free of English domination. Throughout the late Middle Ages, as Tudor power in England grew stronger, the Scottish kings continually fought with the English to maintain their nation's independence. The English kings, for their part, regarded the wild land to the north as a seething caldron of turmoil and rebellion.

In 1371 the Scottish king had died leaving no heir, and thus the crown passed to Robert Stuart, whose family ruled Scotland and, at times, even England during the Reformation period. The Stuart and Tudor families were united in 1503 when King James IV of Scotland married the sister of King Henry VIII of England, Margaret Tudor.

Despite this dynastic marriage, however, Scottish kings still felt themselves bound to their traditional alliance with France, on whom Scotland had long relied as a comrade-in-arms in its struggle against the English. Thus when Henry VIII joined in an alliance against France in 1511, King James IV of Scotland turned against his Tudor brother-in-law. Killed in battle, James IV was succeeded by his son, James V, who in 1538 married a French princess.

By this point Henry VIII's revolt against Rome was well underway in England, and the Scottish nobles began to envy the freedom from Roman control which Henry had won for his English lords. Thus the Scottish nobility turned against their Catholic king, James V, and hired themselves out to Henry VIII, promising to keep the French at bay.

When James V died in 1542, he was succeeded by his six-day-old daughter, Mary Queen of Scots. Cardinal-Archbishop David Beaton of St. Andrews began to act as Mary's regent while at the same time pledging loyalty to the French. At this, Henry VIII invaded Scotland and sacked the country with the aid of Scottish nobles hostile to the Catholic Church. Two of these nobles led a band of lords to Beaton's episcopal palace and murdered him.

Thus began the Reformation in Scotland. As in England, political motives were uppermost in the minds of the Scottish revolutionaries. Unlike in England, however, it was nobles rather than the monarch who initiated the revolt. The Scottish crown remained allied to French and Catholic interests, while the nobility turned Protestant and harbored suspicions of the monarch.

The Scottish nobles' main interest was to free Scotland from the French alliance. By doing this they hoped to destroy the political power of Catholicism in Scotland while consolidating their own power and wealth by confiscating Church lands.

The famous Catholic historian Hilaire Belloc (d. 1953), in his work *How the Reformation Happened*, wrote, "The corruption of the Church, bad everywhere throughout Europe in the 15th century, had in Scotland reached a degree hardly known elsewhere."[7] This unchallenged judgment will suffice to summarize the Scottish Church's condition on the eve of the nobles' revolt. We will not catalog the long list of Scottish clerical vices.

John Knox

Well before the nobles' political revolt, Scottish polemicists had called for reform of the Church. As elsewhere in Europe, would-be reformers had met with unyielding and sometimes violent resistance from the Scottish hierarchy. Archbishop Beaton had tortured and executed the popular Calvinist preacher George Wishart in 1546. One of Wishart's disciples, John Knox (1514-1572), assumed the leadership of the Calvinist movement in Scotland.

Knox had been a priest and a canon lawyer. When he converted to Calvinism he renounced his previous faith with a fury surpassing that of any reformer we have studied thus far. Knox assisted the nobles who assassinated Beaton, writing later that the crime had been easily accomplished because the conspirators broke in on Beaton "busy at his accounts with Mistress Ogilvy that night."[8]

Knox soon became both leader and symbol of the Protestant cause in Scotland, adopting Calvinism as the vehicle for his revolt. According to Knox, Calvin's theocracy in Geneva represented "the most perfect school of Christ that ever was on earth since the days of the Apostles."[9] Like Calvin in Geneva, Knox supervised the Calvinist Church in Scotland with an iron fist, believing that he too was directly guided by divine command. Under Knox's leadership, a Scottish synod of Protestant elders met in 1552 and adopted a purely Calvinist theology.

Like Calvin, Knox found more solace in the Old Testament than in the New, and it was the angry, vengeful God of the Pentateuch whom Knox preached. Drawing his strength from this wrathful God, Knox turned all his attention to the condemnation of Catholics. Since Catholics were children of Satan rather than of God, he wrote, the biblical injunction to love one's enemies did not apply to Catholics. Knox reveled in what he called the "perfect hatred"[10] for Catholics which the Holy Spirit had put into Protestants' hearts. Whereas Luther and Calvin had limited their attacks to the Catholic *system* and its hierarchy, Knox damned all Catholic *believers*, lay and clerical alike.

When Queen Mary Tudor of England ("Bloody Mary") married the Spanish king, Philip II, Knox became increasingly involved in Reformation politics. Fearing the spread of Mary's Catholic policies to Scotland, Knox wrote an inflammatory pamphlet condemning the marriage (1554).

He combined his hatred of Catholics with his mistrust of women when in 1558 he wrote another pamphlet, *First Blast of the Trumpet Against the Monstrous Regiment of Women*. Calling Mary Tudor "Jezebel," Knox said that a woman ruler was contrary to nature and a violation of God's law. "Woman in her greatest perfection," he wrote "was made to serve and obey man, not to rule and command him."[11] (It was perhaps Knox's predestined misfortune to live in an island dominated by strong females.)

Like Luther and Calvin before him, Knox could tolerate freedom of conscience only for those who accepted his own interpretation of the Bible. All others were heretics who merited burning at the stake. When voices of protest were raised against Knox's views, he condemned his critics as pagan rationalists who perverted the pure word of God by their logical arguments. For Knox reason and faith were completely incompatible. (At least Luther and Calvin, by their reasoned analyses, acknowledged their indebtedness to humanistic rationalism). "For what impudence is it," Knox asked, "to prefer corrupt nature and blind reason to God's Scripture?"[12]

Kirk and State

In a book written in 1560—his *First Book of Discipline*—Knox showed himself a skilled organizational thinker. For Knox, Church and state were to be completely united. He called for state regulation and supervision of the Scottish "Kirk" (the Scots' word for "Church"). In his book Knox called for the division of Scotland into ecclesiastical provinces, each ruled by a superintendent. At an annual "Kirk Session" the superintendents and their deacons were to elect new deacons and elders. Although the Scottish nobles never fully supported Knox's presbyterian form of Church government (see p. 92), the groundwork was nonethless laid for the future Presbyterian Church of Scotland, the forerunner and model of the various modern Presbyterian denominations.

Also in 1560, Knox and his associates formulated the "Confession of Faith" which, when approved by the Scottish Parliament, became the official Scottish Creed. The Creed acknowledged belief in the Trinity, original sin (by which the image of God in human beings was "utterly defiled"), predestination, two sacraments (accepting Calvin's sacramental theology) and, highly significant for the future, the union of Church and state. The Scottish nobility, uninterested in religion except as a support for their own interests, rejected Knox's request for the donation of state-supported Church land. At this, Knox's Church broke with the nobles and sought to gain control of the Scottish government by electing Presbyterians to the Scottish assembly.

When Knox died in 1572, the Catholic Church in Scotland still existed, but its influence was nil. Catholic bishops were appointed by the annual Synod of the Scottish Kirk, and most of them simply followed the Kirk's directives. In theory there were two Churches; in practical effect only one. The Scottish bishops eventually lost all contact with Rome and organized themselves as their brothers in England had done—that is, into a national episcopacy supervised by the crown.

Knox was succeeded as head of the Kirk by Andrew Melville (1545-1622). Melville in his *Second Book of Discipline* exceeded Knox's theory of Church-state relations by demanding that the state bring all its activities into line with Kirk doctrine. Melville's doctrine would of course have eliminated princely authority, and thus the nobility rejected his theories.

Catholic King James VI of Scotland (1567-1625) tried to institute an episcopal form of Church government similar to England's in which Church and state would achieve a reasonably balanced division of authority. In 1584 he secured the parliamentary passage of the "Black Acts," which reasserted the supremacy of the state over Church affairs. Through state-controlled bishops King James hoped to destroy (or at least minimize) the power of the Presbyterians.

Thus began in Scotland a struggle between Episcopalians (those who accepted the episcopal model of Church organization) and Presbyterians. The result was a major victory for the latter in 1592. James was forced to abolish the episcopate and restore the Kirk to supreme ecclesiastical power. In 1597, however, after a Presbyterian attempt to dethrone James had failed, a compromise was reached in which Episcopalians and Presbyterians agreed to mutual toleration.

When Queen Elizabeth of England died in 1603, King James VI of Scotland (great-grandson of Henry VIII's sister, Margaret Tudor, see p. 90) was the only available heir to the English throne. After promising to support the Anglican Church, James was crowned as King James I of England, uniting in his person both the thrones of Scotland and England and the dynasties of Tudor and Stuart. Since James' Stuart ancestry was linked to Catholic France, however, neither the English nor the Scots ever lost their suspicion that he harbored pro-Catholic sentiments. Ironically, it was King James, the crypto-Catholic, who authorized the publication of the King James Bible, English-speaking Protestants' most prized possession.

Since Stuart ties with France were always a point of Protestant suspicion and thus highly significant for the future, this is a good time to discuss the effects of the Reformation in France.

CATHOLIC FRANCE

When Luther's revolt began in Germany, Francis I (1515-1547) was king of France. Francis and the Holy Roman Emperor Charles V were bitter rivals, despite their common Catholic religion. Each tried to advance the interests of his respective dynasty at the expense of the other. When Charles got bogged down in Luther's revolution, Francis sent his troops into territories claimed by Charles in Spain and Italy. But when Francis' most powerful vassal, the Duke of Bourbon, betrayed Francis and became general of Charles's Italian army, Francis was taken prisoner and forced to sign a treaty favoring the Empire. (It was during this war that an obscure Basque soldier named Ignatius Loyola was seriously wounded—an event, as we shall see, of immense significance for the future.)

Charles's victory over Francis was too much to bear both for the pope (see p. 64) and the Protestants; each feared the enormous aggrandizement of Charles's power. When Pope Clement VII joined France and several Italian cities in an alliance against the emperor, Charles's troops invaded Rome (1527) and gave it the worst sacking since the days of the Visigoths, imprisoning the pope in the process (see p. 102).

For the next 20 years France tried unsuccessfully to oust the emperor from the leadership of Catholic Europe. When Francis died, he left his country virtually bankrupt. One of his last official acts was to send a huge gift of money to German Protestants as a bribe to induce them to overthrow his Catholic rival, the emperor.

Francis I and the French Church
The French Church suffered from the same abuses which characterized Catholic decadence elsewhere in Europe. Yet, thanks

largely to the strength of the French university system (especially the prestigious Sorbonne in Paris), Luther's theology was quickly refuted by Catholic theologians even in the face of the widespread clerical abuses. Protestantism *as a system of thought* thus never acquired a significant foothold in France. When a few heretics were burned at the stake in 1526, the French people generally supported the authorities instead of the persecuted radicals.

Another reason why France did not teeter toward religious revolution lay in this fact: For two centuries the French Church had achieved a large measure of independence from Roman domination. The debacle of the papal schism (see *The People of the Faith*, p. 137 ff) had meant that the French crown controlled the papacy rather than the other way around. Only a year before Luther's revolt, Pope Leo X had entered into a *Concordat* with King Francis I in which the pope ceded to the king the right to name bishops and abbots in the French Church. Thus, unlike the situation in Germany, there was no climate of curial oppression in France; the French Church, although Catholic in theology, was virtually a state-controlled body well before Luther.

At the outbreak of the peasants' rebellion in Germany (see pp. 58-60) Francis I decided to repress the weak Protestant movement in France. In need of the clergy's money to finance his wars with Charles V, Francis willingly heeded the clergy's demands to eradicate heresy. Yet Francis' attitude toward Protestants *outside* of France depended on his political interests. He frequently allied himself with Protestant princes in Germany while jailing Protestant polemicists in France.

The greatest atrocity resulting from Francis' two-faced religious policy occurred in 1545. Francis' troops attacked some 20 villages in the region of Provence (southern France) which were linked religiously to the medieval Waldensians (see *The People of the Faith*, pp. 95, 96). When these people drew up a profession of faith based on the views of German and Swiss reformers, Francis authorized their massacre. News of the mass murder shocked Christians throughout Europe; it even motivated many French Catholics in the region to convert to the Protestant faith. These new French Protestants adopted the same name used by the Swiss revolutionaries in Calvin's Geneva—*Huguenots*.

Toward Religious War
After the Provence murders, Huguenot power steadily grew in France, particularly in the Atlantic coastal town of La Rochelle.

And as had happened in Scotland, ambitious French nobles began to envy the wealth and power which the spread of Protestantism had brought to their brothers in other countries. Some of the greatest

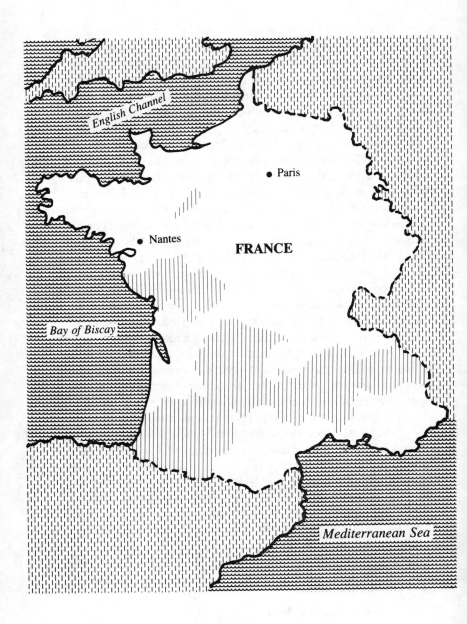

CATHOLICS AND HUGUENOTS IN FRANCE (c. 1562)

Huguenot areas   Catholic areas

Catholic lords in France deserted their king, most notably Gaspard de Coligny, Prince Louis de Condé and Antoine de Bourbon. Henry II (1547-1559), who succeeded Francis I, was dominated by his mistress Diane de Poitiers. Diane feared the growth of Protestant power in France because it conflicted with her family's interests. Her son-in-law the Duke of Guise and his brother Cardinal Lorraine controlled the French Church. King Henry II thus began to persecute the Huguenots, fanning the fires of religious hatred.

Henry's son, Francis II (1559-1560), reigned for only a year—just long enough to intensify the religious strife. Along with prominent nobles, a large portion of France's middle class had by now accepted Calvinism. One Catholic observer placed the French Protestant population in 1559 at one-fourth of the nation's whole.

When Francis II stepped up the royal persecution, the Huguenots prepared for civil war. Francis II died abruptly and was succeeded by his 10-year-old brother, Charles IX (1560-1574). The government of France was once again dominated by a woman: the young king's mother, Catherine de' Medici.

The Huguenots, by now no longer a loose collection of Calvinist radicals, were a major political faction seeking a substantial voice in the French government. The Huguenot leaders were well-organized and well-financed; perhaps as many as half of the French nobility were now Protestant. The Huguenot and Catholic factions aligned themselves geographically as follows: The southwest of France became Huguenot country (except for the peasantry, which everywhere stayed Catholic); while Paris and the northeast generally remained Catholic (see map, p. 96).

St. Bartholomew's Day

Between 1562 and 1598 a total of eight religious wars were fought in France. The most villainous incident of these wars took place on August 24, 1572—St. Bartholomew's Day. This incident has come to be known as the "St. Bartholomew's Day Massacre," an event which still stands out as one of the saddest moments in French history. Ironically, the massacre took place only four days after Catholic and Protestant parties had tried to compromise their differences by arranging a dynastic marriage between Charles IX's sister Margaret and the Bourbon Prince Henry of Navarre, titular head of the Huguenots.

While the Huguenot leaders who had attended the wedding were still in Paris, Queen Catherine de' Medici persuaded the Catholic Duke of Guise to assassinate the Huguenot leader, Gaspard de Coligny. Since Coligny was only wounded in the attempt, Catherine feared her son the king would discover that she had masterminded the plot. Panicking, she convinced her weak-kneed son to authorize the wholesale slaughter of Huguenot leaders in Paris and the provinces as the only means of preventing Huguenot retribution. Perhaps as many as 10,000 Huguenots were murdered in the ensuing massacre.

The deed was exceeded in disgrace only by the official Catholic response: Four days after the murders the royal court celebrated the Huguenot deaths by attending a Mass of thanksgiving. Pope Gregory XIII in Rome did likewise, praising God in a homily for the murderers' success.

The St. Bartholomew's Day Massacre naturally provoked the Huguenots to stiffen their resistance to Catholic persecution. Religious war erupted again. Although the Huguenots had been deprived of most of their leaders by the massacre, they fought on through five more wars, each interrupted by brief periods of peace.

Neither King Charles IX (who died in 1574), nor his brother King Henry III (who died in 1589) was survived by any descendants. The crown thus went to the very Henry of Navarre whose wedding had been the prelude to the St. Bartholomew's Day murders. (Henry's marriage had earned him a share in his wife's inheritance of her dead brother's—Charles IX's—right of succession.)

'Paris Is Worth a Mass'

Henry's religious sentiments were by no means stable; he had vacillated back and forth from one faith to the other depending on the momentary advantage to be gained. During the fifth religious war, when it looked as though the Huguenots would prevail, he reembraced Calvinism. But when he realized that the throne of France had fallen into his hands, he pledged not to harm the Catholics should he be crowned king. For Catholic leaders this assurance was not enough. They crowned their own man Charles X king (Cardinal de Bourbon), and fortified themselves inside the walls of Paris. Although Henry besieged Paris, he realized that the defeat of the Catholic party would not bring lasting peace to a country whose lower classes were still overwhelmingly Catholic. Thus, in a practical resolution of the imbroglio, Henry decided to reconvert to Catholicism, uttering his famous rationale: "Paris is worth a Mass."

On this opportunistic premise France remained Catholic. Henry was crowned King Henry IV (1589-1610), the first king of a Bourbon lineage that would extend into the 19th century.

Henry's greatest contribution to the Reformation was his promulgation in 1598 of the *Edict of Nantes*. By this Edict, the

Huguenots were given *political* rights equal to those enjoyed by Catholics, but not completely equal *religious* rights. Only certain specified cities and provinces were to tolerate the Reformed religion. The Huguenots were forbidden to practice their faith in all episcopal and archepiscopal sees, in the city of Paris and its suburbs, and in the royal court itself.

By 1598 the Huguenot population had shrunk considerably from its height at the beginning of the religious wars to perhaps only one-twelfth of the population.[13] War and massacre had effected utilitarian reconversions and had prompted many Huguenots to emigrate to freethinking Holland or to England. The savage hatred unleashed by the war, the hypocrisy of Henry's conversion to Catholicism and the atrocious behavior of the Catholic leadership all combined to give French Catholicism a cynical and anticlerical coloring which has affected the French Church to this day. In response to this ethos, some French Catholics overreacted and turned fanatically puritanical, as we shall see when we discuss French Jansenism in Chapter Ten.

CHAPTER SEVEN

THE CHURCH RESPONDS

Reintegrating the Catholic Tradition

When Pope Leo X died in 1521, Luther's revolt was becoming a breakaway success in Germany and was gradually infiltrating the other nations of Europe as well. Leo had looked upon the events in Germany as a monks' squabble and had taken Luther's movement seriously only in the latter days of his pontificate. But the cardinals who met to elect Leo's successor realized that the new pope must give first priority to Catholic reform.

THE POPES AND REFORM

Adrian VI

The man elected to succeed Leo X was as different in personality and temperament from the gay and carefree Leo as one could imagine. In a highly unusual decision, the cardinals bypassed the Italian candidates and elected a stern Dutch cardinal, Adrian Dedel, who had been bishop of Tortosa in Spain since 1515. From 1516 he and Cardinal Francisco de Cisneros Ximenez, archbishop of Toledo, had acted as regents for the young emperor Charles V and, thus, virtually governed Spain.

When informed of his election as pope, Adrian set sail for Rome, determined to reform the Church. In his first speech to the Curia he repeated the words of St. Bernard of Clairvaux, to complain of the filthy stench arising from the Curia's sins. Immediately Adrian began to make enemies. Many cardinals wanted reform—but for others, not for themselves. As for the Roman people, they considered the cardinals' election of the pale, ascetic Dutchman madness.

As Adrian continued to speak in his blunt Dutch way, it became increasingly obvious to the Curia that the new pope represented a serious threat to their interests. Consider, as an example of Adrian's intentions, his letter to a Diet of German princes and bishops meeting at Nuremberg:

> Holy Scripture loudly proclaims that the sins of the people have their source in the sins of the priesthood....We are well aware that even in this Holy See much that is detestable has appeared for some years already—abuses in spiritual things, violation of the commandments—and that everything has been changed for the worst....All of us, prelates and clergy, have turned aside from the road of righteousness and for a long time now there has been not even one who did good....You must therefore promise in our name that we intend to exert ourselves so that, first of all, the Roman Court [the Curia], from which perhaps all this evil took its start, may be improved. Then, just as from here the sickness proceeded, so also from here recovery and renewal may begin.[1]

As the Curia's opposition rose, Adrian turned elsewhere for support. He begged Erasmus, his former classmate at the University of Louvain, to come to Rome and direct a corps of Catholic polemicists who would refute the heretics' writings and spearhead clerical reform. Erasmus declined because of poor health, but encouraged Adrian to disband the Roman hangers-on and form a body of Catholic scholars who would enter into peaceful dialogue with the Lutherans.

Had Adrian lived long enough to follow Erasmus's advice the entire course of the Reformation would no doubt have been different. Instead, Adrian died on September 14, 1523, verifying the words he left for his epitaph: "Oh, how much depends upon the time in which the work of even the best man falls."[2]

Clement VII

After a conclave that lasted seven weeks, the cardinals elected a Medici, an illegitimate cousin of Pope Leo X whom the family patriarch Lorenzo had raised along with his other children. Pope Clement VII took the papal throne at age 45, raising the Curia's hopes that the policies of the monastic Dutchman would be reversed.

Clement's reign got off on the wrong foot when he reinvolved the papacy in a conflict with the emperor, a policy which distracted papal attention from reform and led to the disastrous sack of Rome in 1527. Emperor Charles's soldiers tore the city apart in a rampage which lasted for eight violent days. Clement was taken prisoner and confined in Castle Sant' Angelo. He escaped, disguised as a servant, seven months later. His dream of restoring papal supremacy in Italy shattered, Clement resigned himself to accepting imperial sovereignty.

The pope's thirst for political power had sidetracked the reform initiative begun by Pope Adrian VI. At Clement's accession in 1523, reconciliation with the Lutherans was still possible; at his death in 1534, England had seceded from the Church, as had a portion of Switzerland, most of Germany and the crowns of Denmark and Sweden. Clement's was unquestionably a calamitous pontificate; his desire to increase the power and wealth of his Medici relatives resulted in the total collapse of the papacy's reputation.

Paul III

Clement's successor, Alesandro Farnese, was raised in the same environment as Leo X and Clement VII. He had studied at the court of Lorenzo de' Medici in Florence. A cardinal at 25, Farnese was unanimously elected pope and took the name Paul III.

Paul was torn between restoring the Renaissance papacy and fostering reform. He desired the former but realized the Church desperately needed the latter. Paul vacillated, hoping to enjoy the best of both worlds.

Twice Paul sent representatives to Germany to invite Lutheran leaders to a council. But, when his legates informed the Lutherans that the pope refused in advance to compromise on questions of doctrine or on papal authority, the Protestants naturally refused to consent to a council.

In 1541 Paul sent Cardinal Gasparo Contarini to the town of Ratisbon in central Germany to discuss the possibility of doctrinal compromise with Melancthon and other Protestant leaders. According to Contarini, agreement was reached on the key issue of justification, proving that in the central element of Luther's theology the two sides had never been as distant as Luther had imagined. Yet the conferees were divided over eucharistic doctrine—Catholic transubstantiation versus Lutheran consubstantiation—and thus the Ratisbon meeting came to nothing.

Shortly after the Ratisbon conference, when dialogue with the Lutheran princes over religious matters was sorely needed, the pope chose instead to support the Protestant princes in their war with Charles V. Paul decided that religious reconciliation with the Lutherans, which would unite the divided Germans under the emperor, would mean political disadvantage for the papacy in Italy. Paul therefore deserted the emperor during a critical stage of Charles's civil war with the

Protestant princes (see p. 64). Encouraged by Paul's treachery on their behalf, the Lutherans no longer had a motive for considering compromise with the Catholics.

Although Paul's struggle to gain supremacy over the emperor meant the destruction of reform efforts in Germany, Paul III did make some headway in Church reform in Italy. He began by appointing cardinals of unquestioned sanctity and loyalty. Contarini, for example, became the leader of Catholic reform in Italy; and Gian Pietro Carafa, the future Paul IV, cofounded the Theatine Order, which transformed the lives of priests all over Europe. Paul III thus undertook to reform the Church as a whole by reforming the cardinals. (As if to balance out his good appointments, however, the pope also appointed two of his relatives to the College.)

Another important aspect of Paul's reform involved the mendicant orders. Both the Dominicans and Franciscans—the glory of the late medieval Church—had long since succumbed to spiritual and moral decay. Pope Paul's reform-minded cardinals appointed equally reform-minded minister-generals for the two orders. Luther's own order, the Augustinians, likewise received a new general dedicated to reform.

These generals in turn appointed provincials throughout the rest of Europe. They called their orders back to simple life-styles. The ownership of private property by individual friars and monks was condemned, regular visitations of friaries and novitiates were reinstituted, and the decentralization of control (so that the Curia in Rome had less to say about the mendicants' lives) were all tools which zealous provincials used to prune away the dead branches from the mendicant vines.

In 1536 Paul III appointed a reform commission comprised of eight neutral prelates. In daring boldness, they reported to the pope on March 9, 1537, that the root of all abuse was the papal office and its Curia. As remedies, the commission called for the reform of procedures by which dispensations were granted, better supervision and screening of candidates to the priesthood, and an overall reform of the hierarchy's private lives.

When the commission called for an end to the sale of curial offices, however, Paul III resisted, refusing to allow reform to deprive him of a principal source of revenue. Nonetheless, Paul did implement one of the commission's key recommendations: He required 80 bishops who lived permanently in Rome feathering their political nests to return to their dioceses and become shepherds of their local flocks.

The Call for a Council

Despite Paul's somewhat ambivalent reform efforts, he did take one step of immense significance for the future of Catholicism. In 1535 the pope announced a general council which was to meet in Mantua in northern Italy. When Mantua failed to please the diverse elements whom Paul invited (including various Protestant princes), the pope declared his intention to move the council to Vicenza, northeast of Mantua and closer to Germany. When Paul's legates opened the "council" of Vicenza, however, no bishops appeared, and Paul's proposal for a council was momentarily shelved.

In 1541 the emperor intervened, suggesting as a site for the council the city of Trent, over the Italian border in German territory. War between Charles V and Francis I again delayed the start of the council (politics always superseded religion) until 1543, when a mere 10 bishops heeded the pope's summons to Trent. Finally, on Paul's fifth attempt to get the bishops to respond to their own demand for a council, the first session of the Council of Trent convened on December 13, 1545, with 25 archbishops and the generals of five orders in attendance. It was an inauspicious beginning for what would become the most important council of the Church since the early Middle Ages.

THE COUNCIL OF TRENT

The 30 men who came to Trent milled around for weeks waiting for more delegates to arrive and for someone to propose an agenda. The pope himself was not present, but sent three legates to preside over the Council. The delay in setting an agenda was due in large part to conflicting theories about the purpose of the Council: The emperor wanted simply to reform abuses, thereby allowing his Protestant princes maximum opportunity both to vent their spleen and to present their own discussion of doctrine; the pope wanted to focus on a restatement of Catholic doctrine and delay discussion of clerical abuses.

In response to Paul III's constant call for support of the Council, the number of delegates steadily increased. The second session of the Council had 70 delegates and the third 225. At the Councils of Constance and Basle (see *The People of the Faith*, p. 144) the delegates had voted in "nations," that is, according to national groupings, with each group having one vote. These national groups had included not only prelates but lay nobles as well. At Trent, however, Paul III forbade the participation of laymen. Only cardinals, bishops, generals of religious orders and abbots could vote—and they voted *individually*, each delegate having one vote.

Thus, the Italian bishops, heavily indebted to the pope for their offices, controlled the voting. This was due to two facts: There were more bishops in Italy than in other countries, and more Italian bishops attended the Council than did the bishops of other countries.

Further, it was the pope, acting through his appointed advisers in Rome (whom he collectively called "congregations"), who submitted the issues to the delegates. Thus, the delegates did not choose their own agenda. Right from the start, Trent was destined to be a Council in the medieval mold, controlled by the pope lest the delegates assert their independence.

The emperor and non-Italian delegates won a partial victory at the Council's second session (January 1546) when the Council voted to discuss both the reform of clerical abuse and the restatement of doctrine. The Council generally adhered to this twofold agenda throughout its duration.

With the agenda established, the Council delegates began to address the various ecclesiastical and doctrinal issues that had been raised during the years since the start of Luther's revolt. Since the Council met in 25 sessions spread out over a period of 18 years (1545-1563), an exhaustive analysis of every issue discussed is impossible here. Instead, we will simply summarize the Council's teachings on the most important issues. First we will look at what Trent said about two issues related to the Bible: canonicity and the role of Tradition.

Trent on the Bible

At the fourth session (1546) the Council ruled that the canon of the Bible must include the seven Old Testament books—Tobit, Judith, Wisdom, Ecclesiasticus, Baruch, and 1 and 2 Maccabees—in addition to the Greek portions of Daniel and Esther which the Protestants had excised. The Council likewise declared Jerome's *Vulgate* translation the only authoritative text and the Catholic Church as the only authoritative interpreter of Scripture.

In addressing itself to Luther's doctrine of *sola scriptura*, the Council stated that the Bible contains God's revealed Word and that Church Tradition consists of the authentic interpretation of that Word. On the relationship between Scripture and Tradition, the Council stated that it "receives and venerates with a feeling of piety and reverence all the books both of the Old and New Testaments, since one God is the author of both; also, the traditions, whether they relate to faith or to morals, as having been dictated either orally by Christ or by the Holy

Ghost, and preserved in the Catholic Church in unbroken succession."[3]

Thus the Council reformulated the Church's ancient belief in God's continuing revelation throughout time. The Council did not separate revelation into Scripture and Tradition but, following the understanding of the early Church (see *The People of the Creed*, pp. 48-49), continued to teach that revelation is an ongoing and holistic process begun by God and continued through the Church in its postbiblical teachings.

After *sola scriptura*, the other major Lutheran doctrine was justification by faith. When the Council turned to address this issue, it entered into one of its most prolonged debates.

The emperor's legates opened the discussion by posing the question of the interplay between the justifying grace won for humanity by Jesus' death on the cross and the sanctifying grace which inheres in the soul as a result of the sacraments. This question, which lay at the very heart of Luther's break with the Catholic Church, rose in response to the doctrine taught by some Catholic theologians known as "twofold justification." Since we now have reached the point where Catholicism addressed the key Lutheran challenge, let's digress and explore the central issue of Luther's revolt.

A Necessary Digression: Grace, Faith and Justification

The theory of twofold justification grew out of the Scholastic understanding of grace, in which God's own life was said to be infused into the soul through the sacraments. It was thought that through the sacraments one could "accumulate" grace, as it were, and thus transform the condition of one's soul from sin to holiness. Twofold justification, therefore, contained the notion that grace depends on both human initiative and God's initiative because humans were thought to merit salvation by their actions in accumulating grace.

Notice that Catholic teaching on sanctifying grace did not necessarily *presuppose* the theory of twofold justification. The way in which some theologians *applied* the concept of sanctifying grace, however, led to the theory of twofold justification.

According to Thomas Aquinas, the best of the medieval theologians, when God justified a person in Baptism (or "cleansed the soul of original sin"), God infused into the soul sanctifying grace—that is, the grace which sanctifies or makes someone holy. Luther rejected sanctifying grace because it seemed to him to place the responsibility for justification on people's actions—going through the various sacramental rituals—rather than on God's initiative. He insisted that, since it is people, not God, who choose to receive the sacraments, people thus believe themselves graced for having done something on their own initiative. For Luther, therefore, the pursuit of sanctifying grace in order to free one's soul of sin's stain was simply a "work," something human beings did on their own initiative in order to merit salvation.

Traditional Catholic thinking had always taught that once a person accepts God's gift of salvation in Baptism, the Church and the other sacraments then become efficacious means by which Christ *continues* to maintain his graced relationship with the justified believer. Luther denied this. For him, once a person says yes to God, such a person is assured of salvation and no longer has need of this "habitual," or sanctifying grace, which Christ gives through the sacraments. That is why Luther and other Protestants redefined the sacraments simply as *actions* whereby one *testifies* to Christ's justifying grace, not *means* whereby one actually participates in grace—or, in Scholastic terminology, *receives* grace.

Protestant theology since the Reformation has moved beyond Luther's position just as Catholic theology has moved beyond the Scholastic position. Thus the dichotomized views of grace presented above don't always hold true today. Scripture scholars today, for example, have shown that the Greek word *charis*, usually used for the word *grace* in the New Testament, is also used for the word *reward*; thus God's grace is seen in Scripture in several places to be related to human action. Also, some Protestant theologians today speak of the sacraments as sources of "cooperating grace" by which justifying grace is, as it were, restimulated.

Further, Catholic theology since the Middle Ages has moved away from the static view of grace as an entity or thing to a more accurate view of grace as a dynamic *relationship* with God. In our own century, for example, the Jesuit theologian Karl Rahner (d. 1984) did much to correct the Scholastics' inadequate understanding of grace. Thus Catholic and Protestant (or *some* Protestant) positions on grace are closer together today than at the time of Luther.

Trent on Justification

This digression relates to our present discussion as follows: Had the Council of Trent defined sanctifying grace according to the theory of twofold justification (justification by both God's efforts and humanity's efforts), it would have proved Luther right to criticize Catholicism for teaching salvation by works. But in fact Trent specifically rejected the theory of twofold justification. Instead it decreed that God alone, through his own initiative, justifies humanity through Jesus' sacrificial death on the cross. Trent thus taught that sanctifying grace is God's unmerited free gift, not something one earns through one's own merits by receiving the sacraments. Trent thus reaffirmed traditional Catholic belief in the power of the sacraments to confer sanctifying grace, but also stressed that this grace is, in the last analysis, always a result of God's initiative.

In a distinction of immense significance, Trent did not teach that it is *faith* which justifies. Rather, Trent emphasized it is *Christ* who justifies and faith which enables one to receive justification.

Luther had been so concerned with condemning the Scholastic view of grace that he had, in effect, replaced Christ with faith as the *source* of justification. This of course simply substituted one type of "work" for another—*believing* one's way to heaven instead of *working* one's way there. In other words, Luther made it possible to "earn salvation" in another way, through *my* faith, *my* acceptance of Jesus as Lord, *my* decision to follow Christ.

Yet these attitudes can be every bit as self-centered and "work"-oriented as the Catholic abuses which Luther rightly condemned. Protestantism can easily become as distorted as certain aspects of late medieval Catholicism if it emphasizes only the believer's faith decision, rather than that faith decision *plus* the continuing life of grace Christ gives us in and through the ministry of his Church.

Through the sacraments and our shared life in the Church we nurture our gift of justifying grace and enhance it, deepen it and enrich it. But we do not "earn grace" either by proclaiming "I believe" or by being baptized. Luther was right to steer Catholicism away from its distorted emphasis on human effort. Yet Luther was wrong, in my estimation, to reject the Church as the means by which God continues to grace his people even after they have been justified.

In actuality, then, both Luther and the Council of Trent taught that justifying grace is God's free gift bestowed on humanity independent of human initiative. Trent, however, went on to say that the human will plays an essential role in justification: Human will must decide whether to accept or reject justifying grace. Thus Trent spoke both of God's prior initiative as the key to justification and also of the human *response* as a necessary adjunct to God's initiative. In defining these two elements the Council wrote, "Without any merit on their part they [sinners] are called; that they who by sin had been cut off from God, may be disposed...*to convert themselves to their own justification* by *freely assenting to* and cooperating with the grace"[4] (emphasis added).

The emphasized words are not the same as twofold justification; human response to God's grace is not the same thing as meriting or earning justification. The Council clarified this when it said, "nor is man able by his own free will and without the grace of God to move himself to justice in His sight."[5]

Both Luther and Trent emphasized the gratuity of justification. Their respective teachings on justification differed, however, in the following respect: Whereas Luther spoke of God's justice as being *imputed* to the sinner (see pp. 38-39), Trent made it clear that, "not only are we *reputed* just, we are truly called and *are* just...."[6] Thus Catholicism held fast to the Church's traditional belief in objective justification and rejected Luther's subjective justification. Trent took the Apostle Paul at his word when he wrote, "...if anyone is in Christ, he is a new creation. The old order has passed away; now all is new!" (2 Corinthians 5:17).

As for Luther's condemnation of Catholicism's "works," Trent taught that it is only after one has become justified that one's good works can be said to receive merit. In this sense, then, Trent could speak of salvation (the end product of the Christian's graced life) rather than of justification (Christ's initial gift of sanctification) as requiring both faith and works. Salvation, Trent wrote, is both a "grace mercifully promised to the sons of God through Jesus Christ, and a reward promised by God himself, to be faithfully given to [the justified believers'] good works and merits."[7]

Trent on the Sacraments

The discussion on the sacraments began during the Council's seventh session (1547), with reaffirmation of the medieval view of seven sacraments as instituted by Christ and efficacious in and of themselves to give grace aside from the sanctity of the minister. The sacraments were declared to be necessary for salvation. But as the delegates began to debate the decree on the Eucharist, an epidemic of typhus broke out and the delegates voted to adjourn to Bologna. This decision infuriated the German delegates, who considered the adjournment a ruse to consolidate Italian control of the Council (an erroneous opinion—the epidemic was a reality).

The imperial party remained in Trent while the majority opened the eighth session in Bologna (April 1547), a situation which threatened to produce a schism. In the meantime, Pope Paul III had died (November 10, 1549). The new pope, Julius III (1550-1555), imitated the papacy of Leo X by reintroducing Renaissance hedonism to the papal office. Julius cared little for tedious matters like the appropriate venue of a council. He therefore rejected the plea of the majority, who wanted to remain at Bologna, and returned the Council to Trent (1551), thereby endearing himself to the emperor.

The size of the imperial delegation had by now grown to such an extent that Italian control of the Council was broken. At the first reconvened session even German Protestants were present as observers. The Protestants' call for a decree asserting a Council's superiority over a pope was rejected, and the Council returned to its interrupted debate on the Eucharist.

In the 13th session the delegates reaffirmed traditional teachings on the Real Presence and transubstantiation as defined during the Middle Ages, particularly at the Fourth Lateran Council of 1215. A motion to debate the propriety of allowing the laity to receive Communion under both species was permanently tabled.

In its decree on Baptism, the Council once again restated traditional Church doctrine by declaring that Baptism effects what it signifies: It removes the stain of original sin or, in the terminology used above, it bestows sanctifying grace as the water is being poured. This was a purely legalistic way of defining Baptism, however, since nothing was said of its role in conferring new spiritual life.

On sacramental Penance the Council reformulated three traditional elements: (1) contrition (which Trent defined as "sorrow of heart and detestation of sin committed, with the purpose of not sinning in the future"), (2) confession to a priest (declared to be essential for absolution) and (3) satisfaction (or the actual penance).

The Reform of Abuses

So far the Council had proceeded as smoothly as could be expected in the area of redefining doctrine. When it attempted to address the issue of clerical abuse, however, tempers began to erupt. One bishop opened a session of the Council by blaming Luther's revolt entirely on the corruption of priests and bishops. Two other bishops disagreed over this remark so violently that one snatched a handful of hair out of the other's beard, prompting the emperor to threaten to throw them both in a nearby river until they cooled off. When a debate on monastic abuses began, one delegate was shouted down by another, leading the first speaker to ask, "Is this still a free council?"[8]

The debate over clerical reform threatened to be the most intractable which the Council would face. All that was achieved in the early sessions was a decree prohibiting bishops from controlling more than one diocese or from ruling their dioceses *in absentia*, and such regulations had already been promulgated by various popes.

The impulse toward clerical reform was strengthened when Julius III named several reform-minded cardinals to the Curia. When

Julius died these cardinals, controlling the balance of power in the electoral conclave, spearheaded the election of the saintly Marcellus Cervini. As Pope Marcellus II, he expressed his ardent desire for reform this way: "For 20 years people have talked about reform and openly admitted that it was necessary, but nothing has resulted." [9] It was a tragic blow to the reform party when Marcellus died only 22 days after taking office.

Marcellus was succeeded by Cardinal Gian Pietro Carafa, Pope Paul IV (1555-1559). Although 79 when he ascended the papal throne, he was described by a contemporary diplomat as "a man of iron;...the very stones over which he walks emit sparks." [10] Paul was a pope in the best tradition of the Middle Ages. His severe demeanor, sternness and unyielding quest for papal power reminds one of the greatest pope of the Middle Ages, Innocent III. Unlike Innocent, however, Paul IV eventually succumbed to the power of the emperor in the political arena. Ironically, Paul's failure to achieve political supremacy in Italy freed him from the demands of warfare and enabled him to concentrate on his real interests: ecclesiastical reform and eradicating heresy.

PAUL IV CHARTS HIS OWN COURSE

Paul was too jealous of papal autonomy to trust the Council of Trent to achieve his reform. He therefore refused to convene another session of the Council. Instead he appointed a reform commission made up of leading cardinals and bishops. Paul sought to force his brand of morality on clergy and laity alike, beginning with the papal court and the city of Rome. For example, the governor of the city was empowered by Paul to punish immoral conduct as a violation of the civil law. Rome became another Geneva—at least temporarily. Paul also used two infamous tools for the suppression of heresy: the Index of Forbidden Books and the Inquisition.

Neither institution was new; both traced their origins to the Middle Ages. But Paul IV "sharpened" these tools to fit the circumstances of the Reformation.

The Index
In 1516 the Fifth Lateran Council had prohibited the publication of books which had not first received ecclesiastical approval. Paul IV expanded that decree by requiring all permissible books to be first certified with the *imprimatur* (Latin for "let it be printed") and a seal of approval granted by a designated censor. (Catholics were not the only ones to use such seals. In England, for example, the crown likewise

112

required prior censorship of books and likewise affixed its *imprimatur* to permissible literature. The Reformation, as we have repeatedly seen, was not the season for freedom of thought.)

In 1559 Pope Paul IV published the first papal *Index of Forbidden Books*. The writings of the Protestant reformers, all the writings of Erasmus (perhaps the only Catholic who could have won European intellectuals to Catholicism), any works published anonymously during the preceding 40 years and any books published by 61 specified printers were listed as forbidden reading.

In addition Paul ordered mass book-burnings. It was said that 10,000 books—an enormous amount in those days—were burned in a single day in Venice.

Along with the many versions of the Bible, even volumes containing the works of the apostolic fathers were placed on the Index. The Jesuit theologian Peter Canisius complained, "Even the best Catholics disapprove of such rigor."[11]

The Inquisition

As for the Inquisition, it had actually been restored under Pope Paul III in 1542 (For the origins of the Inquisition, see *The People of the Faith*, pp. 99-100). But Paul IV made it a truly effective means for suppressing heresy. Here too, however, Paul exceeded prudence and became fanatical. He once remarked, "Even if my own father were a heretic, I would gather the wood to burn him."[12]

The Inquisition was a judicial process for gathering evidence against suspected heretics and prosecuting them when sufficient evidence was amassed. Yet one should not conclude that the Inquisition possessed procedural safeguards like probable cause and due process; those were part of later jurisprudence. In the Inquisition the accused was presumed guilty until proven innocent, rather than the reverse.

As a cardinal, Paul IV himself had drawn up the rules for the Inquisition. Here are some samples:

> When faith is in question, there must be no delay, but on the slightest suspicion vigorous measures must be taken with all speed....No consideration is to be shown to any prince or prelate, however high his station....No man must debase himself by showing toleration toward heretics of any kind, above all toward Calvinists.[13]

Under Paul IV the Inquisition gained renown for its merciless pursuit of heretics, suspected heretics and those who simply looked or sounded suspicious. Eventually the Inquisitors (prelates who acted as judges in the Inquisition) prosecuted not just heretics but common

113

criminals as well. The ecclesiastical court virtually became a means to implement state-sponsored terrorism. In countries where it succeeded, it put even Calvin's Geneva to shame. Cardinal Seripando said of the Inquisition that "from no other judgment seat on earth were more horrible and fearful sentences to be expected."[14]

At one point Paul IV even began to accuse cardinals of heresy. When Cardinal Giovanni Morone, bishop of Modena, was cleared of heresy by an Inquisitors' court, Paul refused to acknowledge the verdict and burned Morone's brother Cesare at the stake in the cardinal's stead.

Perhaps in no other country was Paul's Roman Inquisition imitated as zealously as in Spain. The Spanish Inquisition, directed principally against Jews and Moslems since the late Middle Ages, had become proverbial as an instrument of brutal oppression by the time of the Reformation. For reasons of expediency many Spanish Jews and Moslems pretended conversion to Christianity.

By the time of Paul IV the Spanish Inquisition was led by a "Grand Inquisitor" who supervised 14 local Inquisitors. The tentacles of the Spanish Inquisition spread throughout Spain, becoming in effect the equivalent of our century's Gestapo or KGB. Under King Philip II (d. 1598), the Spanish Inquisition became a major source of revenue as it confiscated heretics' property and funneled penalties and fines into the royal treasury. The Spanish Inquisition—like the elders in Calvin's Geneva—attempted to enforce morality, or rather a caricature of morality, on the Spanish people.

The Reformation in Italy and Spain

Because of the Inquisition, the Reformation in Spain and Italy never involved the diverse discussions over doctrine or the sectarian warfare which characterized the Reformation in other countries. In both countries the hierarchy was closely allied to the secular power—or actually *was* the secular power, as in Rome—and in both countries the Inquisition intimidated dissenters into submission. In both Italy and Spain the word *reformation* meant almost entirely the reform of clerical abuse rather than the process whereby new Christian doctrines and new models of Church organization were absorbed into the social fabric of the nation.

Yet the Spanish and Italian forms of the Reformation, though not as diverse as that of other countries, were not characterized simply by brutal repression of dissenting opinions. There was much real reform undertaken by the clergy itself in both countries and, although Spain was notorious for its Inquisition, it would nonetheless produce the three greatest names in Catholic Reformation spirituality (as we shall see in

Chapter Eleven). One of these, Ignatius Loyola, would found the Society of Jesus, the principal organ for Catholic reform throughout Europe. And had it not been for the Italian clergy, the Council of Trent would never have accomplished anything like the tremendous doctrinal restatement of the Catholic faith which it actually achieved.

Trent's 'Catholic Package'

When Pope Paul IV died in 1559 reaction against his repressive policies came swiftly. Roman citizens destroyed the offices of the Inquisition and rejoiced when the tyrannical Paul was succeeded by a Medici lawyer who took the name of Pius IV. Pius warned the Inquisitors that henceforth they should "proceed with gentlemanly courtesy rather than with monkish harshness."[15] In 1561 Pius called for the reconvening of the Council of Trent, which had not met since 1552.

Beginning about 1562 Pius IV increasingly entrusted his reform program to his nephew, Charles Borromeo (1538-1584), whom he had named cardinal-archbishop of Milan. Borromeo brought to the Catholic Reformation an educated mind and an impeccable moral life—two qualities which had seldom served Catholic reform at the highest levels of the hierarchy. Borromeo became a key participant in the final sessions of the Council, helped to draft a Catholic catechism which served as the basis of Catholic education for four centuries and, by spending his spare moments as bishop serving the poor and the sick, did more than anyone to motivate Council delegates truly to attend to ecclesiastical reform.

When the Council reopened in 1562, it was perhaps for the first time truly a reform council. More than 100 bishops attended, prompting one cardinal to remark that the opening session of 1545 had been by comparison simply a diocesan synod.

During the final 11 sessions, the delegates addressed both issues of reform and of doctrine. In the 22nd session, for example, the Council defended the sacrificial character of the Mass (the reenactment of Christ's sacrifice on the cross which applies the merits of that sacrifice to Christians throughout time). At the same session, the delegates approved the recommendations of a reform commission which had called for several technical changes in ecclesiastical discipline.

In the 25th and final session (1563) the Council concluded its work by approving decrees confirming the Church's traditional teaching on purgatory, the use of religious images and relics, the veneration of saints and—coming full circle to the issue which had precipitated Luther's revolt—indulgences. Bishops were admonished to eliminate in their dioceses the "criminal gain" and "grievous abuse" which had grown up around the granting of indulgences.

In all of doctrinal decrees throughout the Council, the delegates restated traditional beliefs and redefined traditional practices. With the exception of the decrees on ecclesiastical discipline, Trent made few substantial changes in Catholic practice or belief. Thus the Council's decrees were a reintegration of former doctrinal positions rather than the formulation of new positions. The Council was essentially a reform based on *going back* rather than on *going forward*.

Yet in defining traditional beliefs and in choosing certain expressions of those beliefs rather than others, Trent authenticated an expression of Catholicism which necessarily excluded streams of thought and belief formerly considered Catholic. What came out of Trent was a Catholic "package" which, until Vatican II, was considered by Catholics and Protestants alike as the only possible embodiment of authentic Catholicism.

Trent thus sacrificed pluralism and diversity for doctrinal unity and precision. For 400 years after Trent, Catholics grew up believing that Tridentine Catholicism was the only historical form Catholicism had ever assumed—as if the apostles had offered unswerving allegiance to the pope, gone to confession inside a dark box and celebrated Mass in Latin. Precisely because of Trent's success at defining Catholicism in inflexible terms, many Catholics had difficulty accepting a revised model of the Catholic faith after Vatican II.

Trent's doctrinal definitions clarified Catholic faith in opposition to Protestant doctrines. It accepted and elaborated on the medieval Church's hierarchical model, assuring the continued centralization of all Church authority in the hands of the pope (an organizational device useful in the Church's ongoing struggle to reverse the splintering effects of religious revolution). Trent also reversed the moral decay of the clergy by demanding the elimination of abuses and the reinstitution of ecclesiastical discipline. From Trent onward, there were still scoundrels and fools aplenty in the institutional Church, but for the first time such persons could be seen for what they were against the objective criteria of conciliar decrees approved by the pope.

Now that Trent had finished its agenda, there remained the practical question of implementing the Council's decrees and achieving vigorous support from Catholics throughout Europe. Needed to accomplish this was a veritable army of preachers and teachers zealously dedicated to the Gospels, staunchly obedient to the pope and fiercely loyal to the cause of Catholicism.

THE JESUITS SPREAD TRIDENTINE CATHOLICISM

Ignatius Loyola, the founder of the Jesuits, was born in 1491 in the Basque country of northern Spain. By disposition he was similar in many respects to Martin Luther. Like Luther, the young Loyola trembled with fear that his soul was lost; also like Luther, Loyola desperately sought assurance of his salvation. Had he been born in Germany rather than in Spain, he might have joined the Protestant cause. But given his ancestry, he was destined to become the single most important exponent of Catholic reform in the history of Christianity.

Wounded in the battle for Pamplona in 1521 (see p. 94), Loyola was forced into a long period of convalescence in a castle where the only reading material available was a life of Christ and the lives of the saints. The soldier in him was attracted to these courageous exemplars, and for the first time his nominally Christian conscience began to accuse him of his youthful sins. His conversion may be dated to this period when, after seeing a vision of Mary and the Christ Child, he fell to his knees and vowed to become a soldier for Christ.

Yet Loyola could not shake the doubt that his sins were unforgiven. With a soldier's severity he embarked on a program of fasting, mortification and poverty in hopes of proving to himself the sincerity of his recent vow. Then, after months of the most demanding austerities, he was granted a vision which freed his mind of all doubt.

Like Augustine (and like Luther) Loyola later wrote of his transforming experience, describing it as "an illumination so great that these things appeared to be something new. He seemed to himself to be another man and to have an understanding different from what he had previously."[16] (Like Paul in 2 Corinthians 11:2-6, Loyola wrote of his experience in the third person.)

Gradually Loyola reentered the real world and began to formulate a plan to win it for Christ. He devised a program called *The Spiritual Exercises*, a 30-day regimen of introspection and successively deeper conversion to the Gospels in which the participant is guided in prayer and discernment by an experienced spiritual director. Ignatius practiced the *Exercises* himself and then persuaded his two roommates at the University of Paris, where he had gone for study, to allow him to direct them in his new method of prayer. These two associates, Peter Faber and Francis Xavier, soon became dedicated both to Loyola and to his desire to convert souls to Christ. In 1534 Loyola, his roommates and seven other students took vows of poverty and chastity and pledged themselves to serve as soldiers of Christ in a war against sin and unbelief.

The Society of Jesus was born.

The Mission

The first Jesuits, as the Society of Jesus was colloquially known (Loyola despised the nickname), initially had no desire to combat Protestantism. Their first intention was to travel to the Holy Land and convert Moslems. Loyola and his band set out in 1536, walking from Paris to Venice and living as beggars along the way. Their plans for the Holy Land never jelled, and Loyola proposed that the men simply put themselves at the service of the pope for whatever menial task he might devise.

In 1538 these first Jesuits thus found their way to Rome, hoping for nothing more than to become orderlies in hospitals or servants of the city's poor—tasks to which they did in fact begin to devote themselves. Loyola, for example, undertook a ministry to Rome's many prostitutes. Gradually the men's reputation for sanctity spread, and many novices joined them. Loyola at this point required his Jesuits to take a new and unique vow: "to serve the Roman pontiff as God's vicar on earth [and] to execute immediately and without hesitation or excuse all that the reigning Pope or his successors may enjoin upon them for the benefit of souls or for the propagation of the faith."[17]

Loyola elsewhere explained the seriousness with which he regarded this vow when he said, "We ought always to be ready to believe that what seems to us white is black if the hierarchical Church so defines it."[18] For the Jesuits the most serious obstacle to the Christian life was self-will and individual discernment. Loyola's *Exercises* and the training of the Society were thus designed to eradicate self-will from the novice and lead him to substitute his superior's judgment for his own. Such single-hearted obedience was the precise opposite of the Protestant spirit of individual discernment which had captured the hearts of many Christians throughout Europe.

The usefulness of such a band of enthusiasts to the Church's program of reform eventually appealed to Pope Paul III, who in 1540 issued the bull *Regimini Militantis Ecclesiae* ("For the Rule of the Church Militant"), officially establishing the Jesuits not as an "order," but as a new and unique "society" dedicated to reforming the Church and evangelizing unbelievers. Paul III could hardly have realized the significance of his bull for the future.

Although not initially conceived of by Loyola as an educational society, the Jesuits soon attracted the most educated men in Europe into their ranks. Within 25 years of their foundation, over a thousand Jesuits supervised a hundred colleges throughout Europe and in the New World.

RELIGIONS IN EUROPE (c. 1600)

 Catholic

 Lutheran

 Orthodox

Anglican

 Islamic

 Calvinist

Their students imitated their teachers by excelling in scholarship and learning. The Jesuits conquered souls by first winning minds. They became the greatest teachers of the entire Reformation period and, some have said, of all future western civilization.

The Jesuits' Effect on Catholic Reform

When Paul IV became pope in 1556 Loyola, as he remembers it, trembled from head to foot, perhaps sensing the conflict which the Jesuits' unique vow of obedience would produce in the Society should its members be called upon to implement Paul's despotic policies. But Paul IV not only did *not* call upon the Jesuits for service, he actively harassed them. Paul IV was suspicious and hateful toward anything Spanish, and Loyola's birthplace stirred the pope's paranoia.

Despite Paul's animosity the Jesuits flourished, sometimes by entering into peaceful dialogue with their Protestant opponents—and sometimes simply by out-preaching them. Peter Faber in Germany with his new recruit Peter Canisius, Francis Xavier in the East Indies, Francis Borgia in Spain, James Laynez in France (the Society's second general upon Loyola's death)—all were spectacularly successful in spreading the Society and founding schools and colleges. In lands where they were outlawed, Jesuits carried on their activities in secret.

Wherever Jesuits went, Protestants reconverted to Catholicism and Catholics stood firm in their faith. In Luther's homeland, for example, Peter Canisius met Protestant polemicists head-on, composing several catechisms which explained the Catholic faith in an easily understood question-and-answer format. By Canisius' death in 1597 the tide of Luther's revolt had been turned; no further principalities joined the Protestant ranks.

By the start of the 17th century, because of the Council of Trent and the spread of Tridentine Catholicism by the Jesuits, the religious map of Europe was fixed essentially into the shape it would assume until the present day (see map, p. 119). Luther's religious revolution had failed to sweep Catholicism from its path. Christians now faced the challenge of living in a house which threatened to be irrevocably divided.

CHAPTER EIGHT

OF POPES AND KINGS

An Overview of 17th-Century Politics and Religion

In the next two chapters we will discuss Protestant and Catholic theological developments after the death of Luther and Calvin. Since the period we are about to enter was one in which theology continued to be politicized and politics continued to be theologized, it is difficult to get a grasp on the developing theologies without first understanding at least a little about the changing European political climate. In this chapter, therefore, we'll discuss the 17th-century political situation as it was influenced by religion. This will serve as background for the next two chapters.

ENGLAND: COUNTERING THE CATHOLIC THREAT

When King James I (1603-1625) ascended the English throne, he found his new subjects every bit as difficult to rule as his fellow Scots had been. When he made the mistake of announcing that he intended to rule England as "God's lieutenant on earth," some members of Parliament felt they had made a mistake in inviting James to take the English crown. The House of Commons was now made up not only of Anglicans but of a large Puritan faction as well, and James's theory of the divine right of kings violated their belief that God makes an individual convenant directly with each believer, rather than through one's king. Further, Commons had become increasingly middle-class. The newly rich merchants and lawyers in Parliament had no place in their political philosophy for James's elitist views.

James was undeterred, however, and increasingly asserted himself as virtually the pope of the English Church. He insisted that England should be united under its king in religion as in politics. In 1605 certain Catholic fanatics decided to put an end to James and his state religion. The conspirators placed 31 barrels of gunpowder under the hall where the House of Lords and the royal family were to convene for the opening of Parliament. One of the plotters got cold feet, however, and revealed the plan to the authorities.

The king's soldiers entered the underground chamber and arrested one of the ringleaders, Guy Fawkes, who was tortured and executed. (The English still celebrate "Guy Fawkes Day" on November 5.) The discovery of the plot led Parliament once again to pass repressive anti-Catholic legislation. Catholics were now required, for example, to take an oath repudiating papal authority. Some took the oath, but many didn't. The jails were filled with recalcitrants.

Despite the king's pursuit of these anti-Catholic measures, the Puritans could not shake the old suspicion that a Catholic heart beat within the breast of their Stuart king. England became more and more divided. The north was generally poor, agricultural and Catholic; the south industrial, Protestant and middle-class. In 1625 King James died, succeeded by his son Charles I (1625-1649). Charles further stirred Puritan suspicion because he was married to the sister of Louis XIII, the Catholic king of France. Protestant-controlled Parliament intensified its anti-Catholic policies.

When William Laud, Anglican archbishop of Canterbury (chief bishop of the Anglican Church), began to restore many Catholic externals to the Anglican liturgy, Puritans in Parliament took this as a sign that King Charles intended to restore his wife's faith in England. Thus began a bitter feud between the crown-sponsored Anglican Church and the Puritans. (Catholics were still only able to worship clandestinely.) The Puritans grew ever more critical of English society.

Scottish Presbyterians likewise became enraged when the king and Archbishop Laud revoked the authority of the Kirk and made the Scottish bishops supervisors of the Presbyterian clergy. The Kirk rebelled and declared itself free of king and bishops, and King Charles dissolved Parliament when it sided with the Kirk.

The Puritan Revolt

A new Parliament convened in 1640 (the famous "Long Parliament") and was controlled by the Puritans. One of their number, Oliver Cromwell, sponsored a bill which abolished the Anglican episcopacy. When King Charles reinstated and promoted two of the

122

deposed Anglican bishops, Cromwell and his allies (who virtually equated Anglicanism and Catholicism) accused the king of plotting a Catholic takeover of England.

Parliament then asserted the right to govern the English Church, warning the nation that Charles's new "Catholic" policies would lead to a massacre of Protestants and the destruction of the pure Church. When Puritan radicals seized a royal munitions warehouse, civil war erupted between the king, Anglicans and Catholics on one side, and Puritans and Scottish Presbyterians on the other. Oliver Cromwell gained control of the Puritan army, defeated the royalist forces and, in 1649, had King Charles I beheaded.

In 1653 Cromwell became "Lord Protector of the Commonwealth of England, Scotland and Ireland." Under his leadership the Puritans began England's second religious revolution (Henry VIII's had been the first). Until his death in 1658, Cromwell attempted to turn England into a theocracy governed along the lines of Calvin's Geneva. The Puritans, who had formerly demanded toleration for their own beliefs, now persecuted Catholics and Anglicans alike, outlawing the Anglicans' cherished Book of Common Prayer.

Some Puritans objected to their leaders' tactics. For example, when a Puritan named George Fox began to preach a religion of peace based on the direct divine guidance of the "Inner Light," many joined him and the Quakers were born. Meanwhile the rest of England wearied of Cromwell's Calvinist ways; "Merrie England" was no place for Old Testament theocracy. Cromwell died before his many enemies could make good on their threats to assassinate him.

In 1660 Parliament, now overwhelmingly Anglican and royalist, declared as king the Stuart prince Charles (son of the executed Charles I). King Charles II reigned from 1660-1685. England rejoiced at the restoration of its monarchy and the end of the Puritan experiment. Charles, who had lived in France during Cromwell's rule, resisted the attempts of his Catholic mother and sister to convert him to Catholicism; he chose to be an ostensible Anglican. (On his deathbed, however, he converted to Catholicism.)

Under Charles II the Anglican-controlled Parliament restored the Book of Common Prayer and required all preachers to swear allegiance to its doctrine. When the Puritans refused, it became their turn to be persecuted. King Charles himself was tolerant of all religions, but for political reasons he dared not stop Parliament's repressive legislation.

Charles's Portuguese Catholic wife and his brother James's conversion to Catholicism in 1668 once again aroused English fears of a Catholic restoration. In 1677 a defrocked Anglican priest and opportunist named Titus Oates announced his discovery of a papal plot to assassinate Charles, elevate the king's Catholic brother to the throne and force Catholicism upon the English. Oates was later proved to be a liar; but in the meantime he was cheered as the savior of Protestant England.

One Catholic leader after another was put to death. Parliament passed an exclusionary bill prohibiting James from inheriting the crown should his brother Charles die. A wave of anti-Catholic paranoia swept England; it once again became a capital offense to be a Catholic priest. When Oates's deceit was eventually discovered, however, England repented and agreed to Charles's demand that his brother James succeed him as king.

The Last Catholic King

James II (1685-1688), the last Catholic king of England, succeeded his brother Charles and announced a policy of religious toleration. James foolishly flaunted his Catholicism in public, however. He installed a papal legate and Catholic priests at his court, built up a private army led by Catholics, and otherwise alienated his largely Anglican subjects. When James elevated four Catholic bishops to a position of equality with the Anglican hierarchy, Parliament could no longer tolerate the king's patent attempt to restore Catholicism. It offered the crown of England to James's Protestant daughter Mary and her husband, the Dutch prince William of the House of Orange.

James was overthrown and William and Mary were crowned king and queen of England (1689). Parliament, declaring that "it hath been found by experience that it is inconsistent with the safety and welfare of this Protestant kingdom to be governed by a popish prince,"[1] forever forbade the succession of any Catholic to the throne of England. From that moment on the supremacy of the Anglican Church was never again threatened, and England became resolutely Protestant.

THE DECLINE OF PAPAL INFLUENCE

Pius V

Pope Pius IV died two years after the Council of Trent concluded its agenda. He was succeeded by a Dominican who had held the rank of Grand Inquisitor: Pope Pius V (1566-1572). According to popular account, Pius turned Rome into a monastery. Like Paul IV, Pius V used the Inquisition as a tool for reform. Despite his repressive measures, the new pope achieved the moral reform which Trent had urged. Pius became the true pastor of Rome, inspiring his brother bishops to return to their episcopal callings. During his pontificate the Confraternity of Christian Doctrine (today's CCD) was founded by "the Apostle of Rome," Philip Neri. This organization, dedicated to the care of pilgrims and the sick, attracted hundreds of priests to its apostolate.

Meanwhile Charles Borromeo motivated clerical reform by his saintly example. "He in his own person does more good at the Roman Court than all the decrees of the Council together,"[2] wrote the Venetian ambassador. As bishop of Milan, Borromeo earned a reputation as "the paragon of the Tridentine bishop."[3] Under his leadership diocesan synods were extended throughout the Catholic world as a means of improving clerical discipline, and his seminary in Milan served as the pattern for ever-improving priestly education.

Pope Pius V followed Borromeo's example by instituting strict guidelines for the examination and nomination of episcopal candidates. Toward the end of his life Pius regularly walked on crippled legs to Rome's seven basilicas to celebrate Mass for his parishioners. Rome's Catholics watched in amazement as their pope became once again an exemplar of the gospel.

Gregory XIII

Pope Gregory XIII (1572-1585), who gave us the Gregorian calendar, did not share Pius V's reforming zeal. He dabbled instead in international politics. It was he who rejoiced at the news of the St. Bartholomew's Day Massacre (see p. 98). Gregory pursued a policy calculated to suppress heretics in Catholic lands and to restore Catholicism in Protestant lands. His political ambitions got the better of him when, in violation of Trent, he allowed a Catholic prince in Germany to own five episcopal sees at once. Gregory's most notable accomplishment was the founding of several colleges in Rome for priestly education. He richly endowed the Jesuits and made them the educators of a new breed of Tridentine seminarians. The Jesuit college in Rome—the Gregorian—bears his name to this day.

Sixtus V

Pope Sixtus V (1585-1590), like Paul IV and Pius V, imposed reform by force. His cruel policies included burning a homosexual priest at the stake, hanging a woman for selling her daughter into prostitution and ordering capital punishment for priests and nuns found guilty of fornication. In foreign affairs Sixtus (like Gregory XIII) hoped to win Protestant lands back to the Catholic Church. One historian has called Sixtus "by far the greatest statesman who has ever sat on the papal throne."⁴ Sixtus reorganized the Roman Curia so that it functioned more efficiently, built a new Vatican Library, started the Vatican Press, beautified Rome and supervised the revision of the Vulgate into the form it would keep until modern times.

Clement VIII and Urban VIII

Two of Sixtus's most notable successors, Clement VIII (1592-1605) and Urban VIII (1623-1644) served as popes in an era dominated by increasing animosity between Catholic and Protestant nations. The popes thus became increasingly involved in European politics. Yet it was *papal* rather than *Catholic* interests that guided these politician-popes. Urban VIII, for example, supported the Protestant king of Sweden in his war against the Catholic emperor; Urban also raised a papal army to fight the Catholic Duke of Parma in the Netherlands. Catholic reform, nevertheless, continued to spread during this period, thanks to the zeal of saints like Philip Neri, Francis de Sales, Vincent de Paul and Aloysius Gonzaga. Under their spiritual leadership, new religious orders arose based on the promotion of Catholic education and apostolic service.

Papal Influence at an End

Until the close of the 17th century, the popes could not decide whether to pursue internal Church reform or external ecclesiastical politics. Under Pope Alexander VII (1655-1667), the Curia lapsed into its old ways. One cardinal observed that papal taxation exceeded in severity the oppression suffered by the ancient Israelites under Pharaoh. Alexander himself was a saintly man who simply had no talent for converting Church bureaucrats to Christianity. He thus gave more and more power to the cardinals, who during the tenures of Clement IX (1667-1669) and Innocent XI (1676-1689), virtually wrested control of the Church bureaucracy away from the popes. Yet, perhaps because of the decline in papal autonomy, even Voltaire was to have kind words for Innocent XI, calling him "a virtuous man, a wise pontiff, a poor theologian, a courageous, resolute and magnificent prince."⁵

Innocent cautioned King James II against proceeding too fast with the reestablishment of Catholicism in England. Constantly at odds with the French, the pope looked favorably on the succession of William and Mary to the English throne; by uniting the interests of Holland and England their marriage provided a more secure barrier against French aggression. When Innocent died in 1689 Europe was a new reality—a continent dominated by nationalism, science and secularism. The age of papal influence in affairs of state was at an end.

CATHOLIC SPAIN

At the close of the Council of Trent in 1562, Spain was the greatest power in the world; by the accession of William and Mary in 1689, it had become the looting ground of Europe. King Philip II (1556-1598), son of Emperor Charles V, was an able ruler but a religious fanatic. His reign was characterized by the pursuit of heretics and by intrigues against the Protestant rulers of Europe. As a result he kept Spain involved in nearly constant warfare, a policy which eventually bankrupted the country.

His son King Philip III (1598-1621) would have perhaps been happier as a monk. He devoted himself almost entirely to the spiritual well-being of the Spanish Church. Catholic Spain then counted 9,088 monasteries, 32,000 mendicants and a large corps of Jesuits,[6] all put into the service of the state-controlled Church. It is estimated that one-third of the Spanish population served the Church. Philip left affairs of state to the unscrupulous Duke of Lerma, who further corrupted Spain's political system and hastened the government's economic collapse. Even the wealth from Spain's colonial empire in the Americas could not save the country from economic ruin.

Under King Philip IV (1621-1665), the Spanish army's exhaustion surfaced in a humiliating defeat at the hands of the French (1643). With the Peace of the Pyrenees in 1659, Spain surrendered its control of European politics to France. King Louis XIV of France now ruled the world's most powerful nation.

FRANCE IN TURMOIL

King Henry IV (who said, "Paris is worth a Mass"; see p. 98) was assassinated in 1610 by a Catholic fanatic who doubted the sincerity of his king's religious convictions. France, like England, was deeply divided by religious hatred. Henry's successor, Louis XIII, was only nine years old and hardly able to rule the divided nation; thus his mother began to serve as regent.

The French Reform

The French clergy had still not responded to Trent's call for reform. As the saintly priest Vincent de Paul (1580-1660) observed of the period, "the worst enemies of the Church are her unworthy priests."[7]

Yet there were notable exceptions to this rule. Pierre de Berulle (1575-1629), for example, founded both the reformed Carmelites and the Oratorians in France. (His preaching on the Incarnation earned him the nickname "Apostle of the Incarnate Word.") Another priest, Jean Jacques Olier, founded the Sulpician Order for the purpose of reforming the lives of priests; his congregation eventually blessed France with many dedicated bishops. John Eudes (1601-1680) founded an order to care for destitute women as well as a society of priests who devoted themselves to seminary education. Eudes, along with Margaret Mary Alacoque (1647-1690), gave the French Church its cherished devotion to the Sacred Heart of Jesus.

Women reformers also made their presence felt. Jane Frances de Chantal (1572-1641) founded the Order of the Visitation, dedicated to serving the poor and the sick. By her death de Chantal's order could count 400 convents. Some 80,000 nuns became the glory of the Church and the ancestors of thousands of religious sisters who made Catholicism in the New World possible.

Vincent de Paul (1580-1660), founded perhaps the most famous women's congregation, the Sisters of Charity. With Francis de Sales (1567-1622), persecuted bishop of Geneva, Vincent inspired a rebirth of French piety and spirituality. Mysticism began to appeal to many French as the only suitable response to the religious and political strife which divided their country. At Port Royal, in an event full of significance for the future (see Chapter Ten), a religious community dedicated to asceticism and contemplation was founded.

Richelieu

Into the power vacuum left by Henry IV's assassination stepped a powerful French bishop, Armand de Richelieu, who became the most cunning statesman in Europe. Gradually worming his way to power, Richelieu persuaded the young Louis XIII to promote his election to the College of Cardinals and, eventually (1624), to name him prime minister of France. Cardinal Richelieu believed he best served his king and country by serving his own interests.

Richelieu insisted on the "Gallican liberties" of the French Church, a slogan used by French prelates in asserting their independence from Rome in the movement later know as Gallicanism. Richelieu thus resisted the efforts of "Ultramontanists"—that is, clergy whose interests lay "beyond the mountains" in Rome. These clergy wanted to bring the reforms of Trent and its centralized discipline to bear on the French Church. Under Richelieu the French Church became every bit as much state-run as the Anglican Church under King James I.

When the Huguenots revolted against the cardinal's anti-Protestant policies, Richelieu himself led a Catholic army that laid siege to the Huguenot capital of La Rochelle. Defeating the Protestants, he then shocked the Catholic nobility by granting the rebels a general amnesty. Richelieu needed the Protestants and their middle-class economic potential for his political struggle with the Catholic nobility. "Differences in religion," he said, "never prevented me from rendering to the Huguenots all sorts of good offices."[8]

Richelieu's true interests continued to manifest themselves during the Thirty Years' War (see below, p. 136) between the German Catholic emperor and his Protestant princes. The cardinal maintained alliances with the Protestants and continually fed them French money, large portions of which came from the tithes of French Catholics. At the cost of a cruel and costly tyranny that would eventually backlash into the French Revolution, Richelieu united French Catholics and Protestants in a marriage of necessity that he manipulated for his own political and economic gain. His was no way to achieve a reconciliation among the faiths; French Christians grew increasingly embittered and cynical. When they united again to overthrow the "Old Regime" in 1789, many of them did not care whether any religion existed in France.

The Church of Louis XIV

Under King Louis XIV (1643-1715) France became the dominant power of Europe. The French Church, dramatically reformed in comparison to its condition a century before, entered into a new and troubling phase of its existence.

In 1663 Louis, seeking to consolidate the French Church's independence from Rome in opposition to Ultramontanist bishops, declared himself free to choose which papal bulls would be published in France. Then in 1682 the king convened an assembly of handpicked clergy who promulgated "The Four Articles." These articles denied the pope's jurisdiction in certain temporal affairs, asserted the superiority of councils over popes, reasserted the king's ancient right to name French bishops and denied the infallibility of the pope except when his teaching agreed with that of a council.

Pope Innocent XI (1676-1689) protested feebly; he could not run the risk of driving Europe's greatest Catholic nation into the arms of the Protestants. Louis eventually softened his position. By 1693 he was no longer insisting on the Four Articles, and Pope Innocent XII (1691-1700) compromised with the king by guaranteeing him the right to name French bishops.

Under Richelieu's successor as prime minister, Cardinal Mazarin, France's one and one-half million Huguenots enjoyed a high degree of religious liberty—largely because Louis XIV's finance minister understood how important middle-class Protestants were to the economy of France. When Mazarin died in 1661, however, Louis became increasingly more suspicious of his non-Catholic subjects. Like James I of England, Louis advanced the divine right of kings. This gradually came to mean the imposition of one state-sponsored religion chosen by the king.

Louis took seriously a slogan coined by one of his most famous bishops, Jacques Bossuet: "one king, one law, one faith." When some of his most devout clergy began to call for repression of the Huguenots, Louis started a full-scale persecution.

In a series of edicts issued between 1661 and 1685 Louis deprived Huguenots of religious and civil liberties and made it increasingly difficult for them to earn a living. In 1681 the king instituted the "dragonnades," the housing of French troops in Huguenot homes. Terrified Protestants fled from France in such huge numbers that Louis's counselors were able to convince him that the Edict of Nantes (see pp. 98-99) no longer served any purpose and should be revoked.

After this the few Protestants who remained in France suffered indignities and oppression rivaling the plight of Catholics in England. The exodus of Huguenots across French borders deprived the French economy of its most skilled artisans and merchants; Protestant Europe gladly welcomed the French emigrants into its shops, factories and banks.

The king's chaplain and court preacher, Bishop Bossuet (1627-1704), became virtually a French pope. Bossuet defended the divine right of kings and attacked Protestant doctrines in learned treatises. Another bishop, the royal tutor Francois de Fénelon (1651-1715), challenged Bossuet's hold on the king. Fénelon wrote for the king's grandson a novel, *Télémaque*, in which he questioned Bossuet's absolutist theories. After Fénelon published a treatise on mysticism, Bossuet began a campaign to discredit him, and Fénelon was eventually banished from Louis's court.

The court rivalry between these two leading bishops was for many French Catholics simply one more sign of the corruption of their religion. The Huguenot persecution, the conflict between Jansenists and Jesuits (which we will discuss in Chapter Ten) and, above all, the growing skepticism of the intellectual community—all contributed to the decline in religious belief.

The signs were present everywhere. Vincent de Paul, for example, had bemoaned the steady drop in Mass attendance. The philosopher Pierre Bayle (1646-1706) correctly attributed the large growth in atheism among former Catholics to the controversies which divided Christians. A German princess remarked, "One now rarely finds a young man who does not wish to be an atheist."[9] And the Protestant ecumenist and philosopher Gottfried Leibniz (1646-1716) wrote of Paris that "piety is there turned to ridicule...and the disorder of religion has gone beyond anything ever seen in the Christian world."[10]

The religious decline was matched by social and economic degeneration. Louis's wars had despoiled half the continent and contributed to a population drop of some four million people. Bishop Fénelon wrote anonymously that the king's ministers "have impoverished all France to establish at the court a monstrous and incurable luxury....All France is now but a vast hospital, desolate and without provisions."[11] On this note Louis died, leaving French Christians a horrible legacy of bitterness and cynicism.

THE DIVISON OF THE NETHERLANDS

Emperor Charles V placed his son Philip II of Spain in charge of the family's Netherlands possessions in 1555; Philip, in turn, named his half sister Margaret of Parma as regent. When King Philip persuaded Margaret to crush heresy among the open-minded Dutch, both Catholics and Protestants demanded toleration. Holland was not Spain.

King Philip pressed on, however, driving many noble families to Protestantism. A "Calvinist fury" broke loose as Protestants, many of whom had come to Holland because of religious persecution elsewhere, ransacked churches and destroyed monasteries. The Catholic Prince William of Orange ("William the Silent," great-grandfather of the future English King) decided to convert to Calvinism and thereby ride the crest of revolution to a position of leadership.

At this King Philip's new regent, the Spanish Duke of Alba, declared William an outlaw. This action made the prince simultaneously a Protestant hero and the leader of a Dutch independence movement. In a war for independence marked by barbarity of a kind seldom witnessed elsewhere, William of Orange successfully united the seven northern provinces (colloquially called "Holland" in distinction to the southern provinces of "Flanders") into a unified country independent of Spain (1579). These "United Provinces" were largely Calvinist (under the "Dutch Reform Church"), while the southern provinces remained largely Catholic.

A threefold religious struggle between Church and state, between Catholic and Protestant, and between various branches of Calvinists gripped the Netherlands during the early 17th century. At the Calvinist Synod of Dort (1618) the Dutch Reformed Church formalized its doctrine (more on this in Chapter Nine) and expelled dissenters.

The cause of national unity became increasingly critical in the second half of the century. During various Dutch wars with England and France, the Netherlands momentarily forgot religious differences and allowed a degree of religious and intellectual freedom to develop that was unknown elsewhere in Europe. The southern provinces (today's Belgium) remained in Spanish hands until 1713—and remained Catholic thereafter. The northern provinces sent their leader William III of Orange to England to become its king.

SCANDINAVIA, POLAND AND RUSSIA

King Christian III of Denmark (1534-1559) chose Lutheranism both for his own country and for Norway, which the Danes controlled. Sweden too accepted the Lutheran faith. The Reformation came to Poland very early, so that until the Council of Trent the nation veered toward Calvinism. After Trent, however, with the success of Jesuit reconversion efforts, Poland was restored to Catholicism.

From its earliest days Russia had maintained close ties to the Orthodox Church, whose chief bishop was the Patriarch of Constantinople. When Constantinople fell to the Ottoman Turks in 1453 (see *The People of the Faith*, p. 145), the Greek Orthodox Church and its bishops came under the domination of Moslem sultans. Consequently the Orthodox Patriarch of Moscow assumed the leadership of his Church and called his episcopal see "the Third Rome."

Like the Byzantine emperors in Constantinople, the czars of Russia supervised the Russian Orthodox bishops as if the latter were civil servants. Well before the Reformation, then, the Russian Church was a state-controlled Church. This fact is well illustrated by the title which a leading 16th-century Orthodox churchman conferred on the Russian czar: "Czar of all the Christians."

State control of the Russian Church tightened during the reign of Ivan the Terrible (1533-1584), who centralized virtually all power in Russia into his hands. From 1589-1700 the 11 patriarchs who theoretically led the Russian Church were in fact as subservient to the czars as were dukes or princes. At one point, Czar Michael Romanov (1613-1645) and Patriarch Fedor Romanov (1619-1633), a son and his father, ruled state and Church. Under Czar Alexander Romanov (1645-1676), a state office for Church affairs was set up, further subordinating the Church to the czar.

In 1667 the Orthodox Patriarch Nikon instituted a number of liturgical reforms which made the Russian liturgy virtually identical to the liturgy celebrated by Greek Orthodox Christians in former Byzantine lands. This change angered a Russian party called "the Old Believers," many of whom refused thereafter to follow the Patriarch of Moscow and elected their own superior. Under Czarina Sophia (1682-1689), the Old Believers were subjected to persecution; thousands were either put to death or committed suicide. Russian monks by and large led the faction; they therefore came to be regarded as enemies of the state.

Czar Peter the Great (1689-1725) opened Russia to the West, introducing western cultural and religious innovations. Both the Old Believers and the mainline patriarchal Church denounced Peter's westernization program, asserting that *anything* associated with the West was heretical. The traditional Orthodox view of Church-state relations was challenged during this time by Patriarch Stefan Jaworski. He proclaimed in a treatise sent to all Russian bishops: "Czars are the guardians of the laws of God and of the Church, but they are not legislators; it is not theirs to determine what should be part of the faith."[12]

The Patriarch's resistance made Peter determined to gain absolute control of the Russian Church. He thus established a "Most Holy Governing Synod" comprised of 11 men who, as a supervisory body, replaced the patriarchs as leaders of the Russian Church. In 1722 Peter created the office of Chief Procurator of the Synod, to ensure that the policies of the Czar and of the Synod were synonymous. From that point on the Orthodox bishops became little more, to quote a contemporary critic, than "mute dogs who look on without barking."[13] The process by which the Orthodox Church became completely absorbed into the secular government was finalized in 1797 when Czar Paul I (1796-1801) induced the Holy Synod to declare him "Head of the Church."

Although Peter the Great had encouraged Protestant immigrations to Russia, he suppressed Catholicism. This was in keeping both with the ancient Orthodox dislike of all things Roman and the Czar's belief that Protestantism better encouraged freethinking and secularism, the twin pillars of the only religious belief to which the Czar himself subscribed. The Jesuits in Russia were expelled, thereby depriving the Catholic Church of its principal force for evangelization. Catholicism was crushed under Catherine the Great (1762-1796) and Protestantism, which preferred more independence than Russia would tolerate, never gained a foothold. The Russian Orthodox Church has remained until the present day an appendage of the state. Yet the Old Believers never died off; they continued to inspire a vigorous Russian spirituality.

THE EMPIRE'S ANGUISH

After 1555 (the year of the Peace of Augsburg, see pp. 64-66), the Holy Roman Empire continued to suffer the anguish of religious disintegration. Switzerland (theoretically a part of the Empire) was, practically speaking, an independent state divided into Catholic and Protestant enclaves. Hungary, constantly besieged by Turkish Moslems (two-thirds of the country paid tribute to the sultans), expelled its feuding Protestant sects and returned under Jesuit tutelage to the Catholic fold. Bohemia (today's Czechoslovakia) contained a substantial Protestant minority which traced its origins to John Hus, and Bohemian Protestants and Catholics had separated into increasingly hostile factions. In Germany only Austria was a Catholic bastion.

Nowhere was there more religious variety than in the various principalities of Germany. Generally speaking, the north of Germany was Protestant and the south was Catholic. In Lutheran territories Catholics were often less persecuted than Calvinists; thus Catholics managed in many places to practice openly. Likewise, in Calvinist lands Lutherans were often more quickly expelled than Catholics.

A Frankfurt bookseller wrote in 1592, "We have noticed for several years past that the books written by Protestants against Protestants are three times as numerous as those of Protestants against Catholics."[14] Philip Melancthon characterized this Protestant vituperation as "theological rabies." As Protestants grew increasingly hostile toward each other, the Jesuits steadily regained converts for Catholicism. Many Christians longed for the certainty and stability provided by Catholicism, and many princes feared Protestant anarchy.

Meanwhile, religious hatred in Germany grew to a peak unmatched elsewhere. German theological treatises began to read like pornographic novels; texts were peppered with four-letter words and lurid descriptions of the other side's vices. Catholics wrote of Lutherans' taste for incest, while Lutherans created "Popess Joanna," a satanic woman who had mothered all the popes into existence. Her sons were said to dance with devils in the streets of Rome. Calvinists delighted in pillorying Luther as the new pope, while Lutheran theologians called Calvinists "baptized Jews and Muhammadans." In the year 1618 alone, 1,800 bigoted tracts circulated throughout Germany condemning Christians of every stripe.

This fury of hatred naturally led to increased fear and suspicion. In 1608 Protestant princes formed a Protestant Union. A year later Catholic rulers responded with the Catholic League. Both alliances were

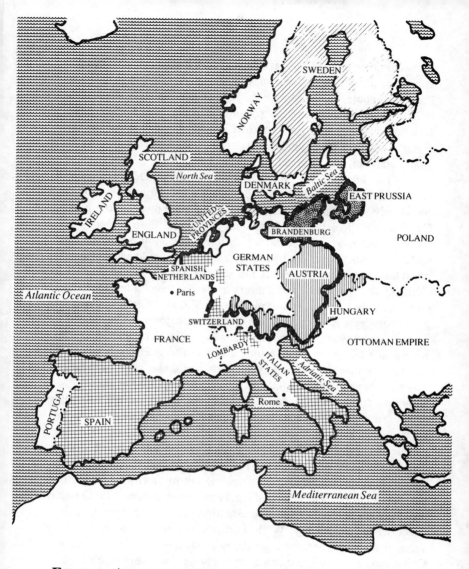

EUROPE AFTER THE PEACE OF WESTPHALIA (1648)

 Territories of Spain

 Austria

 Brandenburg-Prussia

 Sweden

▬ ▬ ▬ ▬ **Boundary of the Holy Roman Empire**

formed, of course, in the name of defense. All that was needed was a spark to ignite the tinder. Bohemia provided the catalyst in 1618 when Protestant nobles expelled both the Jesuits and the archbishop from Prague and threw two imperial-appointed Catholic governors from the fifth floor of their headquarters onto a heap of manure. The governors, though uninjured, could not bring themselves to laugh at their fall from grace, and war soon erupted.

The Thirty Years' War (1618-1648) was a patchwork quilt of brutality, atrocity, treachery and degradation. Religious interests were completely subordinated to the lust for political power on the part of Catholic and Protestant heads of state throughout Europe. Many historians estimate that, had the population and technology equalled the mid 20th-century situation, the Thirty Years' War would have inflicted twice the casualties and destruction suffered during World War II. In Germany and Austria the population was slashed from 21 million to 13 million, and in Bohemia from 3 million to 800,000.[15] These are greater percentage decreases in population than in any major war ever fought.

Germany after the war was literally in ruins. Thousands of farms were either laid waste or idle for lack of workers. Peasants in many places were reduced to eating dogs, cats and grass; even cannibalism was not unknown. Destroyed roads halted transportation and communications; industry and commerce were crippled; stacks of rotting corpses spread disease everywhere. All of this carnage and destruction, created by self-styled Christians seeking to force their faith on others, produced a frightful backlash of religious cynicism throughout Europe.

The Peace of Westphalia (1648), which settled the war, remade the political map of Europe by parceling out territories to the victors (see map, p. 135). Politically speaking, France was the winner and Germany the loser. In terms of religion, Protestantism gained equal footing with Catholicism in Germany. While Luther's revolution had not fully succeeded, he did achieve a posthumous stalemate. From his grave Calvin too had scored a major victory: Calvinism was for the first time granted recognition as a lawful religion. From 1648 until the present, the religious map of Germany would remain essentially unchanged.

The real loser of the Thirty Years' War was European Christianity. In the minds of most European intellectuals, Christianity had utterly discredited itself. Everywhere great thinkers began increasingly to question religious traditions and authority. Could Jesus Christ really have been God, people wondered, when his disciples enforced his gospel of peace and love at the point of a sword? In the minds of many intellectuals a Christianity which chose to live by the sword could just as well die by the sword.

CHAPTER NINE

AFTER LUTHER AND CALVIN

The Growth of Protestant Tradition

In this chapter we will discuss Protestant theology in its second phase of growth, the period after the death of the revolutionaries Luther and Calvin. In this period we will see that Luther's theology is not necessarily identical to *Lutheran* theology, and that Calvin's theology is not always the same as *Calvinist* theology. We will also see a marked development of religious thinking in England following the death of Queen Elizabeth I.

Our discussion in this chapter focuses on the growth of the Protestant *tradition*, something which would have horrified Luther and Calvin. For Luther and even more for Calvin there was no such thing as a doctrinal tradition outside of Scripture. Each insisted that his theology (and his alone) was the pure reflection of Scripture with nothing else added. The inherent weakness of their respective positions was itself revealed by the fact that Luther and Calvin adamantly disagreed with each other over what Scripture meant on certain key doctrinal issues. Nonetheless, each stubbornly clung to *sola scriptura*.

Lutheran and Calvinist theologians during the second phase of the Reformation reluctantly admitted—although not saying so in so many words—that the acute doctrinal controversies between Protestants required further elaboration of their respective founder's theology. Thus the advocates of *sola scriptura* began to redefine their doctrinal positions in creeds, confessions and catechisms, exactly as the Catholic Church had done during the first Christian centuries. In short, theologians for whom the word *tradition* was an abomination began to develop their

137

own Protestant traditions. These traditions rivaled each other as well as the Catholic tradition from which their founders had seceded precisely in hopes of doing away with tradition. Protestants themselves thus discovered that *sola scriptura* was not so "*sola*" after all.

LUTHERAN THEOLOGY

As we saw in Chapter Four, Luther's theology began to change even before he died. As the Lutherans' greatest theologian, Philip Melancthon, systematized his master's thought, he added his own ideas to Luther's. Thus we could say that the first phase of post-Luther theology began with Melancthon. This phase culminated with the adoption in 1577 of a compromise document known as the *Formula of Concord*. A compromise was needed because some Lutheran theologians had developed ideas that were squarely opposed to Luther's teachings; Lutherans as a body wanted to set the record straight.

Compromise was also needed because the Lutherans were in danger of splitting into two factions: those who believed that Melancthon truly represented Luther's views and those who did not. We will first discuss the work of Lutheran theologians who were repudiated by both pro- and anti-Melancthon factions. Then we will discuss the conflict surrounding Melancthon's thought.

Antinomianism and Osiander: Rejected

Early in Luther's career some theologians interpreted his writings to mean that Christians, having been completely liberated from the law by faith in Jesus Christ, could thus ignore all moral precepts such as the Ten Commandments. This school of thought was known as *antinomianism* from the Greek for "against the law." This view of Christianity was actually as old as the first century. Paul himself had to caution his recent converts against turning liberty into license, and both Luther and Melancthon rejected antinomian tendencies in their theological circle. By 1577, when the Formula of Concord was published, nearly all Lutherans were agreed that even after justification the law had a positive value in guiding Christians to virtuous living.

Another teaching rejected by the majority of Lutherans was the theology of Andrew Osiander (1498-1552). He taught that justification occurred not by the imputation to fallen humanity of Christ's holiness, but by the rejuvenation of the indwelling Word who lives within us. According to Osiander, after Christ died for sinful humanity, he came to dwell in fullness in the believer's soul, absorbing all sin and returning humanity to the state of Adam's original purity. Melancthon rejected

Osiander's theory because it sounded too much like Catholic teaching on sanctifying grace. To Melancthon, Osiander seemed to be saying that God made humanity objectively just by inhering within the soul.

Osiander was also rejected because, in denying the concept of imputed holiness, he went instead in the direction of medieval Catholic mysticism, with its emphasis on the indwelling Christ who could be experienced in contemplative prayer. In rejecting Osiander, Lutheran theologians not only rejected the Catholic mystical tradition but the Orthodox tradition as well, which for centuries had developed a mystical theology of the indwelling Christ. The Formula of Concord denied that salvation is in any way related to Christ's divine nature dwelling within humanity. Rather, continuing Luther's purely legalistic theory of justification, the Formula said that justification stems solely from Christ's filial obedience in going to the cross.

'Adiaphora' and 'Works': A Compromise

Most Lutherans agreed on the Formula's settlement of the antinomian and Osiander controversies. When it came to Melancthon's systematization of Luther's theology, however, there were broad divisions among Lutherans.

A major point of controversy involved the externals of Catholic liturgy. Some Lutherans, like Melancthon, regarded these as harmless elements which Lutherans could accept or reject as they saw fit. These *adiaphora* (Greek for "indifferent things") were not, for Melancthon and his followers, fundamentally opposed to Luther's theology. For those who opposed Melancthon, however, the *adiaphora* gave scandal to the weak in faith and thus had to be dropped. To this party, eliminating the *adiaphora* was part and parcel of Luther's doctrine.

The Formula of Concord settled this controversy by acknowledging the validity of both points of view: As long as the externals in question are not forbidden by Scripture they can be maintained, but whenever they seem to deviate from Scripture they must be abolished.

Another controversy within the Lutheran ranks involved the role of good works in salvation. Melancthon was less suspicious than Luther of works as a means to salvation. One of Melancthon's disciples, George Major (1502-1574), even taught that good works are as necessary for salvation as faith. The Formula of Concord took a mediating position on this controversy also. It rejected Major's teaching, but added the cryptic statement: "We also reject...that bold statement that good works are detrimental to salvation."[1]

Had the Lutherans come squarely into line with the Council of

Trent? Cardinal John Henry Newman in the 19th century and Protestant theologian Karl Barth in the 20th would write that Lutheran and Catholic positions on justification (represented by the Formula of Concord and the Council of Trent) were virtually identical.

The 17th Century: 'Protestant Scholasticism'

After the Formula of Concord was signed in 1577 by over 8,000 Lutheran theologians and more than 50 Lutheran princes, Lutheran theology became increasingly academic. Theology moved from the battlefield, as it were, into the university. The 17th century became for Lutherans what the high Middle Ages had been for Catholics: a time for writing synthetic treatises and systems. Indeed, this has been called the period of "Protestant Scholasticism."

Competing universities vied with one another to present authentically Lutheran theology. The University of Wittenberg in Luther's hometown, for example, continued to teach what it thought to be the "pure Luther"; other Lutheran theologians considered their colleagues at Wittenberg dogmatically inflexible and conservative.

Contrary to Luther's own hostile views concerning Aristotle (and philosophy in general), Lutheran theologians now used Aristotle almost as freely as Thomas Aquinas had. At the University of Helmstedt, Aristotelian metaphysics was first put into the service of Lutheranism. There George Calixtus (1585-1656) founded the first ecumenical movement by attempting to define the fundamentals of Christian faith in a way that Lutheran, Calvinists and Catholics alike could support. Calixtus's liberal wing of Lutheran theology was condemned by traditionalists like Abraham Calov (1612-1686), who wrote that it was heresy even to suggest that Catholics or Calvinists could be saved. At the University of Jena, Professor John Musaus (1613-1681) tried to mediate between the Wittenberg hard-liners and the Helmstedt liberals.

Biblical 'Dictation'

Seventeenth-century Lutherans elaborated further upon Luther's doctrine of *sola scriptura*. Some of them went so far as to identify God's revealed Word with the actual page of Scripture; God was said not simply to have revealed the *truths* of Scripture but the actual *words*—even punctuation, grammar and style.

This led to the twofold theory of "full and verbal inspiration": (1) that God has not and will not reveal anything other than the words of the Bible; and (2) that God used the writers of Scripture simply as *amanuenses*—that is, passive, uninvolved copyists for his verbal dictation. Some Lutherans even claimed that God inspired the "vowel points" of the Hebrew text of the Old Testament. (Biblical Hebrew had no vowels; later editors added vowel marks above the Hebrew text so that non-Jews could pronounce the Hebrew words.)

THE ELABORATION OF CALVINISM

The Reformed theology which developed after Calvin's death owes as much to Zwingli and other theologians as to Calvin. The writings of these other theologians were lumped together as "Calvinism" largely due to the derogatory labeling process which occupied theologians during the bitter feuds of the 16th and 17th centuries. For both Catholics and Lutherans, to be a "Calvinist" was to be a heretic; thus the label "Calvinism" was intended as an insult.

Yet it is nonetheless true that Reformed theologians had more in common with Calvin than with any other Protestant reformer. It is also true that his theology came to be regarded by 17th-century Reformed theologians as the essence of pure doctrine. Thus in this sense it is valid to equate Reformed theology with Calvinism, even though Reformed theology departs from Calvinism in significant ways.

Points of Departure

The core of 17th-century Calvinism was predestination. Reformed theologians seemed fascinated with Calvin's infamous theory. One of 17th-century Calvinism's most influential systematic theologians was Francois Turretin (1623-1687), who lived in Switzerland. Turretin advanced a doctrine known as *infralapsarianism*, in opposition to another doctrine called *supralapsarianism*. (One could argue that the degree to which theological doctrines diverge from the simplicity of Scripture is directly proportional to the complexity of their spellings.)

Supralapsarians held that God, even before he willed that Adam fall from grace, willed for some souls to be saved and others to be damned. Turretin argued the reverse: that God first willed Adam's fall and then willed the election or damnation of Adam's descendants. (It evidently never occurred to Calvinist theologians that their debate over speculative, non-scriptural minutiae such as this was exactly like the Ockhamist nitpicking Luther and Calvin had condemned.)

Later generations tended to forget that predestination was only one aspect of Calvin's theology, not the whole of it. Reformed theologian Jerome Zanchi (1516-1590), for example, set the tone for the later Calvinist discussion of predestination when he wrote, "Whatever comes to pass, comes to pass by virtue of this absolute omnipotent will of God, which is the primary and supreme cause of all things."[2] Zanchi stressed not that God *foresees* and thus allows, but that he *wills* both salvation and damnation. The consequence of this teaching, as Zanchi points out, is that Christ died not for all human beings, but only for those whom the Father had predestined to salvation. This became the Calvinist doctrine of the "limited atonement," a doctrine which Calvin himself had not mentioned.

Reformed theology departed from Calvin's teachings in other ways. The *Second Helvetic Confession* is a good example. This confession of the Reformed faith in Switzerland, written by John Bullinger (1504-1575), developed a doctrine of biblical inspiration very similar to the Lutheran position already mentioned. Calvin himself, however, was too much of a humanist to believe that God had dictated the Bible word for word to writers who simply "transcribed" it. For later Calvinists, however, the printed Bible itself became more and more of a divinely dictated manuscript which faithfully recorded God's past oracles verbatim.

While neither Luther nor Calvin advanced such a theory, they nonetheless are at least partially responsible for the later development of an inflexible fundamentalism. They both removed the Bible from the context of God's ongoing revelation in and through the Church, turning the Bible itself into the Church.

The Dutch Reformed Church

The development of Reformed theology gained impetus from the argument over predestination in the Dutch Reformed Church. The debate originated in an argument between two Dutch Calvinist theologians, Jacob Arminius (1560-1609) and Franciscus Gomarus (1563-1641). Gomarus taught that God first willed damnation and election, and then willed the fall as a means to carry out his first decision. He also taught that Christ died for the elect only and that humanity remained "totally depraved."

Arminius, on the other hand, rejected predestination as related to God's will. He taught instead that predestination "has its foundation in the foreknowledge of God."[3] A doctrinal feud erupted between the two men and, when Arminius died, a number of his Calvinist supporters issued the *Remonstrance*, which defended his teachings.

Arminius's critics accused him of destroying the Protestant doctrine of unmerited grace. They argued that if God saves people because he foresees their faith in Christ, then it is their faith which saves them, not Christ. In this, of course, the strict Calvinists were right. Arminius's position was more like Luther's than Calvin's: Luther too had so stressed faith that he (unintentionally) made *it* rather than

142

Christ the means of salvation.

The Synod of Dort: 'Five Heads of Doctrine'

The argument between strict Calvinists and Remonstrants was settled by the Synod of Dort (1618-1619), which condemned the Remonstrants as heretics and greatly influenced future Calvinist thought. Let's analyze Dort's decisions briefly by using the word TULIP. This acronym serves to summarize Calvinist theology (each letter refers to the first letter of a key doctrine) and to remind future Calvinists of their debt to the Dutch Church.

T: Total Depravity. Both the Remonstrants and the delegates to the Synod of Dort (all of whom were opposed beforehand to Arminius's teachings) agreed that fallen humanity is totally depraved—that is, since the fall humanity exists in a state of irremediable corruption. This doctrine was essential to the Calvinist belief that it is impossible for humanity to accomplish anything good without God's prevenient grace. Yet the Remonstrants and the Synod shared this belief for different reasons.

Since the former believed that God's salvation was achieved for all people, damned and elect alike, they also believed that even some totally depraved people could choose to accept—or refuse—God's grace. The strict Calvinists who controlled the Synod of Dort, however, insisted that total depravity meant people must be unable to make any response at all to God's grace. The fact that some people *were touched* by God's grace meant, therefore, that grace is irresistible (see below).

U: Unconditional Election. Arminius and the Remonstrants had taught that the theory of predestination depends on God's foreknowledge rather than on his will: Foreseeing the people who will reject him, God refuses them in advance the gift of faith. The Synod of Dort, on the other hand, declared that God "was pleased out of the common mass of sinners to *adopt* some certain persons as a peculiar people to himself, as it is written."[4] Dort thus rested predestination on God's will, not on his foreknowledge.

L: Limited Atonement. As we have seen, the Remonstrants believed that Christ died for all people. Dort rejected this position and instead declared that "it was the will of God that Christ by the blood of the cross should effectively redeem all those, and only those, who were from eternity chosen."[5]

I: Irresistible Grace. As discussed above, the Remonstrants believed that grace was capable of being accepted (by the elect) or rejected (by the damned). The Synod, on the other hand, declared that God "produces both the will to believe and the act of believing also."[6]

For the delegates to Dort there was no such thing as free human will; there is only God's will, forcing the damned to choose hell and the elect to choose heaven. Dort in effect destroyed human freedom and turned people into so many robots programmed to perform God's will. Dort, then, represents Protestantism's ultimate repudiation of the Renaissance belief in human potentiality.

It is difficult to see how this Calvinist teaching could be squared with Calvinism's stated belief in *sola scriptura*. Scripture seems to argue for another view of human freedom:

> You have made him [human beings] little less than the angels,
>   and crowned him with glory and honor.
> You have given him rule over the works of your hands,
>   putting all things under his feet. (Psalm 8:6-7)

P: Perseverance of the Saints. The Remonstrants refused to teach that someone can never fall again from grace once he or she is recognized as one of the elect. Dort, on the other hand, formulated a doctrine of once saved, always saved, by declaring that the saints (the elect) persevere unfailingly toward heaven. Those who disagreed with this doctrine were condemned by the Synod as "ignorant... hypocrites...and heretics."[7] (Once again, it would appear impossible to reconcile this position with the principle of *sola scriptura*. See, for example, Hebrews 6:4-6.)

The Synod of Dort was the Calvinist equivalent of the Council of Trent. The "five heads of doctrine" established at Dort soon became normative Calvinist theology both in Europe and America. The American colonial Calvinist Jonathan Edwards (1703-1758), for example, spoke of Dort's doctrines as the starting point for all of his theology. Edwards told his audiences that their chief joy in heaven would come from watching the damned toss about forever in unquenchable fire.

On such an attitude much of the American nation was built. Dort's theology provided ample justification for depriving the (unelect) Indians of their land, enslaving Africans, or ignoring the doomed poor while the wealthy elect enjoyed God's prosperity. Never mind that the five doctrines, none of which are found in the Bible, were proclaimed by proponents of *sola scriptura* who claimed to be acting on behalf of a loving God.

PURITANS, CONGREGATIONALISTS AND BAPTISTS IN ENGLAND

In Chapter Eight we saw that English Puritans were essentially Calvinists; yet in certain aspects they differed from continental Calvinists. The first Puritans adhered to the *presbyterian* form of Church government adopted by their Scottish brethren, the formally designated Presbyterians. Other Puritans, however, rejected the presbyterian form of Church government and adopted a *congregationalist* form. In congregationalism each local Church is autonomous and governed by the democratic rule of all its members. In presbyterianism, on the other hand (at least in Knox's version of it), the various presbyters or pastors of several congregations govern their flocks and are in turn supervised by a council of elders. Congregationalists became an increasingly organized group which, like the mainline Puritans, exerted a great deal of influence on the founding of the American nation.

The congregationalist movement in England coincided with the birth of the Baptist Church. This denomination was similar in certain respects to the Anabaptist movement of the early Reformation (see pp. 60-61). One of the first English Baptists was Thomas Helwys (1550-1616). While in exile in Holland, Helwys broke with Dutch Calvinists by insisting on adult Baptism as the only authentic Baptism. When he returned to England, Helwys and his associates organized Congregationalist Churches based on Arminius's brand of Calvinism. Thus the English Baptists were somewhat of a hybrid of Anabaptists, Arminians and Congregationalists.

The Westminister Confession

In 1640 the Puritans convened the Westminster Assembly, a synod of 51 delegates who wrote the *Westminster Confession*. The Confession differed from Calvin's theology in certain respects.

Calvin (and Luther) had spoken of Scripture principally as the proclaimed Word of God constituting the body of believers—that is, the Word was said to serve as a sign of the Church. The Westminister Confession spoke rather of Scripture as the *individual's* moral guide. The Confession also proclaimed the Bible to be *inerrant*—correct in every detail of science, history and geography—whereas Luther and Calvin had never taught this.

SUMMING UP THE CENTURY

By the 17th century Lutheran and Calvinist theology had departed in several significant respects from the positions of their respective founders. A well-developed Protestant tradition had established itself at the start of the 18th century. This tradition was represented most notably by Lutheran theology as taught in German universities and Calvinist theology as defined by the Synod of Dort. Several major splinter groups had developed within Calvinism, most significantly Scottish Presbyterianism and the English Puritans, Baptists and Congregationalists.

CHAPTER TEN

THE GOD OF CONTROL

The Negative Side of Reformation Spirituality

The role of the human will in God's divine plan was seen very differently by Protestants and Catholics. The very essence of the Protestant position was its insistence on God's free decision to save sinful humanity apart from human effort. We will call this the "grace-only" viewpoint. The Catholic position, articulated by The Council of Trent, contained two main points: First, God's prevenient grace is necessary for salvation. Second, the human will can, through its own effort, respond to God's grace (see pp. 109-110). We will call this the "grace-plus-human-response" viewpoint.

It was with this second part of Trent's decree that many Protestants had difficulty. As we saw in the last chapter, Calvinists in particular increasingly came to believe that, because of humanity's total depravity, God must in essence *force* his grace on those whom he has predestined to salvation. Several Catholic theologians were nonetheless attracted to the Protestant "grace-only" viewpoint in contrast to the Council of Trent's teaching. Catholic debate on this subject was initiated when two Dominican theologians at the University of Salamanca in Spain took positions which seemed very near to Calvinism.

THE CATHOLIC DEBATE OVER GRACE

The Dominican Position

Bartolomeo Medina (1527-1580) and Domingo Bañez (1528-1604) were somewhat suspicious of the human will and its ability to cooperate in Christ's work of salvation. Medina taught that good works are not necessary to dispose a person to salvation (a teaching compatible with the Council of Trent), but he also taught that good works cannot even *prepare* a person to receive grace (a teaching that seemed to clash openly with Trent). Bañez argued from the divine nature, asserting that nothing external to God can influence God. Thus, Bañez concluded, no human response can move God to save anyone. Like Zwingli and Calvin, Bañez also said that God withholds his grace from those whom he wills to damn and gives grace to those whom he wills to save.

A Flemish theologian at the Catholic University of Louvain in Belgium, Michael Baius (1513-1589), taught much the same doctrine as Medina and Bañez. Like the Calvinists who lived up the road in Holland, Baius believed in the total depravity of human nature. For Baius, humanity lacked the capacity to turn toward God and accept grace. The Sorbonne in Paris condemned Baius's teaching in 1560, but because he was a favorite of the Spanish crown, Baius nonetheless represented the University of Louvain at the Council of Trent in 1563.

In 1567 (after Trent) Pope Pius V condemned Baius's writings and in 1585 the Jesuits took an interest in the matter, appointing their own man at Louvain, Leonhard Lessius, to write a rebuttal to the grace-only teaching, which threatened to subvert Trent's doctrinal definition on the role of human effort.

The Jesuit Response

Lessius got nothing but trouble for his efforts. The faculty at Louvain stood overwhelmingly behind Baius. In contradiction to Lessius, the faculty declared that God must move the human will to accept grace, and that God does this only for those whom he has decided ahead of time to save. At that point another Jesuit entered the fray. Luis de Molina (1535-1600) from Portugal, added to the controversy his treatise: *The Harmony of Free Will With the Gifts of Grace*. Like Lessius, Molina argued for the grace-plus-human-response position, but in a much more comprehensive way.

Molina, basing his work on Thomas Aquinas's teaching, argued from the premise of God's twofold knowledge. By "natural knowledge" God knows all things without being the cause of them (such as who will go to hell and who to heaven). God's "free knowledge," on the other hand, is directed by God's will and actually causes things to happen. The first type of knowledge has to do with possibilities, Molina said; the second with actual realities.

Humanity, according to Molina, is the only part of God's

creation with the ability to choose from among possibilities and make a reality, because only humanity possesses free will by nature. Original sin destroyed Adam's supernatural capacities but not his natural capacities including his will. Therefore, even ungraced humanity after the fall possesses the ability to choose between belief and unbelief.

Molina argued that if the human will were not truly free to accept or reject God's gift of grace, then this "gift" was neither gift nor grace. "The freedom of the will must be preserved," Molina said, "so that in all things the grace of the Giver may stand out."[1] Thus for Molina God's grace and humanity's free will were not opposed, but two parts of the single organic process—"two parts of a single integrated cause of the act of believing,"[2] as he put it. God's grace, then, does not predetermine the will to choose belief rather than unbelief, as the Calvinists taught, but instead cooperates with the free human decision to believe.

Molina's treatise caused a furor in Spain. The Dominicans asked the Spanish Inquisition to condemn Molina's works, and he responded by asking the Inquisition to condemn the teachings of Bañez. The debate grew so intense that Pope Clement VIII appointed a commission to study the matter. When behind-the-scenes political maneuvering impeded the commission's work, Clement himself reviewed the case but died (1605) before he could make a decision. Pope Paul V then tried to appease everyone by blandly declaring both Dominicans and Jesuits free from error.

Jansen Enters the Fray

There the matter rested until the Dutch Catholic bishop and theologian, Cornelis Jansen (1585-1638), unleashed his own assault against Molina's doctrine. Jansen's main work, *Augustinus*, was not actually published until two years after his death, but he made his position well-known by arguing against the Jesuits at a disputation held at the University of Madrid (1626-1627).

Jansen was fanatically dedicated to Augustine; he had read all of Augustine's writings 10 times before composing *Augustinus*. And Jansen thought the only way to defeat Protestantism was to prove that its teaching on grace was in fact part of the Catholic tradition.

Since most of what we know about Jansen's doctrine comes from the posthumously published *Augustinus*, we can only presume that his earlier teaching coincided with its principal theses. They may be summarized as follows: (1) Without God's grace human beings can perform no works meriting salvation; (2) for the elect, God's grace is irresistible. Catholic tradition could have accepted the first proposition. But it could not accept the second without defining human nature exactly as the Calvinists had: as the victim of divine necessity.

Jansen feebly protested that his teaching was not Calvinist by saying that human beings do have some natural freedom. Whereas Calvin saw human freedom arising completely out of the graced will, Jansen acknowledged some degree of human freedom existing at the moment the will surrenders to God's grace. This distinction was obviously so ephemeral that it amounted to practically no distinction at all.

Further, Jansen accepted predestination in its most Calvinist form: For him God decided before creation who would be saved and who damned. The Catholic Church, he said, had performed a disservice both to Paul and to Augustine—"the source," as he put it, "of all the conclusions that can be formed about grace"[3]—by allowing their teachings on predestination to be superseded by the Scholastics' teaching on the indispensability of free will. In reality, Jansen said, humans can be saved only by irresistable grace. The Jesuits, with their insistence on free will, were surreptitiously bringing the very religious works which Paul had condemned into the Church. Although reason may recoil at predestination, reason must simply yield without protest to faith.

All of this was completely Calvinist, of course, no matter how much Jansen argued to the contrary. Accordingly, in 1642 Pope Urban VIII condemned the *Augustinus* in its entirety. Since the common people were unsure precisely what the *Augustinus* taught, Pope Innocent X's bull *Cum Occasione* (1653) further condemned as heretical five propositions which were said to be contained in the *Augustinus*:

1) that there are some divine commandments which good people lack the ability to obey;

2) that God's grace is irresistible;

3) that for a human act to be meritorious all that is required is that the human will not be coerced, not that it acts out of necessity (a technical, philosophical argument refuting one of Molina's theses);

4) that Semi-Pelagianism (see *The People of the Creed*, pp. 134-137) taught that the human will possesses "resisting grace" (another technical argument);

5) that anyone teaching that Christ died for all people is a Semi-Pelagian.

Since these five propositions were not verbatim quotes from the *Augustinus* but summaries composed by a Jesuit, the Jansenists protested that the bull *Cum Occasione* had not condemned Jansen's actual work, but only the Jesuits' deceitful rendition of it.

At this point, had Jansen's only disciples been professors locked away in academia, the controversy over the *Augustinus* probably would have died a gradual death. As it turned out, however, Jansenism became associated with a popular French spiritual movement and from there became one of the major controversies in all of French religious history. In addition, Jansenism exerted a great deal of influence on the future course of Catholic spirituality.

FRENCH JANSENISM: 'CATHOLIC CALVINISM'

Jesuit Casuistry

As was true everywhere in Europe, the Jesuits had established themselves in France as the principal force for religious education. As their influence on French education grew stronger, so too did their views on moral theology. The Jesuits had developed a method known as *casuistry*, by which they attempted to evaluate the goodness of a given human action. According to the principles of casuistry, a confessor could judge the morality of an action according to the circumstances under which it had been committed, the degree to which the person had freely assented, the person's age, personality and so on.

By the doctrine of *probabilism*, confessors could decide that a person's action was moral rather than immoral if, in view of all the surrounding circumstances, there existed a doubt both as to the action's evil and the probability of its goodness. Although many French Catholics accepted this lenient approach to moral theology, a small minority vigorously objected to what they saw as a clear compromise with sin.

This anticasuist, anti-Jesuit minority was led by a community of zealots who came largely from the influential Arnauld family and who were affiliated with the convent of Port-Royal, seven miles south of Versailles. Jacqueline Arnauld had become mother superior of Port-Royal in 1602. She had transformed the convent from a comfortable hideaway for wealthy French women whose families were unable to find them husbands into a virtual concentration camp for ascetics. Mother Angelica (as Jacqueline came to be called) walled her nuns off from the world and permitted outsiders to converse with the community only through a latticed window. Twelve women from the Arnauld family as well as several Arnauld men played key roles in the supervision of Port-Royal.

Arnauld and Pascal Rebut the Jesuits

Antoine Arnauld II (1612-1694) became Port-Royal's chief theologian. When the *Augustinus* was published, he wrote a treatise (*On Frequent Communion*) in which he sought to implement Jansen's theology in the day-to-day lives of the nuns. Arnauld warned against receiving Holy Communion without being sufficiently full of grace and otherwise cautioned his readers against imagining that their devotional life did any good without the proper interior purity. He particularly condemned "certain teachers" (without actually naming the Jesuits) who advised Catholics not to worry about going to confession and receiving Communion as often as possible after repeated sinning.

French Jesuits attacked Arnauld's treatise so vehemently that he withdrew from public life and concentrated all of his efforts on defending Jansenism from Jesuit attack. As the feud developed, the Arnaulds, the convent of Port-Royal and its foundation convents became the leading proponents of French Jansenism. And as the Jesuit offensive intensified, Antoine Arnauld asked a young colleague named Blaise Pascal (1623-1662) to help him rebut Jesuit accusations.

Pascal responded in a series of 18 *Letters Written to a Provincial* in which he brilliantly condemned Molina's views on grace as well as the Jesuits' casuist and probabilist moral theology. Pascal also urged French Catholics to become as austere and disciplined as he said the early Christians had been. In his final letter (1657) Pascal criticized the bull *Cum Occasione* by writing that the pope, who had clearly erred in condemning the scientist Galileo, could likewise have erred again.

Louis XIV's War on Jansenism

Pascal's erudite defense made Jansenism not simply respectable but popular among Catholics in France and elsewhere. Even a papal condemnation of Pascal's *Letters* did little good in stopping the spread of Jansenist ideas.

King Louis XIV became concerned about the controversy. He saw Jansenism as the means by which Protestantism, denied direct access to French public opinion, could indirectly influence all of Catholic France. Consequently, in 1661 he ordered the French bishops as well as the Port-Royal fanatics to sign an oath prepared by the pope in which they would condemn "with heart and mouth" the five propositions listed in the bull *Cum Occasione*. When the majority of nuns at Port-Royal refused to sign, Louis locked them up and denied them the sacraments.

After a brief period of reconciliation Louis took up the attack again, forbidding Port-Royal or its affiliates to accept novices. He then cajoled Pope Clement XI to issue another papal bull condemning the Jansenists. In *Vineam Domini* (1705) Clement claimed the prerogative to judge questions not only of faith and morals but also of historical fact, such as whether the five propositions condemned in *Cum Occasione* were actually contained in the *Augustinus*. The pope's appropriation of divine omniscience shocked French Catholics and even disturbed King Louis, who published the bull with a proviso defending the traditional autonomy of the French episcopacy.

Meanwhile, a Parisian priest named Pasquier Quesnel had published a defense of Jansenist theology which became popular among French priests. When Clement XI condemned Quesnel's treatise in the bull *Unigenitus* (1713), he imprudently belittled at the same time much of French devotionalism. At this, Jansenism and Gallicanism (French independence from Rome; see p. 95) came to be united in the minds of most French bishops. As for the Jesuits, their initial successes against the Jansenists were reversed in 1773 when the Society's enemies throughout Europe persuaded Pope Clement XIV to suppress the order. Not until Pope Pius VII restored the Society in 1814 were the Jesuits permitted fully to resume their ministries.

Far from destroying Jansenism, Louis XIV thus inadvertently contributed to the movement's success. While the French Catholic Church had kept Calvinism from entering by the front door, it had welcomed it with open arms through the back.

JANSENISM'S LEGACY

As a result of the Jansenist movement many French Catholics grew up more Calvinist than Catholic. This was especially true of the French middle class who, working side-by-side with Huguenots in the marketplace, imbibed Calvinism's negative teaching on human nature in equal measure with what their own priests were teaching them. "The good town of Paris," wrote an 18th-century journalist, "is Jansenist from top to bottom."[4]

By 1730 Jansenist spirituality had become openly masochistic. Jansenist ascetics called "convulsionaries" beat themselves with rods and encouraged others to beat them as well. Only through such "discipline," it was believed, could one control the totally depraved human spirit. Other Jansenists pierced their extremities with nails or had themselves crucified for several hours. Their mentality—although not their severity—captured an entire age of Catholic spirituality. From Jansen's time onward his unknowing disciples put Jansen's theories into practice by doing all they could to denigrate their own humanity and the humanity of others—all in the name of a Savior who proclaimed, "I came / that they might have life / and have it to the full" (John 10:10).

Jansenism's Appeal

Jansenism grew out of a Reformation-era hunger for the same degree of certainty in spiritual life that the faith of the Middle Ages had generally provided.

Toward the end of the Middle Ages, as the laity had become more and more self-assured in developing its own prayer and devotional practices, the clergy's control over lay spirituality naturally began to diminish. Largely because of this situation, Luther—teaching the priesthood of all believers and the primacy of the individual's personal faith—was able to appeal successfully to ordinary Christians who no longer needed the highly structured and institutionalized religious life provided by the Catholic Church. Yet, there were trade-offs.

It is not always as easy as one may have first imagined to become free and independent. Habits and attitudes built up over generations and lifetimes do not disappear overnight. While Luther preached the freedom of the individual Christian, at the same time he demand obedience to his (and only his) interpretation of Scripture and likewise insisted that Christians stop challenging the established social order and submit to princely authority.

No doubt Luther was reacting in some degree to his own uncertainty over the response his call to autonomy and independence had generated among his people. Grasping for past security, he had responded in the only way he knew: an authoritarian demand for rigid control and order—a response which he had learned only too well from the medieval Church system against which he had himself rebelled.

This same ambivalence over where to draw the boundary between security and autonomy is an important factor behind the success of Calvinist theology and its Catholic counterpart, Jansenism. The early Protestants promised unlimited freedom from clerical control with their theology of the priesthood of all believers, individual discernment of Scripture and personal faith as the sole arbiter of doctrine. But their various doctrines of predestination in actuality returned Christians to a system of infinite and perfect control. There is no greater form of security than that which denies human persons the capacity to act on their own volition in their relationship with God.

Thus Protestant theology, particularly the brand of Calvinism proclaimed at the Synod of Dort, effectively restored the lost security of the Middle Ages by substituting a paternalistic, all-providing God for the paternalistic and all-providing medieval Church. While freedom and autonomy from control were proclaimed, control was nonetheless effectively restored with a doctrine that provided the psychological assurance of God's absolute predetermination of human destiny. Jansenists attempted to incorporate into Catholic theology the precise element of security that Calvin had provided for the Protestants.

A Spiritual Dead End

Yet security is an illusion, and theologies based on security inevitably lead to a spirituality which seeks ever firmer assurances. In the back of every "predestined" Christian's mind lurks the nagging doubt that life may not be as perfectly ordered and controlled as one would like to believe; as a result one begins to construct a spiritual life which assuages the doubt. Thus Calvinists developed a spirituality in which one could unerringly determine the status of the soul by pointing to the degree to which one works hard and achieves the rewards of affluence. Jansenists developed a spirituality of degrading the human body, thereby (it was hoped) emulating in one's flesh the degree of control over human existence which God is supposed to exert from heaven.

Such spiritualities never work. Christian tradition reveals that God is not a God of control but a God of freedom and, ultimately, of mystery. Yet perhaps we should not be too hard on Christians of the Reformation era for attempting to regain some sense of the lost security which the Middle Ages had provided. As we have seen, the Middle Ages went out and the early modern age began with a bang. In the political realm, European society in the 17th century was still in a state of flux (in some cases, turmoil), with even greater turmoil and disorder just over the horizon. On the social level, new classes were seeking to replace established ones, raising a great deal of anxiety about their future role in society. Everywhere there was confusion and doubt as to religious truth.

It was only human for such people to look for security, order and stability; it is not surprising to find a certain strand of spirituality developing in the fashion that it did. Yet Calvinism, Jansenism and other such counterproductive attempts to arrive at spiritual certainty are not the whole story. In order to round out our discussion of Reformation spirituality—in order to get a fuller picture of how Reformation-era Christians attempted to live their faith in the often chaotic world in which they lived—let's take up now a more complete analysis of Reformation spirituality.

CHAPTER ELEVEN

THE GOD OF FREEDOM

The Positive Side of Reformation Spirituality

T he negative side of Reformation spirituality, as we argued at the close of the last chapter, was characterized by an overemphasis on the quest for security and order. Here we will focus on its positive dimension: Reformation spiritual writers' attempt to emphasize the mystery and transcendence of God.

Reformation-era Christians understood as well as Christians of any age that the antidote to excessive concern with the God of control is a spirituality which correctly presents God as a God of freedom. This "antidote" was certainly a feature of Reformation spirituality—both Protestant and Catholic.

ENGLISH PROTESTANTISM SEVERS CALVINIST TIES

The most important of the early Protestant spiritual writers was Johann Arndt (1555-1621). His treatise on the spiritual life, *True Christianity*, is reminiscent of one of the great spiritual writers of the Middle Ages, Bernard of Clairvaux. Like Bernard, Arndt spoke of the inner transformation which union with Christ produces; faith did not simply bring about "imputed righteousness" but an objectively new love relationship with Christ in the believer's heart.

Arndt's student Johann Gerhard (1582-1637) introduced Protestantism to Orthodox spirituality by writing treatises on the mystical theology of Athanasius and other Greek fathers. Following in the footsteps of Pseudo-Dionysius (see *The People of the Faith*, p. 21),

Gerhard wrote that God was beyond comprehension and description, and was thus ultimately mystery.

Anglicanism Reembraces Human Nature

In England perhaps more than in any other country, the negative spirituality implicit in Calvin's theology was subjected to a thoroughgoing reevaluation. The Anglican Richard Hooker (1554-1600) astutely observed that Luther and Calvin, in the name of destroying Catholic "innovations," had created their own. Hooker thus rejected Calvin's teaching that Adam's fall had completely destroyed human freedom. Rather, Hooker said, fallen humanity still possesses the ability to hunger for God.

Perhaps more than anyone, Hooker was responsible for steering Anglicanism away from Calvin's depreciation of human nature. In his spiritual writings Hooker spoke like Aquinas of the role played by grace in *perfecting* human nature, and not, as Calvin had conceived it, of grace *overpowering* human nature.

The theories of Hooker were translated into practice for the average Anglican by Lancelot Andrews (1555-1626). A popular and scholarly Anglican bishop, Andrews was perhaps the first practicing mystic of the Protestant Reformation. Like the medieval contemplatives, Andrews wrote down his prayer experiences in the form of spiritual and devotional guides for others. His younger contemporaries—Izaak Walton (1593-1683), Thomas Browne (1605-1682) and Nicholas Ferrar (1592-1637)—reintroduced Anglicanism to a piety and devotionalism that was in many respects Catholic. Prayer, meditation, asceticism— these became the characteristics of 17th-century Anglican spirituality as it severed its ties with Calvinism.

Puritan Mysticism

Some Puritans also departed from the negative aspects of Calvinist teaching and gave birth to a Puritan mystical tradition which smoothed the rough edges of Calvinist theology. A Puritan named Francis Rous (1579-1669) spoke like the Catholic mystic Teresa of Avila about the soul's mystical union with Christ and like Teresa's contemporary, John of the Cross, about the bride's (the soul's) marriage with her spouse (Christ).

In a statement that is strikingly reminiscent of the "apophatic" mysticism represented by John of the Cross (see below, pp. 168-170), Rous writes, "Christ and his love are better than the seeing and feeling of him and his love;...better for thee that they are thine, than that they appear to be thine;...therefore at all times and in all estates, even in darkest desertions and greatest sufferings, trust in him whose love turns all things to good unto his beloved, even death unto life."[1]

It is hard to imagine such words being written by someone whose theological tradition completely scorned traditional Catholic mysticism and the Catholic belief that the love of God inheres as grace in the believer's soul. Yet, as if to go Rous one step better, we find another Puritan writer, Thomas Goodwin (b. 1600), writing of the heart of Jesus in words that seemed to paraphrase French devotionals on the Sacred Heart:

> The drift of this discourse is therefore to ascertain poor souls that His heart...remains the same as it was on earth, that He is as meek, as gentle, as easy to be entreated, so that *they may deal with Him as fairly about the great matter of their own salvation*, and as hopefully and upon as easy terms *obtain it* of Him, as they might if they had been on earth with Him.[2] (Emphasis added)

This is not Calvinist at all. Yet here a Puritan-Calvinist writes of the believer's quest to "obtain" salvation through mystical contact with the love of Christ as represented by his ever-present heart. If the name and title were removed from Goodwin's treatise, one would easily identify it as typical French or Spanish Catholic piety.

The 'Catholic Soul'

The examples of Rous and Goodwin suggest strongly that in the popular mind opposition to Catholicism was directed not so much at Catholicism's soul—its prayer and devotional tradition—as at such external aspects of its life as clerical abuses. As Louis Bouyer, the preeminent historian of Christian spirituality has written, "Whatever their individual doctrine on other points, when these Protestants were dealing with spirituality they expressed a faith whose substance had become Catholic again."[3] No matter how much Reformation theologians attempted to define God as a God of control, in Christians' everyday spiritual lives the God of freedom always broke through, revealing himself as the same loving God to Protestants and Catholics alike.

As a result, English spiritual writers lapse over and over again into language which leads one to wonder whether they really believed Protestant doctrine at all. The Cambridge Platonist John Smith (1618-1652) wrote, for example, "God hath stamped a copy of His own archetypal loveliness upon the soul, that man by reflecting unto himself might behold there the glory of God."[4] Do those words mean that the Anglican Smith believed in sanctifying grace as the indwelling source of the soul's own life?

The Puritan Richard Baxter spoke of the piety in which the reader was encouraged to "exercise his graces, till he finds his doubts and discomforts vanish."[5] (What has happened to the Calvinist assurance of salvation?) And Baxter's contemporary, Arthur Dent, embraced spiritual "works" by listing eight signs of sanctity in his "Catholic"-titled *The Plain Man's Pathway to Heaven.*

Finally, the founder of the Quakers, George Fox (1624-1691), brought Puritanism full circle into complete harmony with much of late medieval mysticism. He wrote, "For though I read the Scriptures that spake of Christ and of God, yet I knew him not, but by revelation, as he who hath the key did open, and as the Father and Life drew me to His Son by His Spirit."[6]

Spiritual writers such as these gradually eroded the strength of Calvinist thinking. As a result, more and more Protestants reacted against the harsh Calvinist theology which, in the mid-16th century, had seemed on the verge of capturing much of Christian Europe. Christians reacted as well against the dry rationalism of the developing Protestant tradition which we discussed in Chapter Nine.

These two reactions, the mystical and the antirationalist, came together to provide a catalyst for what would become—after Anglicanism and Puritanism—the third religious revolution in England: Methodism.

TOWARD A SPIRITUALITY OF THE HEART

The origins of Methodism lie in a continental spiritual revival called Pietism. Its founder was a Lutheran pastor, Philipp Spener (1635-1705). Like many Lutherans of his day, Spener disliked the academic and rationalistic tone which contemporary Lutheranism had assumed. He yearned for the emotional fervor which had characterized Luther's own style of piety.

In 1669 Spener harshly criticized his parishioners from the pulpit for their moral decline, and he subsequently formed small groups dedicated to regular prayer and spiritual reading. These groups were called *collegia pietatis*, from which we get the English *Pietism.*

In Spener's groups doctrine took a back seat to piety and devotion. His followers read and discussed the Bible in common, seeking from their shared reading practical lessons in day-to-day morality and Christian living. Since for many Lutherans such a practice was simply a return to Catholic "works," Spener was accused of being a Catholic in Lutheran dress. Eventually, however, Spener and his disciples gained the support of the elector of Brandenburg for the establishment—oddly enough—of a theology faculty at the University of Halle in central Germany.

There August Francke (1663-1727) developed a school of bibilical scholarship based on the student's experience of inner conversion rather than on doctrinal and technical analysis. From that point on Pietism (and all Protestantism influenced by Pietism) would develop a conversion-experience theology based on belief in a dramatic, inner spiritual transformation traceable to a specific moment in time. Francke's account of his own conversion experience established something of a pattern that would be replicated virtually word for word in the writings of future Protestant spiritual writers:

> Then all my doubts vanished as if by magic; I had the grace of God in Christ in my heart and I would call God my Father. All sadness and all anxiety were lifted from me and my soul was invaded by a torrent of joy.[7]

This tendency toward a religion of inner experience reached its peak in Germany with Nikolaus von Zinzendorf (1700-1760), the founder of the Moravian Brethren. Zinzendorf described his teaching as "a theology of the heart" in which truth was gained through inner revelation by Christ. Since this inner experience was common to all people, Zinzendorf said, it transcended doctrinal attempts to define God and could thus serve as the basis of a truly ecumenical religion. Zinzendorf attracted a group of Moravian Christians (Moravia is in today's Czechoslovakia) to an estate he had established for the purpose of implementing his new style of Christian community.

When he and his followers came under attack from more traditional Lutherans, the Moravian Brethren (as they were known by then) traveled as missionaries to the English colony of Georgia. There a struggling young Anglican priest named John Wesley (1703-1791) befriended them. Wesley shortly (1735) became convinced of the shallowness both of his own spiritual life and of the Anglican doctrine which he had learned while growing up in England.

John Wesley

Wesley had been strongly attracted to Pietism even before meeting the Moravians. While studying at Oxford, he and his brother Charles had formed a group of students similar in their devotional practices to Spener's *collegia*. Less pious students gave Wesley's group derogatory nicknames such as "Bible Moths" and "Methodists." The latter term was intended to belittle the Wesleyan practice of using "methods" of prayer and spirituality, but it was eventually adopted by

Wesley's followers as their permanent title.

After his contact with the Moravians, Wesley returned to England, struggling to reshape his spiritual life. On May 24, 1738, after seeking prayer and counseling from Moravians in England, he had an experience which changed his life. This "Aldersgate experience" (named for the London street where it took place) was later described by Wesley in this way: "I felt my heart strangely warmed. I felt I did trust in Christ, Christ alone for my salvation; and an assurance was given me, that he had taken away *my* sins, even *mine*, and saved *me* from the law of sin and death."[8]

Methodism

Wesley eventually broke with his Moravian friends on questions of doctrine, principally on matters pertaining to Church discipline. Wesley rejected the Moravians' denial of what he called the "means of grace" in the Church: Holy Communion, fasting, private Bible study, and so on. Although Wesley himself had had a conversion experience, he did not teach as Pietists did that the *only* way to grace was through a conversion experience. Wesley wanted to maintain the organized Church structure and devotional life of his Anglican upbringing. His theology was as sacramental and ecclesiastical as Anglicanism itself.

Trent defined works as the means whereby people cooperate with God's grace. Wesley likewise spoke of justification as a process whereby people—graced by God—accept the gift of faith through their own willed response. "There is no man," Wesley wrote, "that is wholly void of the grace of God. No man living is entirely destitute of what is vulgarly called *natural conscience*....So that no man sins because he has not grace, but because he does not use the grace which he hath."[9] This of course is reminiscent of Molina's teaching. And, in fact, Wesley thought highly of the Jesuits, regarding Ignatius Loyola as "one of the greatest men of Christian history."[10]

Wesley had other Catholic inclinations. Most notably he believed in an ongoing process of sanctification—that is, the gradual perfection of the justified believer through a life of ever-increasing conversion. This placed him squarely in line with the Spanish spiritual tradition which we are about to discuss. Wesley further believed (as did Catholics) in the possibility of the believer's fall from grace, and he thus stressed the importance of continual spiritual effort. As one historian observes, "All this, then, marked a return to Catholic doctrine in its deepest and most traditional form....No one did so much [as Wesley] to rebuild the bridges on the spiritual plane between Catholicism (old and new) and a renewed Protestantism."[11]

Had traditional, upper-class Anglicans been willing to give Wesley a hearing, his views on grace and Church discipline could have found a home within Anglicanism. And, in fact, Wesley did not at first seek to separate himself from the Church of England. Gradually, however, as Wesley began to win more and more converts to his views (mostly from among England's working-class poor), and as many Anglican bishops rejected him, he took the fateful step of ordaining his own ministers. Thus Methodism formally separated itself from the Anglican Church.

The Methodist influence was enormous in both England and America. George Whitefield (1714-1740) and Francis Asbury (1745-1816), for example, contributed to a "great awakening" of spiritual fervor in the American colonies. By Wesley's death there were 79,000 Methodists in England and 40,000 in America.[12] This was a huge number of converts given the population of the day and the means of communication available to Methodist missionaries, most of whom preached out-of-doors wherever an audience would gather.

Methodism's principal contribution to Protestantism was this: It won the ordinary believer to a life of practical morality and piety in an age when much of Protestantism had grown overly rational and dogmatic. Wesley did much to replace the God of control with the God of freedom and mystery, particularly in the lives of the lower classes in the English-speaking world.

THE GOLDEN AGE OF CATHOLIC SPIRITUALITY

The three greatest names of Catholic mysticism were all born in the Spanish peninsula within a 50-year span. None of the three specifically intended to take up the cause of defending the Church against Protestantism. Yet they became in effect the greatest achievement of the Counter-Reformation. In order to understand Catholicism's contribution to Reformation spirituality, we will turn to the writings of Ignatius Loyola (1491-1556), Teresa of Avila (1515-1582) and John of the Cross (1542-1591).

First, however, some distinctions are in order: Loyola's (and Teresa's) *kataphatic* mysticism must be distinquished from John of the Cross's *apophatic* mysticism. "Kataphatic" describes a spirituality that is an *affirmative* mysticism, stressing the role of creation in the mystic's ascent toward God. John of the Cross, on the other hand, promoted a *negative* mysticism that stresses the dissimilarities between God and creation. This "apophatic" mysticism thus focuses on God's transcendence rather than on his immanence.

Ignatius's 'Spiritual Exercises'

Earlier we spoke of Ignatius Loyola's career founding the Jesuits. Here we will focus only on his contribution to Catholic spirituality: *The Spiritual Exercises*. In Ignatius's own words, these *Exercises* are "methods of preparing and disposing the soul to free itself of inordinate attachments, and after accomplishing this, of seeking and discovering the Divine Will regarding the disposition of one's life."[13]

The *Exercises* emphasize three elements: (1) disposition toward God, (2) purgation from one's consciousness of that which is not of God, and (3) a process for discerning God's will for one's life. The *Exercises*, which last 30 days, are divided into four "weeks" (not of seven days) during which the "exercitant" (one who performs the *Exercises*) seeks specific graces from God.

In the first week the exercitant seeks the grace to know in a deeply personal way the reality of sin in the world and in the exercitant's own life. The first week reaches a climax when the exercitant is led by interior grace and the director's guidance to ask, "What ought I do for Christ?"[14]

In the second week, the exercitant seeks the grace of illumination by focusing on Christ's own example through the use of Ignatius's "contemplations." These involve the concentrated focusing of one's mind on Gospel scenes—"as though I were present there."[15] Then, in follow-up "reflections," one seeks to know how the insights gained in the contemplations apply to one's own life.

The exercitant is encouraged specifically to make a commitment to serve Christ as a loyal soldier, in whatever fashion the "Eternal King and Universal Lord" chooses. This commitment, made during the second week, is called an "Election." The exercitant then seeks the grace of perseverance by contemplating Jesus' passion and death (third week) and his Resurrection (fourth week).

Ignatius hoped that at the end of the 30 days the exercitant would have experienced a profound conversion of intellect, will and imagination, so that in the future he or she would be able to experience God in all created things. Through a radical reorientation of thinking, feeling and imagining, the successful exercitant would then serve Christ unswervingly, surrendering everything to him for the sake of his Kingdom. Ignatius hoped that those who completed his *Exercises* would be able to make his prayer their own:

Take, Lord, receive all my liberty,
my memory, understanding, my entire will.

Give me only your love and your grace;
that's enough for me.
Take, Lord, receive all I have and possess.
You have given all to me; now I return it.
Take, Lord, receive, all is yours now;
dispose of it wholly according to your will.[16]

Ignatius's spirituality was entirely incarnational; it was a service-oriented mysticism designed to bring the exercitant from contemplative union with Christ to committed service to Christ's brothers and sisters. Consistent with later Jesuit theology (for example, Molina), the *Exercises* emphasized the necessity for both God's grace and human effort in the spiritual life. In leading Christians to surrender all that is false and illusory in human nature and to center their thought, feeling and imagination on Christ' love, Loyola professed to teach what it truly means to be human.

Teresa of Avila

Teresa was a member of the Carmelite Order, which traced its origins back to the 12th century and perhaps even earlier. The Carmelites had originally stressed living in severe poverty and solitude, but by Teresa's time they had become as lax as most other religious orders. Teresa thus set about reforming her Carmelite sisters while her young disciple John of the Cross undertook reform of the Carmelite friars.

In 1542, while entertaining a vistor to the convent, Teresa experienced a vision of Jesus standing by her visitor's side and collapsed into a trance. From that moment on she regularly began to have extraordinary visions and ecstacies as God gave her insights into the most profound mysteries. Yet years of visions brought Teresa not peace but harassment. At one point she was summoned before the Inquisition as someone possessed by a demon.

In order to assure her examiners of her orthodoxy, she wrote her spiritual autobiography, *Vida*, which so impressed the Inquisitors that they not only cleared Teresa's name but encouraged others to read her book. At this point Teresa, now 57 years old, felt confident to undertake a thorough reform of the Carmelite sisters throughout Spain from her convent in Avila (central Spain). To distinguish themselves from the lax Carmelites, Teresa and her sisters wore sandals rather than shoes; they thus became known as the "Discalced" (unshod) Carmelites.

Teresa's practical, down-to-earth personality came to the fore when her reform efforts were stifled by Church bureacrats who had no sympathy for a woman demanding a return to gospel values. Teresa simply blustered them into submission. Nor was she above calling a bishop a fool when his conduct deserved it. Teresa's sanctity, her zeal for reform and her outgoing, impetuous personality endeared her to Spanish Catholics and made her the most famous spiritual leader of her day. Even men approached Teresa for spiritual direction—unheard of in the Spain of her time.

Teresa details her spirituality in two treatises, *The Way of Perfection* (1567) and *The Interior Castle* (1577). In the latter Teresa describes the soul as a diamond castle containing many rooms. The spiritual life, she says, consists in entering the castle and passing through seven "mansions" (stages of prayer) so as to meet Christ the King in the center of the castle. Teresa defines contemplative prayer as "nothing more than friendly intercourse, and frequent solitary converse, with Him Who we know loves us."[17]

In order to understand how Teresa applied her concept of prayer to her seven stages of spiritual life, let's look briefly at Teresa's seven mansions:

First Mansion. This stage of the spiritual life is where most Christians ordinarily find themselves. This is the "ground floor," so to speak, where one's desire for God and for a life dedicated to the Gospels is overshadowed by everyday cares and the desire for wealth, security and fame.

Second Mansion. Here Christians who realize the shallowness of their lives begin to pray more frequently. They realize that they must stop sinning and turn away from those things which lead to sin, but they also realize they lack the power to accomplish this. In this stage "the spirit is willing, but the flesh is weak." Teresa counsels second-stage pilgrims to be prepared for vicious attacks from the devil and for great dryness in prayer. By perseverence, she assures us, spiritual progress can be made.

Third Mansion. By now one realizes that only positive action can reduce the grip which sin has on one's life. Hence third-stage Christians mortify their bodies by fasting and penance and by performing works of service to others. In spite of their efforts, however, Christians in the third stage may experience even more dryness in prayer. Teresa characterizes this as a time of testing; God must teach one humility in preparation for service to his Kingdom.

Fourth Mansion. For persons who persevere, God begins to grant graces of "infused contemplation," a type of prayer that comes not from human effort but from God himself. Infused contemplation is for Teresa the "second degree of prayer," far superior and infinitely more soothing to the spirit than the first degree of prayer, which is ordinary recollection. Teresa's second degree of prayer is a surrender of one's self to God for the service of his Kingdom. Teresa's mysticism, then, like that of Ignatius, is an incarnational, service-oriented mysticism.

Fifth Mansion. In this stage one experiences what Teresa calls the "sleep of the faculties," a type of infused contemplation in which the intellect, memory and imagination are drawn into God to such an extent that they are no longer aware of sensory input (compare Ignatius's prayer, pp. 164-165). Yet this stage is not sleep; this is not the absence but the fullness of awareness. Teresa calls this stage the "prayer of union." Here the soul and God are joined together as if in an engagement or betrothal. The soul and God delight in each other, finding great joy in the anticipation of their wedding day. At this stage the soul begins to desire sharing the beloved's sufferings. As a result, the impulse to service of others becomes even stronger.

Sixth Mansion. The soul, now prepared for the consummation of its marriage, must still go through one last stage of purgation, the stage of mystical death. In one's active life, Teresa says, one can expect now to be totally abandoned by friends, relatives and worldly consolations. As the last vestiges of sin leave the soul, they wreak havoc. Yet in the midst of this painful process by which the ego dies to itself, God gives the grace of certitude—a certitude, as Teresa describes it, in which "the soul realizes that it has deserved to go to hell, yet its punishment is to taste glory."[18]

Because the soul is no longer trapped by the world's illusions, the body may begin to experience great rapture and demonstrate psychosomatic powers such as levitation or locutions (hearing God's voice audibly). Such phenomena are nothing, however, in comparison to the ever-growing joy which the soul experiences by surrendering totally to God. (Both Teresa and John of the Cross strongly caution against *pursuing* psychosomatic phenomena.)

Seventh Mansion. In this stage the soul consummates its mystical marriage with God. God and the soul in effect now share the same soul, fulfilling mystically the "great foreshadowing" (Ephesians 5:32) of which Paul spoke when he quoted the Old Testament, "...the two of them become one body" (Genesis 2:24). Likewise, this stage is the fulfillment of Jesus' words in John's Gospel, "The Father and I are one..../...[T]hat all may be one / as you, Father, are in me, and I in you" (John 10:30; 17:21a).

The soul now experiences the mind of Christ—"But we have the mind of Christ" (1 Corinthians 2:16b)—so that it now contemplates the greatest of mysteries. Teresa herself was given the ability in this stage to understand the Trinity—that is, to understand how it is that there are three persons in one God.

Teresa exuberantly professed that her own amazing spiritual journey was something that every Christian—not just cloistered monks and nuns—could undertake. As farfetched as it may sound to those of us who have difficulty even walking up the steps to Teresa's first mansion, Teresa stressed that everything she taught was commonplace, everyday Christianity. All Christians, Teresa believed, are called to be mystics—mystics in Teresa's own style, *everyday* mystics who find God within themselves and bring God joyfully to others.

This profoundly human—even earthy—woman proclaimed that union with God is the great adventure of human life, an adventure that draws us out of our own fears and shortcomings and transforms us into laughing, playful children of God. One gets the impression that if Teresa had met John Calvin she would have slapped him on the back and told him not to take himself so seriously. What a pity the two never met; it might have made all the difference in the world!

John of the Cross

When the prior of a Carmelite monastery asked Teresa for assistance in reforming his monastery, he placed at her disposal his own services as well as those of a boyish friar named Juan de Yepis y Alvarez. When Teresa saw the prior's diminutive associate she exclaimed, with her typical sense of humor, "Now I have a friar and a half to begin the Reform with!"[19] The "half friar" would become known as John of the Cross, Teresa's most celebrated spiritual disciple and her only equal as a mystical writer.

Whereas Teresa was jovial and impetuous, John of the Cross was reserved and unassuming. If we could compare the two mystics' treatises to New Testament writings, Teresa reads like Paul while John of the Cross reminds us of John. Teresa's mysticism, like her own personality, was outgoing and vivacious; the mysticism of John of the Cross was lofty and refined.

Like Teresa, John of the Cross suffered greatly for bringing reform to the Carmelite friars. At one point he was imprisoned by a resistant Carmelite superior. Thus, like Teresa, John also found it necessary to form separate Discalced Carmelite monasteries. Even then, however, John found little peace. While serving as prior of a Carmelite house in Grenada, John was banished by the Discalced general when the latter refused to further John's call for ongoing reform.

During all of this turmoil, John was experiencing his own version of spiritual growth. Different from Teresa's, John's mysticism renounced all psychological and spiritual consolations and proceeded by blind faith. John's way is summarized in the following advice which he gave to initiates in the spiritual life:

To reach satisfaction in all
desire its possession in nothing.
To come to the knowledge of all
desire the knowledge of nothing.
To come to possess all
desire the possession of nothing.
To arrive at being all
desire to be nothing. [20]

Like Teresa's, John's mysticism is one of love, but a love that is willing to give up even the sensory consolation which lovers ordinarily share. Consider John's stark and desolate depiction of his own love relationship with God:

Love consists not in feeling great things, but in having great detachment and in suffering for the Beloved....The solitary bird can endure no companionship, even of its own kind....Divest thyself of what is human in order to seek God....Live in this world as though there were in it but God and thy soul, so that thy heart may be detained by naught that is human. [21]

John's major spiritual treatises are *The Ascent of Mount Carmel* and *The Dark Night*, written for beginners in the spiritual life, and *The Spiritual Canticle* and *The Living Flame of Love*, written for the more advanced. In *The Dark Night* John calls for a radical purgation of the senses so that one's desires can be refocused from the world's illusions to God alone. This purgation takes place first in an "active night of the senses" in which one affirmatively seeks mortification. Then, in a "passive night," God himself strips the soul of its illusory attachments. During the active night one's prayer is called meditation; during the passive night one moves to infused contemplation.

Beyond the two nights of the senses are two even darker nights. In the "active night of the spirit" one rejects all interior sensations such as feelings and images. Then, in the "passive night of the spirit" (colloquially called "the dark night of the soul"), one experiences, John says, "a cruel spiritual death." During this latter step (similar to Teresa's "sixth mansion") the mystic is stripped by God of all knowledge or sensation of God's presence. In this stage one simply plods forward in totally naked faith, motivated by love for God. Eventually—after perhaps many years, John warns—the passive night of the spirit gives way to the daylight of spiritual union with God. John describes this union in *The Spiritual Canticle* in astonishing language:

The union wrought between the two natures and the communication of the divine to the human in this state is such that even though neither change their being, both appear to be God. [22]

This state is simlar to Teresa's "seventh mansion." But John goes even beyond Teresa's description of this unitive marriage by writing that the soul is now so "confirmed in grace" by God's love that it is impossible to sin. In *The Living Flame of Love* John develops even one further stage of spiritual life, the "living flame of love." This mysterious state seems to be the equivalent of the beatific vision reserved for all souls in heaven. Here John's language lapses almost entirely into a mystical poetry that is very difficult for the uninitiated to decipher.

In comparison to Ignatius and Teresa, some have criticized John because he does not explicitly urge the performance of apostolic works as a companion to contemplation. In response, we can cite both John's own life of full and active service as well as his teaching that the purest form of service is the surrender of one's very self to God and the transformation of that self into a receptacle of divine love.

In actuality the very purpose of Christian life is this transformation from love of self to complete love of God. Once transformed, it is as impossible not to love and serve others as it is for God to cut himself off from his creation. All service and apostolic activity, in the last analysis, must be measured against the scale of this transformation into Christ which John describes. The true Christian servant is able to repeat the words which John spoke during his banishment as he encouraged his associates to persevere: "Where there is no love, put love and you will find love." [23]

THE LEGACY OF REFORMATION SPIRITUAL MASTERS

Protestant Spirituality

What effect did the writings of the Protestant spiritual masters have on the lives of ordinary Christians?

On the theoretical level, the Protestant writers did much to restore balance to Protestant theology. They countered Calvinism's doctrine of a controlling God who predetermines human action with a more scriptural picture of a God who encourages human freedom. In that sense, then, the Protestant spiritual tradition traced in this chapter represents a higher response to the Renaissance belief in creative human potential than do the theologies of Luther and Calvin.

This Protestant spiritual tradition returned the attention of Protestant Christians to the God of mystery and freedom and turned it away from the God of security and control. In this spiritual climate Protestant Christians could authentically satisfy their aspiration for spiritual autonomy and independence—the very aspiration which had arisen during the Catholic Middle Ages and which had played such a large role in assuring Luther's success.

On the practical level, the writings of the Protestant spiritual masters influenced a whole generation of Protestants to develop prayer and devotional practices which were in many respects similar to Catholic spirituality. John Wesley and the Methodists in particular, along with the continental Pietists, created a spirituality of the heart in which Protestants, like their Catholic brothers and sisters, based their everyday faith on close personal contact with the Jesus they met in daily Bible reading and in spiritual writings of the times.

By the turn of the 18th century there was doubtless much less conflict between Catholics and Protestants on the level of this everyday faith than on the level of doctrine. The God of freedom and mystery met Protestants and Catholics alike in prayer and Scripture reading, without asking for denominational identification.

Catholic Spirituality

What effect did Catholic spiritual writings have on the Christians of the Reformation era? From the 16th century onward, the spirituality of Ignatius, Teresa and John of the Cross made an enormous impact on the training of priests and religious as well as on the lives of ordinary Catholics throughout the world.

The spirituality of Ignatius of Loyola was taken by Jesuits into schools and parishes wherever they went, so that few Catholics were untouched by its influence. Ignatius's emphasis on spiritual discipline, obedience to superiors, the examination of conscience, and the surrender of the heart and mind to Christ became the staple of Catholic spirituality for four centuries.

What pre-Vatican II Catholic, for example, does not remember making the "morning offering" of one's "thoughts, words, desires and actions" to God for the upcoming day? And what pre-Vatican II Catholic does not likewise remember scrawling at the top of school papers the Jesuit motto "A.M.D.G."—an abbreviation of the Latin for "all for the greater glory of God"?

In our own day a rebirth of interest in the *Spiritual Exercises* as well as in the mystical writings of Teresa of Avila and John of the Cross coincides with a revived interest in eastern religions. If Catholics are to take seriously the call of Vatican II to enter into dialogue with Hindus and Buddhists, they would do well to take with them an appreciation for Teresa and John of the Cross.

The Reformation's Finest Hour

Taken together, the Protestant and Catholic spiritual writers of the Reformation era influenced Christianity by underscoring the primacy of personal prayer and commitment to the Lord in the Christian's life. Throughout the Reformation era, Church leaders and theologians on both sides of the religious controversy had too often engaged in doctrinal polemic, either for its own sake or for the purpose of gaining an advantage over the opponent. The spirituality of the Reformation, as we have defined it in this chapter, may therefore be considered the Reformation's finest hour.

We may also look upon this Reformation spirituality as the starting point for a reunification of Christians today. The spiritual masters of the Reformation alerted all Christians to the God of freedom. Only when we let God be the God of freedom will the Spirit left us by Jesus truly be able to transform us. Then Catholics and Protestants together may make an affirmative response to Jesus' prayer "that all may be one" (John 17:21a).

CHAPTER TWELVE

'ÉCRASEZ L'ÎNFAME'

The Reformation's Aftermath

We have thus far been considering the effect of the Reformation on the Christian Church. Except for highlighting here and there its political consequences in Christian Europe, we have not otherwise devoted much attention to the Reformation's effect on the wider European society. In order to conclude and round out our understanding of the Reformation era, we will discuss briefly in this chapter what we could call the aftermath of the Reformation: its general effect on Europeans *as Europeans* rather than *as Christians*.

In particular, we will consider how the Reformation affected the intellectual climate of western society. The Reformation not only helped to create a whole new worldview; it also influenced the way people thought of themselves in relationship to it.

In the Middle Ages Christian thinkers had attempted with some success to construct a harmonious model for human existence out of both theology and philosophy. In this medieval synthesis the Christian's individual existence was integrated into the larger event of salvation history. Distortions of the gospel at times weakened this attempt to make humanity principally religious in its outlook; but the mere attempt nonetheless meant that people found meaning in their lives which transcended the here and now. But this medieval worldview was disintegrating everywhere in the late Middle Ages.

A number of factors combined with this disintegration to ensure that the picture of the world by the start of the 18th century was vastly different from either the medieval worldview of Thomas Aquinas or that of the 16th-century reformers: (1) The Protestant Reformers' suspicion of the Renaissance and of philosophy and reason in general; (2) the religious hatred unleashed by a century of sectarian warfare; (3) the explosion of scientific thought touched off by the discoveries of Galileo Galilei in the 16th century and the theories of Isaac Newton a century later; and (4) the division of theology and philosophy into two separate and often opposed disciplines by the early modern philosophers.

At the start of the 18th century we no longer find a society dominated by the religious consciousness of an Aquinas or a Luther. Instead we see a society dominated by the secular and self-confident spirit of the Renaissance—but with a change in emphasis: The Enlightenment's devotion to human reason has preempted the Renaissance devotion to human power.

THE ENLIGHTENMENT

The thrust of early modern philosophy was to place philosophy on its own foundation, separate and apart from theology and indeed from all religious tradition. Men like René Descartes in France (1596-1650) and John Locke in England (1632-1704) wanted to construct philosophies that were unimpeded by prejudice, superstition and religious authority. While these early philosophers wanted to be free from the influence of nonrational factors, they did not deride or condemn religion as the enemy of reason. As we turn to the philosophy of the Enlightenment, however, we encounter of philosophers who are convinced that established religion is the implacable foe of reason. For the philosophers of the Enlightenment, therefore, philosophy and the traditional faith—in particular Roman Catholicism and the Protestant state Churches—must not simply be segregated but also set at odds with one another.

Yet this is not the whole story. Not all Enlightenment philosophers were determined foes of established religion. Nor were most of them atheists (if one gives a broad interpretation to the meaning of God and theism). The principal purpose of the Enlightenment philosophers was not the undoing of organized religion, but the establishment of reason, over and above nonrational impulses like faith, as the basic principle by which one can understand human civilization, culture and society.

The focus of Enlightenment philosophy was the human person aside and apart from God and uninfluenced by organized religion. Especial attention was paid to moral, psychological and social drives and impulses. Enlightenment philosophers did not start from the premise

174

that the human person is best served by atheism or by this religion as opposed to that. Nor did they start from the premise that there should be no absolute standard of morality. They simply attempted to observe and define the human person apart from the teachings of revealed religion.

As it turned out, of course, most Enlightenment philosophers, particularly the *philosophes* of the French Enlightenment, arrived at conclusions which made organized religion the foe of reason and progress. But they did not start out with the desire to destroy it. They saw themselves extending the discoveries of science to the entire human enterprise—philosophy, religion, arts, education—and, in the process, replacing the intolerance and backwardness of established religion with the light of reason and tolerance.

THE PHILOSOPHES

France is the home of the Enlightenment as it is popularly understood. The philosophes, or principal spokesmen for the French Enlightenment, differed markedly from previous philosophers. In addition to writing abstract philosophy, they embraced certain practical aims including the dethronement of organized religion, the reform of education and the repeal of longstanding social customs. We could characterize their new attitude in this way: Whereas earlier philosophers pursued wisdom for its own sake, the philosophes, in addition to their underlying program of replacing unreason with reason, had "an ax to grind" with the established religious, social and political system.

To a certain extent we could say that the philosophes were "ideologists" rather than philosophers. In fact, it was during the Enlightenment that the word *ideology* was invented. The word suggests a system of belief that inspires social or political action rather than an abstract and impartial analysis of reality. This prosyletizing tendency—toward winning people over to one's point of view in order to achieve certain stated objectives—developed during the Enlightenment in a way it had not ever existed before in philosophy.

The master polemicist and most famous philosophe was Francois Marie Arouet (1694-1778), who changed his name to Voltaire. Voltaire is perhaps unduly associated with his slogan, *"Écrasez l'înfame"* ("Crush the infamous thing"—referring to the French Catholic Church and its intolerance of different religious and philosophical opinions). It is nonetheless true that he was not a philosopher in the strict sense, but something of a pamphleteer engaged in a war of words with the established Church and its hierarchy.

In terms of substantive doctrine, the French *philosophes* believed that all knowledge comes from sense experience; thus it is to that world of sense phenomena that intellectuals and scientists must turn in arriving at an accurate description of the material world and humanity's place in it. Étienne Bonnot de Condillac (1715-1780), for example, did away with the innate faculties of the soul (judgment, willing, desiring and the like). For Condillac such faculties—indeed all mental activities—were purely the result of sensations impinging on the mind from the outside world. Claude Adrien Helvétius (1715-1771) agreed: "Corporeal sensibility is therefore the sole mover of man." And the philosophe Jean Georges Cabanis (1757-1808) wrote, *"Les nerfs—voilà tout l'homme."* ("Nerves are all there is to man.")

In this scheme of things human beings became simply one more object to study, one more phenomenon to be subjected to analytical scrutiny. As a result, the philosophes tended to segregate religion and morality. Human beings were looked upon as autonomous moral creatures who, through the proper use of reason, were capable of arriving at the universally applicable and effective code of moral conduct. The philosophes' outlook was thus positivistic—that is, they believed that the application of empirical research to human relationships could only produce positive growth and progress for the human species. Looking back from the vantage point of the nuclear age, we can realize their naivete, but to the ordinary person of the day the philosophes' writings had great appeal.

The crowning achievement of the French Enlightenment was a multivolume encyclopedia edited by Denis Diderot (1713-1784) and Jean d'Alembert (1717-1783), with contributions from a wide variety of writers. True to the premises of the philosophes' general program, the famous *Encyclopédie* went beyond a mere description of the natural world and of history to attack the Catholic Church and organized religion. It was a work of ideology rather than of philosophy or science in the strict sense.

The basic philosophical presuppositions of the *Encyclopédie* included: (1) the general Enlightenment belief in unlimited human progress based on science and reason apart from the teachings of organized religion; (2) the belief that human beings apart from God can become by their own study and effort perfect moral and intellectual creatures; (3) the idea that the true nature of reality may be understood only through the impartial and systematic observation of phenomena in the material world rather than through deduction from *a priori* first principles as in the systems of philosophy endorsed by the Church (such as Thomism).

We could summarize Enlightenment ideology in this way: (1) It had as its central belief system either skepticism about God's existence or outright atheism. (2) It inspired action against organized Christianity. (3) It asserted a sociopolitical program based on improving human life on earth through the use of reason. It was this third element which most appealed to 18th-century people and which enticed them to accept the other two.

Today we know that reason and science, although improving life on earth in some instances, have also brought about untold human suffering and persecution. And the development of nuclear bombs has even brought humanity to the verge of extinction. In the 18th century, however, such consequences were not as obvious as they are today. Thus the philosophes' ideology appealed to many people as a truly "enlightened" attempt to banish ignorance, superstition and prejudice. Given Christians' bitter warfare with each other; given Protestant theology's often negative depiction of human nature; and given the Catholic hierarchy's repression of Protestant and much secular writing, the philosophes' ideology looked much more "Christian" to many people than official Christianity.

The Attack on Christianity

It's fair to say that the focus of Enlightenment ideology was an attack on organized Christianity and, in particular, on the Catholic Church. Writing in 1753 in his *Journal and Memoirs*, King Louis XV's foreign minister Rene-Louis d'Argenson leaves us a vivid description of both the society in which the philosophes circulated and the target of their program:

> The minds of men are turning to discontent and disobedience, and everything seems moving toward a great revolution in both religion and government....It will be a very different thing from the rude Reformation—a medley of superstition and freedom that came to us from Germany. As our nation and our century are enlightened in so very different a fashion, they will go whither they ought to go: they will expel the priests, abolish the priesthood, and get rid of all revelation and mystery.[1]

One of the strangest supporters of the philosophes' program was Jean Meslier (1678-1733). On the surface this Catholic priest lived the exemplary life of a dedicated pastor, but he secretly kept a journal in which he poured out his doubts and hatred. "The priests have made of God such a malicious, ferocious being," he wrote, "that there are few men in the world who do not wish that God did not exist."[2] Meslier's

Jesus is "a fanatic, a misanthrope"[3] in whose name Christians "have unsettled empires, caused revolutions, ruined sovereigns, devastated the whole of Europe."[4] That such bitterness could inhabit the heart of a priest indicates how completely antireligious sentiment had captivated Catholic France.

The consequence of such hostility was amply reflected in writings like *L'Homme Machine* ("Man a Machine") by Julien La Mettrie (1709-1751). He wrote that human beings are merely higher forms of animals, the human soul being "an empty word, of which no one has any idea, and which an enlightened man should use only to signify that part in us that thinks."[5] The general editor of the *Encyclopédie*, Denis Diderot, revealed what was perhaps the prevailing Enlightenment attitude toward Christianity when he wrote, "I would sacrifice my life, perhaps, if I could annihilate forever the notion of God."[6] And again, "The Christian religion is to my mind the most absurd and atrocious in its dogmas."[7]

Claude-Adrien Helvétius's goal was to devise a philosophical morality that would supplant Christian morality. Helvétius based all behavior on utility, which he called "the principal of all human virtues, and the foundation of all legislation."[8] Paul Henri, Baron d'Holbach (1723-1789), authored *The System of Nature*, perhaps the single most influential book of the Enlightenment. He echoed Helvétius: "Live for yourself and your fellow creature....The friend of mankind cannot be a friend of God, who at all times has been a real scourge to the earth."[9]

These sentiments, which strike our ears as so contemporary, were brought to their culmination by Voltaire. Never had Christianity faced a wittier and more skillful adversary than when it confronted Voltaire. Writing in the Prussian court, in hiding under the protection of noble French patrons or from his estate judiciously located near the Swiss border, Voltaire became the philosophes' spokesman. "Attack, brothers," he urged his fellow philosophes, "skillfully, all of you, *l'infame* [the Church and its antirationalist dogma]. What interests me is the propagation of the faith and of truth, the progress of philosophy, the suppression of *l'infame*."[10]

Voltaire accepted the mantle which Luther had unwittingly placed around his shoulders. In one of the most telling passages in all Enlightenment literature, Voltaire urged his followers to bring to fruition the work which the Protestant revolutionaries had started:

> We are told that the people need mysteries and must be deceived. My brethren, dare anyone commit this outrage on humanity? Have not *our fathers* [the Protestant reformers] taken from the people their

transubstantiation, auricular confession, indulgences, exorcisms, false miracles, and ridiculous statues? Are not our people now accustomed to doing without these superstitions? We must have the courage to go a few steps further."11 (Emphasis added)

Toward the Church in the Modern World

With our consideration of the Enlightenment we conclude our discussion of the Reformation era and its effect on both Church and society at the end of the 18th century. In many respects the Enlightenment was but the culmination of a process which had begun in the late Middle Ages. From that point on Europeans attempted to free themselves from reliance on authority, tradition and received opinion concerning human nature and the nature of the world around them; they worked to establish for themselves an identity in which they could see themselves as autonomous individuals.

The Reformation had itself been a stage in this process; but the Reformation had attempted to address the quest for human autonomy only within the context of humanity's relationship to God (with varying degrees of success, as we have seen). The Enlightenment emphasized human reason rather than divine grace as the principal force underlying human thought and action. Yet the reformers and the philosophes were both inspired by essentially the same purpose—to bring humanity to a point of greater freedom and maturity. Neither the reformers nor the philosophes were completely successful, but we can nevertheless sympathize with their efforts.

The philosophes' attack on Christianity underscored the reformers' failure to answer satisfactorily a fundamental question posed all during the Reformation. This same question had been asked of medieval society by the Renaissance: Where does one draw the boundary between that which is human and that which is Christian?

The various reformers, both Catholic and Protestant, had attempted to answer that question. Generally speaking (and forcing a very complex picture into what is only a rough organizational model), we could say that by the end of the 18th century we are left with these three unsatisfactory answers to this question:

1) The "Protestant Answer," in which human freedom is limited by God's predetermination of human destiny. Here the boundary between that which is human and that which is Christian becomes related to the overall question of who is saved and who is not. In this view Christians are often seen chiefly as the assembly of the elect who must segregate themselves from the world of the unelect, avoiding all contact

179

with the world's false values.

2) The "Catholic View," in which both Protestantism and Enlightenment ideology tend to be identified as "the world." The world, then, becomes the place where error and falsehood originate, and the Church becomes not leaven in the world but a fortress defending the faithful from attack. As we shall see in the sequel to this book, *The People of Hope: The Story Behind the Church in the Modern World*, the popes of the 19th century distinguish the Christian and the human increasingly from a mind-set of "us vs. them."

3) The "Enlightened Liberal View," which defines the human as the entire range of cultural and intellectual pursuits open to reason and scientific study, through which humanity brings itself to fulfillment. In this view the Christian tends to become identified with close-minded and intolerant repression of human progress supposedly epitomized in the medieval Church.

None of these three views was accurate, but Protestants, Catholics and secular intellectuals increasingly segregated themselves into three hostile camps. By the 19th century each of these three views had become somewhat inflexibly established in the minds of many modern individuals as the only way in which to perceive the interrelationship between the Church and the world.

This, then, becomes the problem bequeathed to the modern age by the Reformation: How do Christianity and secular society extricate themselves from their respectively opposed positions and enter into a harmonious working relationship for the common benefit of the human family? Describing modern humanity's attempt to find a solution to that problem will be the subject of *The People of Hope: The Story Behind the Church in the Modern World*.

CONCLUSION

A Tragic Necessity

The story of the Church during the Reformation era is a series of misunderstandings and missed opportunities. The following overview counts them off:

1) Luther reacted (or overreacted) to the perversion of the gospel that he saw all around him. It is too easy for Catholics to say that he should have humbly submitted to Church authority and prayed for change. As bad as things were in many areas of the Catholic world, one can hardly blame a devout Christian like Luther for seeking to return the Church to its authentic mission.

2) Luther was not listened to but was instead condemned without benefit of a hearing conducted in Christian love and trust. This illustrates how corrupt much of the authority of the Catholic Church had become. Shepherds who respond to legitimate questions only with suspicion, fear and anger have ceased to hear God's Word: "...be kind to one another, compassionate, and mutually forgiving, just as God has forgiven you in Christ" (Ephesians 4:32).

3) Yet Luther could have heard these same words. As an advocate of *sola scriptura* Luther was given a unique opportunity to prove the efficicacy of Jesus' teaching: "My command to you is: love your enemies, pray for your persecutors" (Matthew 5:44). Instead of "heaping burning coals" of love upon his enemy's head, instead of "conquering evil with good" (see Romans 12:20-21), Luther responded to Catholic bigotry by heaping hot coals of anger upon his persecutors. His response released a flood of religious hatred into the world. Although we cannot

181

condemn Luther for reacting as he did, we can at the same time lament his failure to have killed his tormentors with kindness.

4) Instead of initiating a true Church reform based on love and forgiveness, Luther simply gave the Christian world more of the same—more anger, more condemnation, more confusion, more scandal caused by Christians fighting with each other. Although Luther certainly did not give birth to modern religious bigotry—there was Catholic bigotry aplenty before his time—he nonetheless failed to check its spread within his own ranks. He therefore lost an opportunity to prove to the world how his brand of Christianity was any different from the distorted Christianity which he condemned.

5) Luther's denunciation of the Anabaptists and his feud with Zwingli and Calvin (and their feud with him) proved two things: the inadequacy of individual discernment and the advantage of a centralized teaching authority to define the broad parameters of Christian orthodoxy Fifty years after Luther's revolt Europe had become populated with Protestant "popes," all claiming absolute truth for their doctrines and damning those who disagreed with them. The doctrinal warfare among Protestants exacerbated the scandal of disunity and contributed both to the general sense of religious confusion and to the growth of secularism which culminated in the Enlightenment.

6) At the Council of Trent the Catholic Church likewise lost an opportunity to conquer evil with good. Instead of issuing a forthright confession of its sins and praying for forgiveness, the delegates to Trent and the Tridentine popes lashed out defensively at the heretics. Instead of responding to Luther's legalistic interpretation of the gospel by promulgating a theology of Christian freedom, Trent likewise advanced legalistic dogma. Thanks to Luther and Calvin on the one hand and to Trent on the other, both Protestantism and Catholicism proclaimed to the world a God reduced virtually to the status of a venal judge. No wonder that the Enlightenment wanted to get rid of this God. The God whom Jesus described in his Parable of the Prodigal Son was lost to Christian theology for centuries.

7) With the developing Lutheran and Calvinist theologies of the 17th century and with the rise of Jansenism, both Protestant and Catholic traditions took on shapes that obscured their roots in either Scripture or apostolic tradition. Stripped of power and authenticity, Christianity appealed to fewer and fewer people. On the one hand this stimulated a rebirth of piety and contemplative spirituality; but on the other hand it encouraged the search for truth strictly in the secular forum.

8) When contemporary Christianity failed to satisfy people's hunger for absolute values, Enlightenment ideology offered itself as a

replacement religion. The philosophes substituted human reason for God as the guiding force of the universe, and they exchanged utility for morality as the criterion for human behavior. The cynicism towards all organized religion that resulted from the way Protestants and Catholics behaved right up to and through the end of the Thirty Years' War in 1648 fed the Enlightenment's recourse to reason. Further, the Protestant Reformers' and the Jansenists' insistence on a God of control and order, as opposed to a God of freedom and mystery, seriously undermined the attempt by Christians of all persuasions to proclaim the Christ of the Gospels. This likewise destroyed Christianity's credibility in the eyes of an increasing number of educated people. As Christianity increasingly lost respect in the eyes of intellectuals and political thinkers, the quest for human perfectibility came to be centered on an earthly utopia rather than on Christianity's promise of a new form of human existence transcending time and space.

Perhaps the best phrase to summarize the progression traced above is "tragic necessity." The Reformation, in both its Protestant and Catholic demeanors, was inevitable. The medieval model no longer adequately served humanity's needs. In the sense that the Reformation brought Christianity forward into a new world dominated by a new model, it was a necessity. But in the sense that it failed to preserve the achievements of previous Christian centuries by integrating them into the new model—even assuming an accurate description of the new model could be made—the Reformation was a tragedy.

All in all, the Reformation was a time of the most profound anguish for Christianity, an anguish whose pain has only now begun to be alleviated. Only in our own day have Christians started again truly to hope for the realization of Jesus' own prayer:

...[T]hat all may be one
as you, Father, are in me, and I in you;
...that the world may believe that you sent me." (John 17:21)

NOTES

Chapter Two

1. *Encyclopedia Britannica*, 15th ed., s.v. "Renaissance."
2. *Ibid.*
3. *Ibid.*
4. *Ibid.*
5. Erasmus, "The Praise of Folly," in Will Durant, *The Story of Civilization*, 11 vols., (New York: Simon and Schuster, 1957) VI: 278.
6. *Ibid.*
7. Erasmus, "Colloquies," Ibid., 282.
8. Erasmus, "Commentary on Mt 23:27," *Ibid.*, 284.
9. Erasmus, "Commentary on Mt 11:30," *Ibid.*
10. Erasmus, "Letter to Cardinal Campeggio" (Dec. 6, 1520), *Ibid.*, 432.
11. Boccaccio, "Decameron," *Ibid.*, V: 572.
12. In Durant, *Ibid.*
13. Guicciardini, "Considerations," *Ibid.*
14. In Durant, *Ibid.*, 572-573.
15. *Ibid.*, 378.
16. *Ibid.*, 379.
17. *Ibid.*
18. *Ibid.*, 388.
19. *Ibid.*, 401.
20. *Ibid.*, 406.
21. *Ibid.*, 411.
22. *Ibid.*, 410.
23. *Ibid.*, 414.
24. *Ibid.*, 417.
25. *Cambridge Modern History*, II, 14, *Ibid.*, 481.
26. *Ibid.*, 482.
27. *Luther's Works*, 1530; 31, I, 226, in Hubert Jedin, ed., *History of the Church*, 10 vols., (New York: The Seabury Press, 1980), V: 18.
28. *Luther's Works*, 47, 392; *Ibid.*
29. *Luther's Works*, Br 1, III; Jedin, V: 47.

Chapter Three

1. *Luther's Works*, Tr 3, 51, no. 2888a; Tr 3, 416 no. 3566A in Jedin, op. cit., V: 12.
2. *Ibid.*, 40, I, 298; Jedin, V: 13.
3. *Ibid.*, 3, 465, 6; V: 23.
4. *Ibid.*, 56, 355; V: 25.
5. *Ibid.*, 56, 274; V: 25.
6. *Ibid.*, 56, 272, V: 27.
7. *Ibid.*, 57, III, 191, V: 32.

8. *Ibid.*, 57, III, 206.
9. *Ibid.*, 56, 274; V: 41.
10. In Jedin, V: 50.
11. *Luther's Works*, 1, 530f; Jedin, V: 51.
12. *Ibid.*, 2, 7; V: 56.
13. Durant, op. cit., VI: 353.
14. *Luther's Works*, II, 302-310; Durant, VI: 355-356.
15. Durant, VI: 356.
16. In Jedin, V: 76.
17. *Ibid.*, 77.
18. *Luther's Works*, Tr 5, 65; Jedin, V: 78.
19. Jedin, V: 79.
20. *Luther's Works*, 8, 164, Jedin, V: 82.
21. *Ibid.*, V: 86.
22. *Ibid.*, V: 88.
23. *Ibid.*, V: 90.
24. *Ibid.*, DB, 7, 385; V: 97.
25. Luther, *Table Talk*, 353, Durant, *op. cit.*, VI: 370.
26. *Ibid.*, 91, 96; VI: 372.
27. *Luther's Works*, II, 391; Durant, VI: 373.
28. *Ibid.*, 40:349, in Justo Gonzalez, *A History of Christian Thought*, 3 vols., (Nashville: Abingdon Press, 1983), III:54.
29. *Ibid.*, 31:355; III:56.

Chapter Four

1. *Luther's Works*, 28, 142-201; Durant, VI:377.
2. *Ibid.*, 3, 258-261; VI:378.
3. *Ibid.*, in Durant.
4. *Luther's Works*, Br 3, 256; Jedin, V:125.
5. *Ibid.*, 18, 152; V:126.
6. *Ibid.*, 15, 210-221; V:133.
7. *Ibid.*, 18, 367; V:137.
8. In Durant, VI:380.
9. *Ibid.*, 389.
10. *Ibid.*, 390.
11. *Ibid.*, 393.
12. *Ibid.*
13. Sebastian Franck (1499-1542), in Jedin, V:190.
14. Jedin, V:243.
15. Durant, VI:438.
16. *Ibid.*, 440. 17. *Ibid.*
18. *Ibid.*, 443.
19. *Luther's Works*, Br 8, 367, 20-23; Jedin, V:266.
20. In Durant, VI:416.
21. *Ibid.*, 416.
22. *Ibid.*
23. *Ibid.*, 419

24. *Ibid.*
25. *Ibid.*, 421.
26. *Ibid.*, 422.
27. *Ibid.*, 449.
28. *Ibid.*, 451.

Chapter Five

1. *Zwingli's Works*, 2, 144, 32ff; Jedin, V:158.
2. *Ibid.*, V:164.
3. Durant, VI:410.
4. *Ibid.*, 413.
5. *Ibid.* 412.
6. Jedin, V:250.
7. *Ibid.*, 251.
8. *Ibid.*
9. Durant, V:474.
10. *Ibid.*, 481.
11. *Ibid.*, 482.
12. *Ibid.*, 485.
13. Jedin, V:383.
14. Calvin, *Institutes*, 2.1.8; Gonzalez, III:131.
15. *Ibid.*, 3.11.2; III:140.
16. *Ibid.*, 3.21.5; III:144.
17. *Ibid.*, 2.21.7; Durant, VI:464.
18. *Ibid.*, 2.21.1.
19. *Ibid.*, VI:466.
20. *Ibid.*, 4.1.7; Gonzalez, III:146.
21. *Ibid.*
22. *Ibid.*, 4.1.4; III:147.
23. *Ibid.*, 4.14.1; III:150.
24. Durant, VI:477.

Chapter Seven

1. Pope Adrian VI, "Instruction to the Diet of Nuremburg" (1522); Jedin V:108.
2. Jedin, V:112
3. In Gonzalez, III:218-219.
4. *Ibid.*, 220
5. *Ibid.*
6. *Ibid.*
7. *Ibid.*, 222.
8. *Acts of the Council of Trent*, XI, 710, 713; *Ibid.* V:478.
9. *Ibid.*, XIII, 1, 315; V:482-483.
10. Durant, VI:922.
11. *Letters and Works of Peter Canisius*, II, 377; Jedin, V:487.
12. Durant, VI:926.

13. *Ibid.*, 925.
14. *Ibid.*
15. *Ibid.*, 926.
16. In Harvey D. Egan, S.J., *Christian Mysticism: The Future of a Tradition* (New York: Pueblo Publishing Co., 1984), 36.
17. Durant, VI:912.
18. *Ibid*, 909.

Chapter Eight

1. Durant, VIII, 298.
2. Jedin, V:498.
3. *Ibid.*, 502.
4. W.E. Lecky, *History of European Morals*, II, 97; Durant, VII:243.
5. Votaire, *Age of Louis XIV*, 135; *Ibid.*, VIII:432.
6. Durant, VII:275.
7. *Ibid.*, 375.
8. *Ibid.*, 382.
9. *Ibid.*, VIII:85.
10. *Ibid.*
11. *Ibid.*, 697.
12. Jedin, VI:195.
13. *Ibid.*, 201.
14. Durant, VII:552.
15. *Ibid.*, 567.

Chapter Nine

1. *The Book of Concord*, 477; Gonzalez, III, 111.
2. Jerome Zanchi, *Absolute Predestination*, 24-25; *Ibid.*, 245.
3. *The Writings of James Arminius*, I:248; *Ibid.*, 256.
4. *Canons of Synod of Dort*; *Ibid.*, 259.
5. *Ibid.*
6. *Ibid.*, 260.
7. *Ibid.*, 261.

Chapter Ten

1. Luis De Molina, "The Harmony of the Will With the Gifts of Grace," 14.23.4, in Jaroslav Pelikan, *The Christian Tradition*, 4 vols., (Chicago: The University of Chicago Press, 1984), 4:378.
2. *Ibid.*
3. Cornelius Jansen, *Augustinus*, 1.5.10; *Ibid.*, 377.
4. Durant, IX:257.

Chapter Eleven

1. Francis Rous, "Mystical Marriage"; in Louis Bouyer, *A History of Christian Spirituality*, 3 vols. (New York: The Seabury Press, 1982), III:137-138.
2. Thomas Goodwin, "The Heart of Christ in Heaven"; *Ibid.*, 140.
3. Bouyer, III:143.
4. John Smith, "Select Discourses," I; *Ibid.*, 152.
5. Richard Baxter, "The Saints' Everlasting Rest," III; *Ibid.*, 156.
6. George Fox, "Journal"; *Ibid.*, 162.
7. Auguste Francke, *Ibid.*, 173.
8. *The Works of John Wesley*, 1:103; Gonzalez III:281.
9. *Ibid.*, 6:512; 285.
10. Bouyer, III:190.
11. *Ibid.*, 192-193.
12. Durant, IX:137.
13. A. Mottola, trans., *The Spiritual Exercises of St. Ignatius of Loyola* (Garden City, N.Y.: Doubleday, 1964), no. 1.
14. *Ibid.*, no. 53.
15. *Ibid.*, no. 114.
16. *Ibid.*, no. 234, as adapted for song by John Foley, S.J..
17. Teresa of Avila, *Vida*, 8:110; in Egan, 121.
18. *Ibid.*, 19:181; Egan, 136.
19. E. Allison Peers, *Spirit of Flame* (Wilton, Connecticut: Morehouse-Barlow Co., 1946), 14.
20. *The Collected Works of St. John of the Cross*, trans. Kieran Kavanaugh, O.C.D., 67, in Egan, 166.
21. John of the Cross, "Points of Love," 36, 42, 54, 61; Peers, 20.
22. John of the Cross, *The Spiritual Canticle*, in Egan, 196.
23. *Letters of John of the Cross*, XXII, in Peers, 94.

Chapter Twelve

1. Rene-Louis d'Argenson, *Journal and Memoirs*, in Durant IX:279, 610.
2. Jean Meslier, *Superstition in All Ages, or Last Will and Testament!*, 66, 192; *Ibid.*, IX:613.
3. *Ibid.*, 90; 614.
4. *Ibid.*, preface; 616.
5. Julien La Mettrie, *L'Homme Machine*, 128; *Ibid.*, 619.
6. Durant, XI:656.
7. Denis Diderot, "Letter to Damilaville" (1766); *Ibid.*
8. Claude-Adrien Helvetius, *On the Mind*; *Ibid.*, 687.
9. Baron d'Holbach, *The System of Nature*, I, 14, Ii, 13; *Ibid.*, 706, 704.
10. In Durant, IX: 739.
11. *Ibid.*, 741.

INDEX

Orange, William of (William the Silent), 131
Oratorians, 127
Original sin, 38, 71, 79
Osiander, Andrew, 138-139
Ottomans, 14-15, 63-64
Papacy, 118-120; abuses, 19, 28-29, 30, 32-33, 94-95; decline of power, 15, 19-20, 95, 102-103, 126, 129; and Henry VIII, 84, 85-86; and Luther, 42-43, 46; militarism of, 30, 32-33, 64; and Protestantism, 42-43, 46, 64, 98; and reform, 19-20, 101-102, 104, 124-126; and Renaissance, 28-29, 33
Papal States, 30; map, 65
Parliament (England), and Catholicism, 89, 122, 124; and Commonwealth, 122-123; and Henry VIII, 85-86; official persecutions, 89, 122, 123, 124
Pascal, Blaise, 152
Paul II, Pope, 30
Paul III, Pope, 103-104, 105, 118
Paul IV, Pope, 26, 104, 112-114, 120
Paul V, Pope, 149
Paul, apostle, 37, 39
Peace of Westphalia, 136; map, 135
Peasants' Rebellion, 58-60
Penance, sacrament of, 48, 111
Perseverence of saints, 144
Peter the Great (Russia), 133
Philip of Hesse, 72
Philip I (Spain), 131
Philip II (Spain), 127
Philip III (Spain), 127
Philip IV (Spain), 127
Philip Neri, 125
Philosophes, 175-177, 178-179
Pietism, 160
Pius II, Pope, 29-30
Pius IV, Pope, 82, 115
Pius V, Pope, 124-125
Poitiers, Diane de, 97
Port-Royal, 151-153
Poverty, evangelical, 27, 117-118

Predestination, 154-155; and Calvin, 79-81, 141, 142; in Catholic theology, 16, 148; and Luther, 37-38, 49
Presbyterianism, 75, 92-93, 145
Priesthood of laity, 46, 50, 154
Probabilism, 151
Protestantism, fragmentation of, 62-63, 64-66; and politics, 62-63, 64-66, 134, 154
Puritans, in England, 89-90, 122-123, 145, 158-160; persecuted, 89-90, 123
Quakers, 123, 160
Quesnel, Pasquier, 153
Ratisbon, 103
Real Presence, 111; and Protestants, 49, 72-73, 89
Recusants, 89
Reformation, concepts of, 2-3, 8-9
Reform, and papacy, 19-20, 32, 101-102, 115, 124-126; Protestant, 56-59; and Trent, 106, 111-112, 115-116; other Catholic reform, 26-27, 114-115, 120, 127-128, 165, 168
Regensburg, 63-64
Regimini Militantis Ecclesiae (Paul III), 118
Religious Peace of Augsburg, 64, 66
Remonstrants, 142, 143, 144
Renaissance, 5, 6-7, 25; and papacy, 28-29, 32, 33
Restitution of Christianity, The (Servetus), 76
Richelieu, Armand de, Cardinal, 128-129
Roman Inquisition, 112-113, 115, 124. *See also* Inquisition
Romans, Epistle to the, 37, 39, 49
Rous, Francis, 158-159
Russian Orthodox Church, 132-133
Sacraments, 107, 108; Luther on, 39-40, 48, 49-50; other Protestant views, 81-82, 89; Trent on, 109, 110-111
St. Bartholomew's Day massacre, 97-98
Salvation, 110; Protestant views, 39, 79-81